The Collected Works
of

EDITH STEIN

Sister Teresa Benedicta of the Cross
Discalced Carmelite
1891–1942

Volume Two

The Collected Works

of

EDITH STEIN

The Collected Works
of
EDITH STEIN

Sister Teresa Benedicta of the Cross
Discalced Carmelite

Volume Two

ESSAYS ON WOMAN

Edited by
Dr. L. Gelber
and
Romaeus Leuven, OCD

Translated by Freda Mary Oben, PhD

ICS Publications
Washington, D.C.
1987

The original of this work was published in German by
Archivum Carmelitanum Edith Stein under the title of (Band V)
Die Frau
Ihre Aufgabe nach Natur und Gnade
Translation authorized.
© E. Nauwelaerts, Louvain 1959.
English translation copyright
© Washington Province of Discalced Carmelites, Inc. 1987

ICS Publications
2131 Lincoln Road, N.E.
Washington, D.C. 20002

Typeset by Wenzel Press

Library of Congress Cataloging-in-Publication Data

Stein, Edith, 1891-1942.
Essays on Woman.

(The Collected works of Edith Stein; v. 2)
Includes index.
Translation of: Die Frau.
1. Women—Education. 2. Feminism. 3. Women—
Religious life. I. Gelber, Lucy. II. Leuven, Romaeus.
III. Title. IV. Series: Stein, Edith, 1891-1942.
Works. English. 1986; v.2.
B3332.S672E54 1985 vol. 2 193 s 86-20051
[LC1481]   [305.4'2]
ISBN 0-935216-08-1

Contents

Translator's Preface

Gilbert V. Hartke's dedication to the priesthood was essential in bringing about my conversion from Judaism to Catholicism in 1960. Two years later, it was he who spoke to me of another Jewess who had become a Catholic: Edith Stein, the noted German philosopher and Carmelite, who had been martyred at Auschwitz.

I went quickly to find what I could about her. In those days, twenty-four years ago, I did not know German. I undertook the study of the language expressly to read Stein's works in the original. The subsequent years have been spent in research and translation in order to make her known through articles and talks to the American public.

The translation of *Die Frau* which I offer here is the fruit of many years of work. You may ask: What was it which drove me with such force through the years? I was convinced that she was the needed catalyst in our society's confusion concerning the role of woman. Her writings helped me, as a wife and mother of five children, to establish an equilibrium in my family and professional life. I knew she could have a similar effect on others.

I have always felt deeply the pain of the human condition; before my conversion, however, I did not know how to confront it. Through Stein's life and her writings, I recognize the unique redemptive role of woman. Stein believes that God combats evil through the power of woman's maternal love. That power exists independently of woman's marital status and should be extended to all persons with whom she comes in contact. Everywhere, there is a need for such love, and it is essential to woman's nature that she give it. Just as the Mother of Christ appeared publicly at the crucifixion, so, too, a woman must be involved today in the struggle between good and evil.

Of course, a factor in my dedication to Edith Stein is our sharing in the Jewish heritage. I share her love for our people. I understand that her fidelity to God, the Holy One both of Israel and of Christ, led her to offer up her life for the chosen people. It is hoped that recognition of her sacrifice will encourage the so desperately needed reconciliation between the two faiths.

I offer my heartfelt gratitude to Father Hartke without whom none of my work could have been done. My thanks, also, to Ferrer Smith, O.P., who instructed me in the Catholic faith, and I honor the memory of his brother Alan Smith, O.P., who was the first to hand me a copy of the German edition of *Die Frau*.

As early as 1974, I was planning this American edition of *Die Frau* in collaboration with Dr. Lucy Gelber, editor of the *Edith Steins Werke* and Conservator of the *Archivum Carmelitanum Edith Stein* in Brussels. Through the years, I have been sustained by her faith and encouragement. I acknowledge the generosity of Dr. Ingrid Merkel of the Catholic University of America who checked my initial translation from the German. I wish to express my deep respect for Dr. John L. Brown, Professor Emeritus of C.U.A., who understood the value of this translation, who never failed to inspire me and spent many hours checking my work. My gratitude to Dr. Thomas Prufer of C.U.A. for his help in the translation of some of the philosophical terms. And my special thanks to Adrian Cooney, O.C.D., for the final editing of the text.

I have tried to tread a middle path by keeping in tension a literal translation and a fluid English style. The latter could have compromised Stein's concepts and some freedom has been taken, but any real sacrificing of Stein's content has been avoided. In doing so, I honor her own rule of translation: fidelity to the text, a value which she herself maintained as translator from Greek, Latin, English, and French writings. Therefore, I have followed her in using the masculine pronoun in broad impersonal generalizations.

Stein developed analytically her philosophical thought, and her style might strike some readers as verbose. It is also to be remembered that what may appear as redundancy is due to Stein's presenting these papers originally as talks in major European cities; although these talks often treated different subjects, many of the key concepts remain the same but without verbal repetition.

The high regard shown her by the Church is well justified. In exercising her feminine nature magnanimously, Edith Stein reveals to us what it is to be fully human. As that rare phenomenon, the woman philosopher, she inspires women to the highest intellectual and professional achievement; and she points to the interior life, the life of prayer and contemplation as the source of her strength. In line with some of the women in scripture, Stein is a Jewish heroine, as well as a holy Christian. Assuredly, she demonstrates that the truths of the Christian faith are more than abstractions; she experienced these and lived them passionately.

How well Edith Stein incarnates the essence of holiness. As a woman of intellectual and spiritual stature, she is a witness to authentic feminism.

Freda Mary Oben
Silver Spring, MD
January 13, 1986

Editors' Introduction

The many-sided literary production of Edith Stein falls into three categories: studies in general philosophy and in the philosophy of religion; studies in pedagogy; and studies in hagiography.

With the publication of *Essays on Woman,* the fifth volume in the authorized edition of *The Works of Edith Stein,* the editors now turn to her pedagogical writings. This volume contains a selection of papers on the theme of woman. This is, indeed, a theme with which Edith Stein was deeply occupied, but it was always in connection with educational problems. For that reason, an insight into Stein's entire work as an educator is necessary for us to understand fully and evaluate her doctrinal concepts concerning the genuine nature of femininity.

I. EDITH STEIN AS AN EDUCATOR

Her Educational Vocation

Edith Stein possessed inborn gifts for the teaching profession, gifts which were expressed in a spontaneous inclination to teach even in her youthful years. She had already attempted to teach less competent classmates when she was seventeen years old. When she began to study at the university level, she intended originally to plunge into psychological and pedagogical studies. In February of 1916, the final year of her doctoral program, she began her teaching career. She

1

was motivated in this by material reasons, but, as she herself explains, her joy and interest in teaching motivated her even more.[1] At that time, her approach in dealing with children and adolescents had become habitually that of the teacher.

Edith Stein's personality, in addition to her inborn gifts for teaching, possessed other character traits which destined her for the vocation of educator.

In her contact with people in general and with her students in particular, Edith Stein possessed an unusual *intuitive faculty* which made it possible for her to find her way into the depths of an unknown soul.

She was single-minded in her personal aspirations and also in her devotion to those entrusted to her guidance. The *strength of her will* rejected all sophistry. This established her authority and protected her from inconsequential actions.

Along with this, Edith Stein was indefatigable, capable of continuous intellectual work. Through long workdays, she habitually kept up a rapid pace. According to her own testimony, she drew this power of *inner concentration* from prayer, the fountain from which strength flows.[2]

From all of this, it becomes evident that in the sense of John Henry Cardinal Newman, nature and grace cooperate in Stein's personality to develop her inborn teaching gifts. Edith Stein knew and put into practice the Cardinal's moral claim "that grace doesn't destroy but perfects nature."[3] "We sometimes forget that we shall please Him best, and get more from Him . . . when we use what we have by nature to the utmost at the same time that we look out for what is beyond nature in the confidence of faith and hope."[4]

Thus, in her inner resoluteness, Edith Stein approached the ideal perspective and conduct of life of the religious educator. In her innermost soul she is open to the working grace, forming herself into a woman marked by complete outer and inner quietude.

As if on wings, she entered the classrooms inspired by the ideal that the noblest function of the professional woman is the education of the person in general and of woman in particular. The fruitfulness of her profession as a teacher was secured by her balanced temperament, her genuine knowledge, and her impersonal love for her pupils.

As a speaker, she appeared on the platform without fear but also without vanity to serve the cause of religious education with electrifying eloquence. She left the speaker's stand without being carried away by the applause of the audience or by the enjoyment of a personal success.[5]

In the evening hours, she would take up her pen, forgetting herself in the study of the eternal question of being and, in perfect self-detachment, giving herself to the Creator and glorifying Him.[6]

Educational Procedures

The educator can affect the pupil in three different ways: by the teaching word; by the pedagogical act; and by personal example.

Each one of these procedural methods serves the teacher in encouraging the student's inner participation in the educational process. For the potentialities of the teacher are limited to extraneous influence. The teacher can strive to elicit a response from the varying, deep spiritual state of the students; he can offer guidance and help to them. But the teacher's role in the formation of the students is an indirect one since all development is self-development. All training is self-training.[7]

It was characteristic of Edith Stein's personality that she made use of all three methods of effectual action. Edith Stein consecrated herself in full surrender to whatever she undertook; she explored it from every angle; she implemented it in every possible way.

She used both the spoken and written word not only in practical teaching in the school and in the teachers' college but also in planning and in bringing about educational reform.

After several temporary appointments at the girls' lyceum in Breslau, she spent a decade in teaching German at the Dominican institute in Speyer, which was a teachers' training college and girls' lyceum.

Then she was appointed as university lecturer at the German Institute for Scientific Pedagogy in Münster; because of the political upheaval in 1933, she was forced to relinquish this position after one-and-one-half years of teaching. She was specifically concerned here with feminine education.

Simultaneously with this professional activity in the junior high school[8] and in the academy, Edith Stein participated actively in the work of the Catholic school movement. In the course of the years, she became the intellectual leader of the Association of Catholic Women Teachers. She delivered lectures constantly at the annual meetings and conventions. She was consulted as advisor for the implementation of plans of reform and for pedagogical discussions with government officials.

Edith Stein's influence on her students as teacher and educator through her personal example can be substantiated by passages taken from her own writings. And corroboration is afforded by multiple evidence of former colleagues and students in this respect.

> The children in school . . . do not need merely what we *have* but rather what we *are*.

> The entire educational process must be carried out with *love* which is perceptible in every disciplinary measure and which does not instill any fear. And the most effective educational method is not the word of instruction but the *living example* without which all words remain useless.

> Whoever resorts regularly to the lessons of Holy Scripture as an apt pupil will take the Savior into *her* group, and the children will perceive that He is pre-

sent and that He assists in their work; thus, He will take possession of their souls. The soul formed by God's word acts spontaneously to form other souls in the same sense.[9]

Basic Educational Concepts

Education and the educator are an organic integrated whole. Education requires a goal-orientation by which the pupils' formation must be accomplished, and it requires a method which makes possible any effectual action on the student. The goal-orientation and method are not of absolute magnitude because education is entrusted to human hands. They vary depending on the educator's individuality. For the individual can never perform the educational process indifferently, i.e., separated from his or her concept of the world and attitude to the pupil. Whether or not they are acknowledged, the teacher's views and principles influence his reasoning and conduct. If these views and principles are lacking, then the teacher stands, as it were, before the anvil without a hammer. Perhaps he can make the iron red-hot, but he cannot forge it.

Thus there are concepts basic to all pedagogical activity which become the educator's leitmotif in the measure that they acquire actual significance for him.

There are three leading concepts in the intellectual background of Edith Stein's pedagogical activity: the necessity of a harmonious education; the religious foundation of educational action; and the proper nature of women's education. These concepts motivated Edith Stein as a teacher and university lecturer and indicate the focal point of her pedagogical interests.

The study of these leading concepts may be a valid introduction to the most profound character traits of her individuality.

Harmonious Education of the Person

The growing child is in radical need of education. He needs bodily and intellectual care. With regard to the former, the exterior and interior organs make their specific demands. As to the latter, the intellect and its aspirations (desires, emotions, and intentions), need guiding help. In the measure that education considers the various aspects of educational need and offers to the student the opportunity for development of his particular potentialities, it approaches the ideal of balance.

The concept of a harmonious educational process implies an all-round and balanced development encompassing all natural physical and psychic powers.

Historically, the ideal of a harmonious education originates from the Grecian ideal of the person formed in harmonious proportions physically and intellectually. In Christian religious thought, this concept results in the Thomistic teachings of God's image in creation and humanity.

From the conclusion of St. Thomas' *analogia entis,* Edith Stein borrowed the concept that God's image is like a seed planted in the human soul. In order to bring this inner form to development, the human creature needs formative help of two sorts: the supernatural aid of grace and the natural help of the human educational process. If pupils receive this help, they can by an inner dedication become more similar to the inborn ideal image.

Edith Stein views harmonious development as the essence of a fruitful educational process; she also views a significance of this harmony in its functional connections which enable all available faculties to exert a reciprocal influence on each other. A balanced development of one faculty is a favorable precondition for a corresponding development of other faculties. The equilibrium of all faculties advances the development of the single faculty.

The particular significance of harmonious development for religious education depends on this factor; the religious perspective furthers a wholeness of personality because prayer and God's service call upon the whole person to participation. An unbalanced development of personality may come about through a one-sided development of faculties and even by the absence of the means for proper development; this situation leads inevitably to conflicts or defects in religious attitude.

The Religious Foundation of Educational Activity

In line with the tradition of Christian Philosophy, Edith Stein considers the teaching profession as a religious calling. The teacher stands as a mediator between God and the student. He is expected to introduce the student to God's teachings and laws of creation and to lead him to the kingdom of God.

In the fulfillment of this role, there is a twofold vocation. The educator is called by God's mandate to open his pupil's soul to the workings of grace and, also, to develop the dormant powers of the soul in accordance with God's image.

The authority of the educator is founded on a metaphysical conception of the teaching profession and, following from this, the religious attitude of the educator to his pupil.

The teacher and the student serve and obey God. The teacher does not command arbitrarily but rather follows orders from above. The student does not submit himself to the teacher as to an arbitrarily fixed worldly authority; rather, he submits to that higher power which bestows on the teacher his position and rank.

Both the teacher's attachment to the student as well as the student's trusting devotion to the teacher are characterized by objective love. Such objective love draws the educator to the child. He wins the love of his pupils not for himself but to direct them to the proper object of the educational process—to the content of the curriculum.

As long as the teacher succeeds in stimulating the student's receptivity, as a person he recedes more and more into the background of the teaching process. From that time onward, the teacher tries with the help of the student to deflect the student's original, personal attachment toward the subject matter itself; thereby, the disciplines gain an enduring educational value for the student.

The Unique Character of Feminine Education

The educational ideal of the harmonious person is conditioned by the nature of the pupil. Therefore, education achieves the ideal of balance only when it is appropriate for the inner form of the pupil. Hence, ideally, the educator needs to adapt his concept of the harmonious person to the personality of the individual student, i.e., to visualize clearly the image that is suitable to the inner form of the student entrusted to him.

Edith Stein approaches the question of girls' education as a secondary teacher but that of the education of women as a university instructor. The aforesaid considerations of a rational pedagogy lead her to examine the nature and vocation of woman; she is able to establish thereby sound guiding principles for the theory and practice of feminine education.

Edith Stein discusses the nature and the vocation of woman concisely and conclusively in terms of " . . . what we are and what we should be."[10]

Her conclusive belief after deep ontological considerations is that the species *human being* is developed in a twofold form: the masculine and feminine species. Their difference is expressed in the whole structural essence of the person: this difference is deepened by individual deviations within both species. This further distinction according to natural predisposition effects the formation of types within the species.

Stein's analyses lead to the perception of

> . . . a threefold goal prescribed by the nature of
> woman: the development of her humanity, her
> womanhood, and her individuality. These are not
> separate goals, just as the nature of a particular
> human individual is not divided into three parts but
> is *one*: it is human nature of a specifically feminine
> and individual character.[11]

It is Edith Stein's view that theoretically the concept of
the perfected, unique type of feminine nature is based on the
truths of faith. This concept can be confirmed by philosophical considerations "insofar as they are qualified to penetrate the intellectual content of faith or to supplement what
this content leaves undecided."[12]

Because the human being possessed a perfect nature before the Fall of Man, Edith Stein concludes that the archetype
of perfect humanity came true in the human Person of Christ,
and the paragon of perfect womanhood materialized in the
form of Mary, the new Eve.

Recognition of the inner form of the feminine soul permits further inferences regarding woman's eternal and particular vocation. This vocation is of a twofold nature.

Woman's natural calling is that of wife and mother. To
be a wife is to be the husband's companion and, as such, to
support and safeguard her husband, her family, and the human community. To be a mother innately means to cultivate,
to guard, and to develop true humanity. "Both spiritual
companionship and spiritual motherliness are not limited to
the physical wife and mother relationship, but they extend to
all people with whom woman comes into contact."[13]

According to her supernatural calling, woman is chosen
"to embody in her highest and purest development the essence of the Church—to be its *symbol.*"[14]

In three different ways, woman can fulfill the mission
accorded to her by nature and grace and suitable to her individual disposition: in marriage; in the practice of a profession
which values human development as the noblest professional

activity of woman; and under the veil as the *Spouse of Christ.*

This in brief is Edith Stein's ideal of woman's spirituality, and she extolls the image of the *strong woman* in the Old Testament:

> A perfect wife—who can find her? She is far beyond the price of pearls.[15] (Prov. 31:10-11)

It is not only from her zealous studies of the Bible that Edith Stein came to know this image of the strong woman. She carried it in the innermost recesses of her heart. It is the image of her mother reflected simultaneously in her own nature as well; she placed this image before herself as a model to emulate in word and in deed from the time of her youth. As a mature woman, this image becomes a polestar for her and, ultimately, a guide for all feminine educational work.

Edith Stein's plans for pedagogical reform rest on these inquiries concerning the nature and the mission of woman. With her customary independence and thoroughness of thought, she develops an educational system which takes into consideration the unique characteristic and the intrinsic value of woman.

The author's statements, briefly summarized, offer the following guidelines and aids:

> The girl must be raised to perfect humanity. For this it is necessary that she be guided to "incorporation into the Mystical Body of Christ."[15]

> She must be educated to perfect womanhood. "Since Mary is the prototype of pure womanhood, the imitation of Mary must be the goal of girls' education."[17]

> Her uniqueness must be developed fully, for authentic educational work must consider the individuality of the person. Its goal is the person " . . . who is what *she* is supposed to be personally, who goes *her*

way, and performs *her* work. *Her* way is not chosen
in an arbitrary fashion; it is the way in which God
leads her."[18]

Two goal orientations are combined in the ideal of the
Virgin Mother *("Mater-Virgo")*: on the one hand, the mould-
ing of the woman's soul as wife and mother and, on the other
hand, as the bride of Christ. Therefore, the central problem
of the educational process consists in this: it must qualify the
girl for both marriage and the single life. It is evident from
Stein's commentaries on spiritual motherliness and on the
bride of Christ that both states cannot be interpreted in the
narrow sense of the married woman and the nun.

The order or precedence concerning subject matter must
be suitable to the specific needs of girls' education. Standards
for their proper evaluation are to be derived from woman's
nature and vocation. Three groups of citations may signify
the pedagogical views of Edith Stein:

> The emotions have been seen as the center of
> woman's soul. For that reason emotional formation
> will have to be centrally placed in woman's forma-
> tion . . .[19] however, such authentic formation is
> related to intellectual clarity and energy as well as
> to practical competence. This education forms a
> proper disposition of the soul in accordance with
> objective values, and it enables a practical execution
> of this disposition. To place supernatural values
> above all earthly ones complies with an objective
> hierarchy of values . . .[20] That is why the essence
> of all feminine education (as of education in general)
> must be religious education . . .[21]

> Because human development is the *most specific
> and exalted mission of woman,* studies in *anthropol-
> ogy* and *theory of pedagogy* are essential in girls'
> education.[22]

> [Subjects which can contribute to an awareness
> of humanity are] . . . history, literature, biology,
> psychology, and pedagogy; of course, these sub-

jects should be presented in a simplified form to meet the student's potential. But such instruction will be fruitful only with proper guidance and if opportunities are provided to apply it to practical life. Necessary to the intellectual development are the predominantly formal educational subjects— mathematics, the natural sciences, linguistics, and grammar. But they should not be overstressed at the expense of the student's capacity or the more essential elements of feminine education.[23]

. . . to extricate the purified valuable feminine character . . . every young girl should receive a basic vocational formation . . .[24] [With regard to the choice of vocation:] It seems right, therefore, that no legal barriers of any kind should exist. Rather, one can hope that a natural choice of vocation may be made thanks to an upbringing, education, and guidance in harmony with the individual's nature; unsuitable elements should be eliminated by strict objective requirements.[25]

In principle, an adequate educational process can be achieved only by persons who are themselves well-schooled and prepared for the teaching profession. Moreover, an indispensable basic principle must be acknowledged in light of woman's nature and vocation: only women and, indeed, only adequately prepared women are able to educate young girls to true womanhood. This is why " . . . the education of girls, which requires theoretical foundation as well as practical applications, is specifically a feminine responsibility."[26]

II. SIGNIFICANCE OF EDITH STEIN'S STUDIES ON WOMAN

Historical

A basic shift in the methods of psychology took place at

the turn of the twentieth century with the transition from Elemental to Gestalt Psychology. It was now preoccupied with the dynamic oneness which integrates objective psychic structures; an attempt was made to demonstrate the factors which bring about the formation of this unity and their coherence of meaning. The mechanistic interpretation of the psyche gave way to studies of the inner laws of intellectual functions. Instead of abstract, general images of humanity, there emerged concrete characteristic forms of the sexes, of varying age levels, of the phases of life, of professional categories, etc.

At the time Edith Stein addressed herself to studies of the feminine psyche as special consultant for problems of girls' education, but few psychological inquiries were available; and there were no preliminary works whatever written from a religious point of view on which she could base her findings. In different passages of her papers, she herself alluded to her first groping and probing as on *terra incognita.*[27]

Edith Stein ranks among those humanistic pioneers who were involved with the unique nature of woman's psyche. A lasting importance is attributed to her essays in the history of Differential Psychology.

Pedagogical

In her work as an instructor, Edith Stein was assigned to an educational system which was totally oriented to and coordinated with the intellectual needs of the masculine psyche. Any existing attempts to consider the expediency of feminine schooling as well were undertaken from the masculine point of view. Their efforts were not concerned with developing a young girl's unique nature but rather in forming her as a suitable companion of man.

Edith Stein's studies are focused on her perception of the unique characteristics and the intrinsic value of woman. The author points out that it is fundamentally necessary to give a girl an all-round education suitable to her feminine uniqueness. This position enabled Stein to challenge the existing system of girls' education: one-sided intellectual development should be replaced by an emotionally formative education; always, the different subjects of the curriculum should be so selected and handled that they advance the girl's spontaneous approach to living reality and to the individual.

Almost twenty-five years have passed since Edith Stein recorded her thoughts on feminine education and assumed her courageous stand against intellectualism in the system of higher education. Nevertheless, her essays remain innovative, and they are still directed fully to reality. She treats problems which more than ever today come to the fore in pedagogical discussions.

Stein's studies on woman offer pedagogical value: in her exposés, we find keen and realistic thought as well as a noble attitude of mind. Yet the full importance of these studies can be grasped clearly only from the religious viewpoint. In further remarks concerning a suitable education conforming to the feminine uniqueness, Edith Stein establishes that the religious factor is indispensable for any educational effort to cultivate the emotions. She points out that a girl's education to true womanhood necessitates a religious foundation and that this need is based on woman's nature itself. With these considerations, Edith Stein contributes decisive ideas to the Catholic school system in its objective: she reveals the motivation for religious education placed in the very nature of the pupil.

The Works of Edith Stein

Edith Stein's studies on woman owe their origin to her activity as a teacher: at St. Magdalena, the Dominican boarding school at Speyer; at the German Institute for Scientific Pedagogy at Münster; within the framework of the associations of Catholic teachers and academics. These essays occupy an intermediate position between the author's austere, scientific works and those written in a popular style.

The papers are the fruit of a long experience in teaching, of a profound and many-sided human awareness, and of a lifelong interest in the lot of woman. Their background is constituted by Stein's teachings on finite and infinite being, on the structure of the human person, and on the basic principles of cultural and educational work.

They form a coherent group of lectures and essays whose preparation afforded Edith Stein opportunity to apply her rare, versatile gifts simultaneously with her expertise. From these papers Edith Stein speaks as philosopher, psychologist, educator, and as a woman who is God-seeking and God-fulfilled.

III. AUTHENTICITY OF THE EDITION

The present volume of *The Works of Edith Stein* is made up of eight self-contained essays brought together by the editors under the title of *Essays on Woman*.

The individual articles are arranged thematically rather than chronologically; and together they present a synthesis of the teachings of Edith Stein on woman, her view of the problem of woman, and also the feminine ideal to which Edith Stein herself aspired.

In 1928, speaking during a pedagogic congress in Ludwigshafen,[28] Edith Stein launched a resounding challenge to educators; the last essay in this collection (dated 1932) reveals how Edith Stein's conceptions of the problems of woman's education had matured in the course of those few years. Even at the beginning of her career as a speaker at Ludwigshafen, Edith Stein's breadth and range of knowledge amazed her audience: her oratorial genius was astonishing; she had already developed a comprehensive system of ideas concerning the motivation and orientation of a system of feminine education.   This lecture at the congress gives a resumé of the problems which she was to treat more comprehensively in the essays which in the text precede the lecture given at Ludwigshafen. In reality, Edith Stein, consciously or unconsciously, drafted in this talk the *Five Years' Plan* of her collaboration with the reform of Catholic schools and with the Catholic Women's Movement.

The manuscripts are made up of the loose sheets retrieved from the ruins of the Carmel in Herkenbosch, Holland.[29]

All of these manuscripts were uncatalogued. After a thematic study of the pages and by a comparative examination of the paper and the handwriting, the original order of the manuscripts was secured.

The manuscripts are in the possession of the *Archivum Carmelitanum Edith Stein*. The essays contained in this volume follow the text of the manuscripts faithfully insofar as it is possible.

The following principles were adhered to in the revision of the manuscripts:

The title and subtitle provided a principle of organization for the text.

Excessively long paragraphs were broken up frequently into briefer ones.

Ambiguous sentence constructions were clarified.

Spelling, punctuation, and notes were standardized in accordance with current German usage.[30]

These changes of the original text have not been cited in the footnotes given for the individual essays.

The notes and explanations verifying the text may be arranged in the following four categories:

Historical provides all the data presently available at the Archives on the origin of the essays.

Archival Property specifies manuscripts, further authentic notes, etc., relating to the article and in the possession of the Archives.

First Publication informs the reader of specific data on the possibly prior publication of the article by the author herself. Further reprints by the original publisher or by other publishers were not taken into consideration. In the case of these reprints as well as their translations, we were consistently presented with the problem of authenticity.

Wording of the text explains the actual editing of the text. Deviations in the first printing from the wording of the text are also indicated here. The comparison was implemented by means of footnotes in this major text.

The Ethos of Women's Professions

Origin

The essay consists of the text of the lecture given by Edith Stein under the same title at the autumn convention of the Association of Catholic Academics. The meeting was held in Salzburg, August 30th to September 3rd, 1930; its topic was *Christ and the Vocational Life of the Modern Person.*

Archival Property

1. The manuscript of the lecture including the following title page:

The Ethos of Women's Professions

by

Dr. Edith Stein (Speyer on the Rhine)

Introduction: Ethos, Professional Ethos, Ethos of Women's Professions

   I.   Women's natural vocation and its corresponding ethos

   II.   Other "natural" feminine vocations

      1. Specifically feminine professions

      2. Formation for specifically feminine professions

III. The supernatural vocation of woman
  1. Development of vocations practiced in feminine conventual life
  2. Existing harmony between the conventual vocation and the feminine spirit; conventual ethos—woman's vocational ethos
  3. Means toward attainment of the feminine ethos
    a. Contradiction between the average woman's life and the feminine vocation to which she is called
    b. Eucharistic life
    c. Liturgical life
Conclusion: Summary and completion

Paper: 46 single pages 21 by 16½ cm.
Script: Roman type written in ink on one side of each page.

2. An outline of the basic plan for this essay dated July 20th, 1930. In substance the outline is consistent with the above-mentioned title page; nevertheless, it also contains a heading for a more extensive passage on the "natural vocation of man."[31]

Paper: a note page from a note pad 19 by 11 cm. with writing on both sides of the page.
Script: Roman type, small ink and pencil.

3. A review of the lecture by Dr. Vierneisel in the October 1, 1930 issue of the *Heidelberg Bote:* This newsclip was discovered during the examination of Edith Stein's posthumous works. Since Dr. Vierneisel's statements provide valuable supplementary information, we cite the following excerpt:

At the Salzburg convention, one woman made an unforgettable impression. By chance, her significant lecture was delivered at the beginning of the session devoted to the topic to be developed, before the discussion centered on individual vocations. This woman is Edith Stein. She lives in our neighborhood.

She instructs future women teachers at a teacher's college conducted by Dominican nuns in Speyer, and she corrects about one hundred essays each month. Her philosophical works are marked by their quality and distinction. When one reads them—for instance, a treatise on the relation of Thomistic philosophy to Husserl's phenomenological philosophy from whose school she stems, one is convinced that this woman is destined to make contributions for Catholic Germany of even greater importance than the significant ones she has already made. Another marvel is that we can expect shortly her translation and adaptation of one of St. Thomas' main philosophical works, *De veritate,* in two heavy volumes. In Salzburg, she spoke on *The Ethos of Women's Professions.* At the end of her direct but consistently captivating exposition of 1½ hours, she wisely mentioned that, properly speaking, the ethos of masculine vocations should also be discussed. Manifesting brilliant reflection, she inferred from a formulated truth of St. Thomas, *"anima forma corporis"* (the soul is the formative principle of the body), that inasmuch as the feminine body is a feminine body, this feminine body must also correspond to a feminine soul just as the masculine body must correspond to a masculine soul. Hence, the feminine psychic attitude with its perceptive and loving focus on the personal and the whole is a necessary attitude for the development of humanity. And it is also needed in order to recognize what lies dormant in the individual, to have an open mind, and to practice a self-effacing love. This is precisely the basic attitude of woman. From this stems her vocation as "man's companion" and also the reality of her maternal attitude toward her husband. Her gift for empathy can also be developed in matters which in themselves are foreign to the feminine nature as long as these matters are of a personal nature. The desire to cooperate in such a beneficial manner exists in every person, and this desire fulfills one of the higher functions of education. But this feminine quality for the personal is often accompanied by well-known femi-

nine defects: an overemphasis on the personal and
the desire to possess people for oneself. The integral
feminine nature lives in Mary as wife and mother:
she never asserts a proprietary right toward her son;
as wife, she has a limitless trust and practices com-
pliant submission suitable to her conviction that her
husband was given to her by God.

Are there feminine vocations other than the
maternal one? All history testifies that a woman can
function in other vocations as well. But if at any
time a woman reveals herself capable of another
vocation, that still does not mean that it is primarily
a feminine one such as, for example, teaching or
nursing. In scholarship, woman is particularly endowed in fields which involve the living personality
as in history, literature, art, etc. Indeed, any vocation which involves service to others can be considered *feminine*. Thus, woman is qualified as editor,
translator, adviser in scientific work, and in university teaching. But the feminine make-up can also
adapt itself to essentially masculine vocations; for
instance, office work affords the possibility for a
utilization of feminine assets, as in the case when the
woman as colleague is supportive, helping the man
to overcome the difficulties of his vocation. Also,
woman is more able than man to keep in mind the
importance of the personal and subjective bent even
in apparently objective work.

Indeed, feminine nature in its purity can embrace all things, and the image of God's Mother at
the Wedding of Cana is a perfect example of this:
how discreetly she prevents the embarrassment of
others; how she discerns where there is need; how
she intervenes without being observed. Such a woman is pertinent at all times like a good genius.

With regard to the vocation of women in religious orders, there is in itself scarcely any difference
between the supernatural vocation of man and that
of woman, for contemplation and solemn praise of
God are above natural differences. To be sure, there
does exist an inner harmony between the ethos of
the religious and the feminine ethos insofar as both

vocations require the renunciation of the individual will. It is only the newer orders with their practical functions which have the appearance of being specifically feminine.

Of course, the average woman today finds herself in a serious situation. She bears the unnatural double burden of marriage and a profession. Moreover, she has a tendency to be guided by her moods at all times, in marriage and divorce, in education, in profession—our perverted feminine educational system carries a share of the guilt here. Finally, woman is often oppressed in the end by a feeling of emptiness and dissatisfaction in a freely chosen vocation because, in most part, she neglects to fulfill her feminine role.

Edith Stein's lecture was most convincing because it was free of the pathos of the *feminist movement* and because the speaker herself markedly and visibly personified her own thoughts. Her bearing when she descended from the podium recalled those paintings in which ancient masters depicted Mary's visit to the temple.

4. The above-mentioned memo pad (see point 2) included an outline (dated 1929) on the Catholic woman's mission. The outline contains the essential ideas which are expressed in this lecture ("Ethos") and which also reappear constantly in later studies.

Nov. 21, 1929

Not a history of the feminist movement nor a critique of its errors but rather an interpretation of woman's mission as performed by the Virgin, Mother, and Queen.

Woman's vocation in the religious life and in marriage; her efficacy in public life.

   I.   Image: *Mary's Offering*

       In a depraved era, to devote one's life to God's priase and liturgical service, to intercessory prayer, and to self-sacrifice as supplication and expiation.

  II.   Image: *Bethlehem and Nazareth*

Marriage for the sake of the child. Obedient to
husband as head of the family. Child not a personal
possession but sent from God for God.

III.   Image: *Mary, Heart of the First Christian Community*
Woman in the school: as teacher and as maternally
oriented mentor.

Social work: Christian service to the troublesome
and burdened.

Delegates, government officials: the maternal perspective in public service.

At home, at the office—woman is to carry the spirit
of Christ everywhere.

Mary unites all women everywhere: her freely chosen virginity which is intended by God, accepted
from Him, and preserved in marriage; her maternal
attitude in every situation; queen as bride of the
King and by her altruistic love. Women of Corinth.
Agents of Christ, chosen not by established custom
but rather freely elected in His love (Gertrude,
Teresa, Margaret Mary, Catherine of Siena, Bridget).
The spouse of Christ.

Paper: a page from a note pad 19½ by 11 cm.
written on both sides.

Script: Roman type, ink.

First Publication

1930 in *Der katholische Gedanke,* 1930 No. 4.
1931 as a booklet by Haas and Grabherr in Augsburg.

Wording of the Text

The wording in the first publication corresponds to the
words in the manuscript.

Headings found in the title page of the manuscript were
utilized in the edition of the main text.

The Separate Vocations of Man and Woman According to Nature and Grace

Origin

As Edith Stein indicates in her essay "Spirituality of the Christian Woman," this essay is based on her research on the goal of education for Christian women.[32]

The name of the author does appear on the otherwise undated title page.

Based on the script, type of paper, and literary data found in the commentary, it may be concluded that the study was written in 1931.

Archival Property

1. The manuscript of the essay.

   Paper: 90 single pages 21 by 16½ cm.
   This appears on the backside of a carbon copy of the typewritten pages of Stein's studies, *Eine Untersuchung über den Staat* and *Des. Hl. Thomas von Aquino Untersuchungen über die Wahrheit.*

   Script: Roman type written in ink on one side of each page.

2. A note pad with the inscription "Man and Woman's Calling According to the Old Testament."

   Paper: 28 note pages from a note pad 12 by 6 cm. written on both sides.
   Script: Roman type, pencil.

Besides excerpts from the Old Testament, the notes contain the outline of her ideas about the particular receptivity of feminine nature for that which is morally good and divine; from this receptivity devolves the function of moral and religious education for women and activities for their formation.

Edith Stein used this material word for word in her preparation of the manuscript.[33]

First Publication

January, 1932, in the journal *Die Christliche Frau* in Cologne.

Wording of the Text

The text of the first publication corresponds to that of the manuscript.

Data concerning the manuscript's title: the manuscript was found in a folder upon which the title was written in Edith Stein's own handwriting; it is labeled in ink "The Separate Vocations of Man and Woman According to Nature and Grace" and in pencil "Dr. Edith Stein" was added. On the first page of the manuscript, there is a heading in ink which was struck out: "The Masculine and Feminine Calling and its Development in Professional Life." Since it is clear that Edith Stein herself crossed out this heading, this present edition makes use of the title appearing on the folder.

Spirituality of the Christian Woman

Origin

The draft of this study is based on a cycle of four lectures given by Edith Stein in Zürich during January, 1932 for the Organization of Catholic Women.

Archival Property

1. Manuscript of the essay with the following title page:
   Spirituality of the Christian Woman

4 lectures
given for the Organization of Catholic Women in
Zürich
in January, 1932
by
Dr. Edith Stein

Paper: 104 single pages 15 by 21 cm.
Script: Roman type written in ink on one side
of each page.

2. Notes and excerpts taken from specialized literature
relevant to the subject.

She cites among others the following:

Hedwig Conrad-Martius, "L'existence, la substantialité et l'âme," *Recherches Philosophiques*
(1932-1933).

Rudolf Peil, *Konkrete Mädchenpädagogik* (1932)

Rudolf Allers, *Zur Charakterologie der Geschlechter* (1930).

Paper: (a) note pages from a note pad 17 by 10
cm. labelled "Girls' Education," written
on both sides.
(b) loose notes written on slips of paper
and on the reverse side of letters or pages
taken from exercise books.
Script: Roman type, ink and pencil.

Penciled annotations and marks in a handwriting other
than Edith Stein's as well as finger prints on the edges and
reverse sides of the pages indicate that Edith Stein's handwritten manuscript was in the process of revision in view of
future publication.

Further specifications are lacking as to why it remained
unpublished.[34]

Wording of the Text

The text is in the authentic handwriting of Edith Stein.

The above-mentioned annotations and changes were not taken into consideration.

Fundamental Principles of Women's Education

Origin

The article is a development of a subject presented by Edith Stein in a lecture to the educational committee of the Federation of German Catholic Women on November 8th, 1930 at Bendorf on the Rhine.

An addition to the lecture is given in the manuscript *Wege zur inneren Stille,* a letter written by Edith Stein in a monthly series for the "Societas Religiosa," a group of working women living by a religious rule.

Archival Property

1. The manuscript of the essay. The title on page one originally read *Women's Education;* this was replaced by *Fundamental Principles of Women's Education* in Edith Stein's handwriting. The conclusion of the manuscript was written on the inside of a double sheet which served also as a folder for the other sheets. The cover page contains the following annotation written in pencil by someone else.

Article in the March, 1931 issue of *Stimmen der Zeit.*
Fundamental Principles of
Women's Education

Proof (3 copies) with manuscript to Dr. Edith Stein at St. Magdalena in Speyer.

One copy for us.

Paper: 41 single pages and 1 double sheet, 21 by 16½ cm.

Script: Roman type written in ink on one side of each page.

2. A separate reprint by Herder in Freiburg im Breisgau of the article from *Stimmen der Zeit,* monthly review of contemporary intellectual life, March 1931 No. 6.

> Description: small separate fascicle, 26 by 17½ cm., numbered pp. 413-424 on one side of each page.

3. Supplementary comments to the lecture dated St. Lioba, January 12, 1932.

> Paper: 10 single pages 15 by 21 cm.
> Script: Roman type written in ink on one side of each page.

4. A note page outlining the following:

September 16

Women's Education

I.   What kind of education is suitable to woman's nature and function?
II.   What demands do our times make
    1.   On woman as an individual
    2.   On woman as a citizen
III. What would be the useful method for us to adopt?

I.   *Attitude Toward the Maternal Role of Woman*
      Practical rather than theoretical training in:
          Hygiene
          Study of adolescence
          Understanding economics
          Understanding political-social life
          The formation of ethical-religious life
III. *An Experimental or Model School:*[35]
      According to Montessori principles applied on every level. Possibility of transferring to vocational schools through special courses.
      Education, woman's natural disposition, the fulfillment of her natural disposition through the educational methods advocated below:

> Housekeeping
> Personal grooming
> Spiritual and intellectual formation:
>> Psychology
>> Training of her faculties
>> Insight into the intellectual world
>> Religious education

> Paper: 1 single page 13 by 8 cm.
> Script: Roman type written in pencil on both sides of the page.

First Publication

1931 Essay in *Stimmen der Zeit,* 1931 No. 6
1932 A supplement to the above essay entitled *Wege zur inneren Stille* in the monthly journal of the "Societas Religiosa," Catholic Women's Movement, Zürich, February 1932.

Wording of the Text

The wording of the separate reprint concurs with the handwritten outline.

As compared to the manuscript of the essay, only a few passages in *Wege zur inneren Stille* were either cut or changed, but these changes were not taken into consideration. The text of the essay in the present edition corresponds to that of the manuscript.

Problems of Women's Education

Origin

When Edith Stein was appointed as lecturer at the German Institute for Scientific Pedagogy (summer semester of

1932), she was commissioned to handle the problem of women's education. The present essay was composed on the basis of the manuscript of these lectures which the author revised for publication subsequently. A note pad of Edith Stein leads us to infer that the course was entitled "Problems of Contemporary Girls' Education."

Archival Property

1. Manuscript of the essay. It contains:
   Chapter 1: the folder contains the table of contents and fragments of the text (pp. 1-2, 32-76).
   Chapter 2: the folder contains the complete text (pp. 1-70), together with the table of contents.
   Chapter 3: the folder contains the complete text (pp. 1-50), together with the table of contents.
   Chapter IV: the folder contains the complete text (pp. 1-47); table of contents missing.
   Chapter V: the folder contains the complete text (pp. 1-48), together with the table of contents.
   Chapter VI: empty folder.

   Paper: 250 single pages, 6 double sheets 21 by 16½ cm., 4 slips of paper (Table of Contents) about 16½ by 10½ cm.
   Script: the manuscript pages are written in ink on one side of each page. On the 4 slips of paper there is writing on both sides.

2. A typescript of the second chapter with the author's handwritten revisions.

   Paper: 20 single pages in 4°.
   Script: there are typed pages and also pages written in ink, Roman type, on one side of each page.

3. A separate printing of Chapters 1, 2 and 3 from the *Benediktinische Monatschrift* zur Pflege religiösen und geisti-

gen Lebens (Benedictine Journal for the Fostering of Religious and Intellectual Life) XIV (1932) No. 9-10 and 11-12; XV (1933) No. 1-2 and 3-4.

Description: separate fascicle 22½ by 15½ cm.

First Publications

1932 in *Benediktinische Monatschrift,* XIV, No. 9-10 and 11-12, Chapter I.

1933 Ibid., XV, No. 1-2 and 3-4, Chapters II and III.

Important Note: Chapters IV and V are as yet unpublished. For Chapter VI see the following essay: "The Church, Woman, and Youth."

Wording of the Text

The text of the essay exists in three forms: the original manuscript of the lectures; the manuscript incorporating subsequent changes for publication; the printed articles in the Benedictine monthly journal.

The editor had adopted the revision intended for publication of the original manuscript. However, differences of content between the original manuscript of the lectures and the printed copy in *Benediktinische Monatschrift* from this revised manuscript are indicated by footnotes. Subsequent revisions of style and structure were not called to the reader's attention. The numbering of chapters follows the original data on the folders and tables of content.

The Church, Woman and Youth

Origin

In 1931, Edith Stein gave a lecture at Augsburg of which

the theme was "The Church, Woman, and Youth." The existing pages are, as we are to understand from the title, the manuscript of this lecture. More approximate historical data is missing.

There exists also the following connection between these pages and the sixth chapter of the essay "Problems of Women's Education."

As noted above, while reconstituting the text of the essay "Problems of Women's Education," a folder was discovered indicating that a sixth chapter with the title "Incorporation of Woman into the Mystical Body of Christ" was envisaged. The pages of the Augsburg lecture correspond to the missing pages of Chapter 6. Irrespective of insignificant variations, the wording of these pages is identical with the publication of Chapter VI under the same title in the Benedictine journal cited below.

Did the author remove the manuscript of her Münster lecture from the folder for the Augsburg presentation? Or did she assimilate the Augsburg paper into her study on the problems of women's education? The paper and type face permit us to presume that the pages originated from the manuscript of the Münster lecture and originally carried the title of the Augsburg lecture.

Archival Property

1. The manuscript of the essay with the following title on the first page:

The Church, Woman, and Youth

      Paper: 50 single pages 21 by 16½ cm.
      Script: Roman type written in ink on one side
             of each page.

2. Printed copy from the *Benediktinische Monatschrift zur Pflege religiösen und geistigen Lebens*, XV (1933), No. 11 -12.

Description: Separate fascicle 22½ by 15½ cm.
numbered pp. 412-425 on one side
of each page.

First Publication

1933   in *Benediktinische Monatschrift*, XV, No. 11-12.

Wording of the Text

This edition of the essay is based on the manuscript.
Deviations from the manuscript in the printed text were
indicated by footnotes.

The Significance of Woman's
Intrinsic Value in National Life

Origin

The pages of the existing manuscript contain the text of
the introductory paper which Edith Stein read at the request
of the executive board of the Association of Bavarian Catholic Women Teachers at its fifteenth convention in Ludwigshafen on the Rhine on April 12, 1928.

Archival Property

1. The manuscript of the lecture entitled:
    The Significance of Woman's Intrinsic Value
    in National Life
    Lecture given at the 15th convention
    of the Bavarian Catholic Women Teachers
    in Ludwigshafen on the Rhine
    on April 12, 1928
    by
    Dr. Edith Stein (Speyer)

Paper: 10 single pages 33 by 21 cm.
Script: Roman type written in ink on both sides
of each page.

2. A typed summary of the lecture with the same title
is quoted below because it gives not only a survey of the
range of ideas in the paper but also gives a glimpse of the
nimble mentality with which the author is endowed, here as
thinker, there as speaker.

The Significance of Woman's Intrinsic Value
in National Life
by
Dr. Edith Stein

In the *beginning of the feminist movement,* it would
hardly have been imaginable to consider this theme. At that
time, the struggle for "Emancipation" was taking place; i.e.,
actually the goal aspired to was that of *individualism:* to enable women's personalities to function freely by the opening
up of all avenues in education and in the professions. The
Suffragettes erred so far as to deny the *singularity* of woman
altogether; thus, it could hardly be a question of woman's
intrinsic value as well. These excesses were resolved with the
fulfillment of feminist claims which became "faits accomplis"
since we now have years of experience in the most diverse
areas of professional life. It is accordingly characteristic of
our times that:

1. The obvious phenomenon of *woman's singularity* is
an accepted reality.

2. There is a conviction that this singularity possesses an
intrinsic value.

3. Contemporary social attitudes indicate the trend
toward *utilizing this intrinsic value in the service of the national community.*

I

Woman's intrinsic value must be investigated in relation
to her unique nature. Only the person who has shut his eyes
to the simplest facts of experience could deny this unique-

ness. And many a woman inclined to do so was perhaps made painfully aware of her singularity if she entered one of the traditionally *masculine* professions and was forced into conditions of life and work alien to her nature. Perhaps, if her nature was strong enough, she succeeded in converting the *masculine* profession into a *feminine* one. We might begin our inquiry of these differences on the basis of practical experience (Differential Psychology has been occupied especially with this line of inquiry), emphasizing essential characteristics of the nature of woman as related to her intrinsic value.

1. Her *point of view embraces the living and personal* rather than the objective.

2. She tends towards *wholeness and self-containment* in contrast to one-sided specialization.

Both characteristics have a twofold tendency. First, the desire to assert her *own* identity is accompanied by an overweening interest in persons *outside* of herself. Moreover, her desire to develop herself and to assume an active role as a complete human being is accompanied by the wish to help others to become complete human beings and to treat them as such.

Both characteristics have their drawbacks: lack of objectivity, too much interest in personalities, and superficiality. Woman's intrinsic value can be developed only when these drawbacks are overcome, and we shall indicate specific means for doing so.

II

This intrinsic value consists chiefly in the ability:

1. To become a *complete person* oneself; i.e., a person all of whose faculties are developed and coexist in harmony;

2. To help others to become *complete human beings;*

3. In all contact with other persons, *to respect the complete human being.*

Certain *maladies of modern culture* such as the dehumanization of the person, fragmentation, and the one-sided development of certain faculties leading to the atrophy of others may be *cured* through recourse to the intrinsic value of woman.

III

Woman's *intrinsic value* can contribute productively to the *national community* by her activities *in the home as well as in professional and public life.*

1. The nation needs her services sorely as *a mother* and as a *professional educator* in helping others to attain to total humanity. Such a woman is like a seminal spore bringing new life to the national body. At the same time, she is protected naturally against the poison infecting the body of our society.

2. The experience of recent years has shown that in addition to those professions which have been recognized traditionally as feminine, other professions must be opened up to woman if she is to perform the service of helping other persons *to become complete human beings.* In the *medical profession,* for example, woman with her desire for wholeness can counterbalance the drawback of one-sided specialization; also, the woman doctor is equipped to give the patient the needed human sympathy while preserving the objectivity required for diagnosis and therapy of the whole psychosomatic system. And then, the social services, concerned with meeting human wants, can succeed only when the whole person is considered in relation to social conditions. Finally, the innate sympathy of woman serving in public life in the legislature or as a member of government is able to counterbalance excessively abstract procedures of the bureaucracy.

3. Quite outside of her professional activity, in *no matter what sphere of life* she finds herself, woman can direct her efforts to the furtherance of total humanity. She finds the opportunity to influence others, no matter where she meets them, through her active interest and her own example.

To attain such good results, first of all, the defects of woman's *unique nature* must be purified in terms of her *intrinsic value* so that she herself is a completely formed human being, a mature and self-contained personality. Every employment which requires objectivity of her is a good corrective for her *hyper-feminine* nature: it cures her from excessive concern with her own personal worth; also, it overcomes errors of judgment leading to an abject surrender to another human being. Therefore, each fundamental vocational formation and professional activity has its validity in obtaining this objectivity. However, such objectivity is insufficient in itself. The danger lies in changing over to the *hyper-masculine* type of abstract objectivity and in suppressing the drive towards total humanity. A certain detachment from oneself and from others as well is needed to gain a clear insight into the proper relation between personal and objective values and to maintain a balanced view of one's personal uniqueness and the possibilities of development of oneself and of others. These results above all are not obtained naturally through learning and will. In order for human faculties to be properly balanced, they must all be drawn together by a magnet which through its own power endows them with harmony. And what is this magnet? It is the highest good, the measure for all objective as well as for all personal values.

Our understanding of the mystery of God made man enables us to overcome all false conceptions and presents to us a human image through which we can measure objectively our own nature and that of others. Our love for Him can give us the strength to withstand the temptation of an abject surrender which denigrates both judgment and will. Thus, only through knowledge of and love for God can the right personal attitude be won, and in this attitude we find woman's unique nature purified to its intrinsic value. However, knowledge and love of God is won only by a continuous, intimate communion with Him, most surely through a liturgical life. *That* woman who, everywhere she goes, brings along with her the Savior and enkindles love for Him will fulfill her *feminine* vocation in its purest form. Basically, therefore, woman's *intrinsic value* lies in making room within herself for God's being and works, and she does so by over-coming the drawbacks of her *unique nature.*

> Paper: 5 single pages 38 by 21 cm.
> Script: copy of typescript with penciled changes made in Edith Stein's handwriting.

3. A copy of the journal *K.b.J.L.,* the edition for young people, No. 5, July 1, 1928 in which the lecture was published.

> Description: 2 double sheets (small fascicle), 32 by 24½ cm.

First Publication

    1928   in *K.b.J.L.,* the edition for young people, July 1, 1928, No. 5.

Wording of the Text

The contents of the publication conform to the manu-script. The present edition is based on the text of the hand-written manuscript.

Challenges Facing Swiss Catholic Academic Women

Origin

Edith Stein gave a lecture tour in Switzerland during January, 1932. The manuscript in question is most likely the rough sketch of her lecture in Zürich.

Archival Property

1. An outline of the ideas in the lecture titled: "Challen-ges Facing Swiss Catholic Academic Women." The manu-

script is both undated and unsigned.

> Paper: 9 single pages 27½ by 21½ cm.
> Script: typescript (copy).

2. An undated draft titled: "Mission of the Catholic Academic Woman." The signature—Dr. Edith Stein, Münster in Westfalen—as well as the paper and typeface allow us to infer that this draft is in the context of the lecture tour in Switzerland.

Wording of the Manuscript

Mission of the Catholic
Academic Woman

Today, the admission of women into the university has become problematic again to a degree which we would have considered completely impossible a few years ago. Its justification was attacked with the old arguments with which we are familiar from the beginning of the feminist movement, and forceful power factions are behind this attack. We witnessed the downfall of the secular feminist movement's idealistic beginnings—idealism, individualism, and liberalism—which had been a source of great inspiration at the time of its inception; since that time, the movement has been progressively crushed by new ideology in the universities as well as in political life.

The roots of the Catholic Women's Movement were somewhat different. Thirty years ago, Joseph Mausbach was one of the first to speak out in public from a Catholic perspective on the feminist issue; he said then, "Although we seem to come later, in reality we were there earlier." And in the same vein, we dare to say "We stand our ground in the arena although no one else does." Our foundation cannot tremble because we have built on solid ground. Our guiding star is not the liberal ideal of humanity and femininity conditioned by time. Rather, our ideal is one which exists prior to all time and which will endure for all time. Woman is created by God to stand by her husband's side, to stand with him over and above all other creatures; she is bound to him as the helpmate who corresponds to him in an enduring, indissoluble coexistence. They are charged—and the woman is in more specific ways—to beget and rear children not only in strength, health, and fitness for life but as citizens of God's kingdom. God has fashioned the conjugal tie as the means of sanctifying both spouses.

The Church expresses the *threefold purpose of marriage* in the words *"fides," "proles,"* and *"sacramentum."* It is necessary today to preserve this traditional conception of marriage against the pressure of public opinion which has undermined mere middle-class morality. It is a vital question for our nation and the entire human race that the Church's conception stay preserved. It can be preserved on no theoretical foundation other than the teachings of the Catholic faith. In order that it be so preserved, women must grasp this concept in the depths of their being and live accordingly; they must brave the onslaught of contemporary opinion and help their sisters to do likewise. Therein lies the mission of the Catholic woman educator, physician, and social worker.

There can be no loftier nor holier concept of marriage than that of our Church. But the Church knows something even more exalted. The woman presented to our vision as the image of maternity for all times had decided to belong to no man; such an attitude was against all traditions of her people. She placed her whole being in the service of the Lord. Thus did she become the prototype of *virginity which is consecrated to God,* the prototype of the *Spouse of Christ.* The highest form of life to which one can be called is a life of eternal union with God. It is the vocation of each human soul, it is the mission of the Church. But no one embodies it more forcefully than the woman whose entire life is devoted to the service of the Lord.

We are not talking simply about those who have embraced the religious life. The lot of more and more women today is to lead a solitary life in the world. Whether they pursue a profession only to earn a living or to lose themselves in work through lack of something better, it is in the long run a grueling, exhausting struggle. But if they perceive in the external providential dispensations God's call inviting them to dedicate all their faculties to Him, and if they follow this call, then their lives as women become full and fruitful. This will be a life of love, a life in which all faculties come to development. It will be a spiritual maternity because the love of the bride of God embraces all the children of God.

This is the second ideal which we must preserve. Again, we need women who dedicate their lives to the purpose of educating youth, women who are fully aware of the teachings of the faith and of its historical background. Their intent will be to form a generation which is happy in faith and strong in spirit, a generation which is prepared and ready for both marriage in the highest and purest sense and for virginity dedicated to God according to the model and under the guidance of the Virgin Mother.

Dr. Edith Stein (Münster in Westfalen).

Paper: 6 single pages 21½ by 17 cm.
Script: Roman type written in ink on one side of each page.

First Publication

Both manuscripts are unpublished.

Wording of the Text

The text of Edith Stein's manuscripts are reproduced literally.[36]

Dr. L. Gelber

Chapter I

The Ethos of
Women's Professions

INTRODUCTION: ETHOS, PROFESSIONAL ETHOS, ETHOS OF WOMEN'S PROFESSIONS

The literal meaning of the word "ethos" in its enduring sense must be understood in its relation to human action. By that I do not mean a decree imposed from without upon the person but rather something which is operative within himself, *an inner form,* a constant *spiritual attitude* which the scholastics term *habitus.* Such constant spiritual attitudes give a definite uniform character to changing behavioral patterns, and the attitudes manifest themselves through this character in external action. Temperament is an *inborn habitus,* a natural basic disposition of the soul such as cheerfulness or melancholy. There are attitudes acquired on the basis of natural tendencies; here all natural proficiencies and virtues are important. There is, finally, the established *habitus:* these are, above all, the divine virtues which constitute the holiness of a human being. And just as these virtues can be acquired, so can they also be lost; they do not belong to the soul permanently since they are modified easily.

Along with ethos, this general concept of *habitus* is made specific by focusing on *values.* To speak of ethos is to designate *habitus,* one or several, which possess positive value and satisfy certain objective requirements or prescriptions.

By *professional ethos* I mean to signify the abiding spiritual attitude or the totality of *habitus* which emerges from within as the formative principle in a person's professional life. We are able to speak of this ethos only when the professional life demonstrates objectively a definite uniform character. Indeed, this character emerges as a moral force from within; it is not imposed upon the professional life from without either by the authenticity of the work itself or other regulations. Loyalty and conscientiousness are among such abiding attitudes which can be decisive for professional life. A person's attitude toward his or her profession clearly helps determine the results achieved in it. Whoever regards his work as a mere source of income or as a pastime will perform it differently from the person who feels that his *profession* is an authentic vocation. Strictly speaking, we can only accept the term "professional ethos" in this last instance.

Finally, we must recognize that every profession has an ethos peculiar to its own purpose. (This is somewhat like the helpfulness of the nurse, the circumspection and determination of the undertaker, etc.) The ethos can be displayed by the person's nature (that is, he has a natural inclination for his profession); or, it can grow in him through constant practice of its required activities; and then it can become a standard of behavior independent of external control.

When this evening's topic was suggested to me, it precluded two suppositions: first, that certain abiding attitudes are unique to the feminine soul and form woman's professional life from within out; second, that the very nature of woman draws her to certain professions. Let us now discuss these two points.

I. WOMAN'S NATURAL VOCATION AND ITS CORRESPONDING ETHOS

Are we able to speak of vocations which are specifically feminine? In the beginning of the feminist movement, the radical leaders denied this, claiming that all professions were suitable for woman. Their opponents were unwilling to admit to this concept, recognizing only *one* feminine vocation, *woman's natural vocation*. Our subject requires discussion of both points of view. To begin with, we must ask: Is there a natural feminine vocation of woman? What spiritual attitude does it demand?

Only the person blinded by the passion of controversy could deny that woman in soul and body is formed for a particular purpose. The clear and irrevocable word of Scripture declares what daily experience teaches from the beginning of the world: woman is destined to be wife and mother. Both physically and spiritually she is endowed for this purpose, as is seen clearly from practical experience. However, it follows also from the Thomistic principle of *anima forma corporis* that such a spiritual characteristic does exist. Of course, woman shares a basic human nature, but basically her faculties are different from men; therefore, a differing type of soul must exist as well. Since the fundamentals of the typically feminine spiritual attitude are quite familiar to us, we will trace it only very briefly.

Woman naturally seeks to embrace that which is *living, personal, and whole*. To cherish, guard, protect, nourish and advance growth is her natural, maternal yearning. Lifeless matter, the *fact*, can hold primary interest for her only insofar as it serves the living and the personal, not ordinarily for its own sake. Relevant to this is another matter: *abstraction in every sense* is alien to the feminine nature. The living and personal to which her care extends is a concrete whole and is protected and encouraged as a totality; this does not mean that one part is sacrificed to another, not the mind to the body or one spiritual faculty at the expense of the others. She aspires to this totality in herself and in others. Her theoretical and her practical views correspond; her natural line of thought is not so much conceptual and analytical as it is directed intuitively and emotionally to the concrete. This natural endowment enables woman to guard and teach her own children. But this basic attitude is not intended just for them; she should behave in this way also to her husband and to all those in contact with her.

This maternal gift is joined to that of *companion*. It is her gift and happiness to share the life of another human being and, indeed, to take part in *all things* which come his way in the greatest and smallest things, in joy as well as in suffering, in work, and in problems. Man is consumed by "his enterprise," and he expects others will be interested and helpful; generally, it is difficult for him to become involved in other beings and their concerns. On the contrary, it is natural for woman, and she has the faculty to interest herself empathetically in areas of knowledge far from her own concerns and to which she would not pay heed if it were not that a personal interest drew her into contact with them. This endowment is bound closely to her maternal gift. An active sympathy for those who fall within her ken awakens their powers and heightens their achievements. It is a concerned, formative and truly maternal function, precisely one which even the *adult* needs. This function will come into play also with one's own children, especially when they mature and the mother is released from their physical care.

Participation in her husband's life requires *subordination and obedience* as directed by God's work. It is in accordance with nature that man serve his concern directly. The wife serves his cause for his sake; thus, it is reasonable that this happen under his guidance. That the duty of obedience extends also to the wife's immediate domain—the household and the upbringing of children—is probably derived less from the feminine individuality than from the *natural vocation of man* as guide and protector of his wife. The natural vocation corresponds also to woman's natural tendency towards obedience and service: "Obedient I feel my soul, always most beautifully free."

At the onset, this presentation of the natural feminine individuality did not include any value judgment. It is evident without further elaboration that the purely developed feminine nature does include a sublime *vital value*.   It is essential for this vital value as well as for *ethical value,* which we will soon consider, that the feminine nature be developed purely, and in no way does this come about as a matter of course.   One can even go so far as to say that it is the case only under particular circumstances.   For the feminine disposition suffers from the joint flaw which human nature retains from original sin, which impedes her pure development, and which, if not opposed, leads to typical perversion.   Usually, the *personal outlook* appears to be exaggerated unwholesomely; in the first place, her inclination to center both her activities and those of others about her own person is expressed by vanity, desire for praise and recognition, and an unchecked need for communication; on the other hand, it is seen in an excessive interest in others as in curiosity, gossip, and an indiscreet need to penetrate into the intimate life of others. *Her view reaching towards the whole* leads easily to the frittering away of her powers: her antipathy for the necessary objective disciplining of individual abilities results in her superficial nibbling in all areas.   And in her relations to others, it is manifested in her complete absorption with them over the measure required by maternal functions: the sympathetic mate becomes the obtrusive mischief-maker who cannot endure quiet, reserved growth; and because of this, she does not foster development but rather hinders and paralyzes it. The dominating will replaces joyful service.   How many unhappy marriages can be attributed to this abnormality!   How much alienation between mothers and growing children and even mature offspring!

Were we to present in contrast the image of the purely developed character of spouse and mother as it should be according to her natural vocation, we must gaze upon the *Virgin Mary*.   In the center of her life stands her son.   She awaits His birth in blissful expectation; she watches over His childhood; near or far, indeed, wherever He wishes, she follows Him on His way; she holds the crucified body in her arms; she carries out the will of the departed. But not as *her* action does she do all this: she is in this the Handmaid of the Lord; she fulfills that to which God has called her. And that is why she does not consider the child as her own property: she has welcomed Him from God's hands; she lays Him back into God's hands by dedicating Him in the Temple and by being with Him at the crucifixion. Should we consider the Mother of God as spouse, we find a quiet, limitless trust which in turn depends on limitless trust, silent obedience, and an obviously faithful communion in suffering. She does all this in surrender to the will of God who has bestowed her husband upon her as human protector and visible guide.

The image of the Mother of God demonstrates the basic spiritual attitude which corresponds to woman's natural vocation; her relation to her husband is one of obedience, trust, and participation in his life as she furthers his objective tasks and personality development; to the child she gives true care, encouragement, and formation of his God-given talents; she offers both selfless surrender and a quiet withdrawal when unneeded. All is based on the concept of marriage and motherhood as a vocation from God; it is carried out for God's sake and under His guidance.

How can woman attain this sublime ethos in thought and in deed when such powerful drives in her fallen nature oppose it and urge her to other ways? A good natural remedy against all typical feminine defects is solid objective work. This demands in itself the repression of an excessively personal attitude. It calls for an end to superficiality not only in her own work but in general. Because it requires submission to objective laws, it is a schooling in obedience. But it must lead neither to relinquishing of the good and pure personal attitude nor to a one-sided specializing and enslavement to a discipline which typifies the perversion of masculine nature. How extremely sufficient this natural remedy of objective work can be is seen in the maturity and harmony of many women who manifest a high intellectual formation or who were trained by the hardship of life in the discipline of strenuous professional work. Here we have the parallel to the image of the perfect *gentleman* which Newman sketches in *The Idea of a University:* a cultivation of personality which somewhat resembles true holiness. But in both cases it is simply a matter of *similarity*. The nature restrained only by the *influence of education* maintains its cultivated exterior only to a certain point; then it breaks through all bounds. Only the power of grace can uproot and form fallen nature anew; it happens from within, never from without. How this takes place in feminine nature we will consider later.

II. OTHER NATURAL FEMININE VOCATIONS

We proceed to the second basic question: Are there feminine vocations other than the *natural* one? Only subjective delusion could deny that women are capable of practising vocations other than that of spouse and mother. The experience of the last decades and, for that matter, the experience of all times has demonstrated this. One could say that in case of need, every normal and healthy woman is able to hold a position. And there is no profession which cannot be practised by a woman. A self-sacrificing woman can accomplish astounding achievements when it is a question of replacing the breadwinner of fatherless children, of supporting abandoned children or aged parents. But, also, individual gifts and tendencies can lead to the most diversified activities. Indeed, no woman is only *woman;* like a man, each has her individual specialty and talent, and this talent gives her the capability of doing professional work, be it artistic, scientific, technical, etc. Essentially, the individual talent can enable her to embark on any discipline, even those remote from the usual feminine vocations. In such instances, one would not speak of a *feminine profession*. In using the term "feminine profession" significantly, it can only denote those objective tasks assigned by the feminine nature. This would mean all vocations depending on sympathetic rapport such as nursing, education, and social work; consequently, also included would be the vocation of doctor and nurse, teacher and governess, housemaid, and the entire range of contemporary social services. In scholarship it would be those branches dealing with the concrete, living personal element, i.e., the arts and positions wherein one may help and serve, such as translating, editing, and, possibly, guiding a stranger's work appreciatively. Basically the same spiritual attitude which the wife and mother need is needed here also, except that it is extended to a wider working circle and mostly to a changing area of people; for that reason, the perspective is detached from the vital bond of blood relationship and more highly elevated on the spiritual level. It is also true, of course, that there may be a lack of many of the natural motivating powers, those which exist in living communion. A greater power for self-sacrifice is indispensable for this spiritual attitude.

However, over and above this, one may say that even the professions whose objective requirements are not harmonious with feminine nature, those termed as specifically masculine, could yet be practised in an authentically feminine way if accepted as part of the concrete human condition. An adjustment to dull material or abstract thought is demanded, as in work in a factory, business office, national or municipal service, legislature, chemical laboratory or mathematical institute. But in most instances, the work is conducted with other people, at least with others in the same room; often it is a division of labor. And with it an immediate opportunity is given for development of all feminine virtues. One can even say that the development of the feminine nature can become a blessed counter-balance precisely here where everyone is in danger of becoming mechanized and losing his humanity. In the spirit of the man who knows that help and sympathy await him in his place of employment, much will be awakened or kept vigorous which would atrophy otherwise. This is a way for professional life to be formed by the feminine characteristic; this differs usually from what the man does. There is another possibility. Everything abstract is ultimately part of the concrete. Everything inanimate finally serves the living. That is why every activity dealing in abstraction stands in ultimate service to a living whole. Whoever can take hold of this view of the whole and make it active will feel himself bound to it even in the dullest abstract employment. And this work will become tolerable by virtue of this view and in many cases even turns out to be obviously better than if one lost track of the whole because of the part. The man would perhaps aim at the most perfect juridical form in law or in ordinance; and, in so doing, he might give little consideration to the concrete circumstances which it would be good to settle; whereas woman, if she remains faithful to her nature even in Parliament or administrative service, will look for the concrete goal and adjust the means to the end.

Thus the participation of women in the most diverse professional disciplines could be a blessing for the entire society, private or public, precisely if the specifically feminine ethos would be preserved. A glance toward the Mother of God becomes indicative for us again. For example, Mary at the wedding of Cana in her quiet, observing look surveys everything and discovers what is lacking. Before anything is noticed, even before embarrassment sets in, she has procured already the remedy. She finds ways and means, she gives necessary directives, doing all quietly. She draws no attention to herself. Let her be the prototype of woman in professional life. Wherever situated, let her always perform her work quietly and dutifully, without claiming attention and appreciation. And at the same time, she should survey the conditions with a vigilant eye. Let her be conscious of where there is a want and where help is needed, intervening and regulating as far as it is possible in her power in a discreet way. Then will she like a good spirit spread blessing everywhere.

III. THE SUPERNATURAL VOCATION OF WOMAN

We have surveyed the activity of woman in private and public life and have found it to be rich and fruitful. But in no way does this activity exhaust her potential. Today as in all times since Christ's Church first existed, the Lord calls from families and professional life whomever He has chosen for His holy service. Can the religious vocation claim to be a feminine vocation? Certainly the call is issued to men and women. And it is a *supernatural* vocation, for it comes from above, from the other world, summoning the human being to raise himself above the natural earthly level. And so it would seem that the natural differences between the sexes are irrelevant here. Yet, on the other hand, the axiom still holds true: "Grace perfects nature—it does not destroy it." Thus it may be expected that the masculine as well as the feminine nature is not abrogated in religious life but fitted into it in a particular way and thereby made fruitful. Beyond this lies the possibility that the religious vocation, similar to worldly professions, has unique requirements and fits both the masculine and feminine nature each in its particular way.

The religious vocation is the total surrender of the whole person and his or her entire life to the service of God. The one called is obligated to use the means suitable for fulfilling his vocation: renunciation of every possession, of every vital human tie and relationship, and even of his own will. This can be done in various ways; that is to say, the service which the Lord asks from His creatures can be of different kinds: quiet immersion in divine truth, solemn praises of God, propagation of the faith, works of mercy, intercession, and vicarious reparation.

Thus the unity of the monastic order is expressed by the diversity of its individual members. When we consider the various kinds of religious activities and participation in them according to sex, we see indeed that each kind of activity is carried on by both men and women: however, the relationship of the activity to the nature of the sexes is different. Essentially, we may well believe that contemplation and participation in the liturgy, a true angelic service, transcends difference of sex. The spreading of the faith, a priestly mission, is chiefly a masculine concern, although it is also carried on by women, especially in the teaching Orders. On the other hand, works of charity and sacrifice offered in the spirit of vicarious reparation are decidedly in keeping with feminine nature.

The rule of older Orders, which have a masculine and feminine branch, so divided the work that efficacious activities on the outside, such as preaching, giving missions, etc., fell mainly to men. Women carried out the silent apostolate of sacrifice and prayer; nevertheless, at an early stage, they were engaged in working with youth as an apostolic duty. And without exception, all the contemporary women's communities are concerned with educational and charitable activities. Thus today, since the work of the prevailing majority of feminine religious communities has an external efficacy, the activity of the Sister is materially scarcely distinguishable from the work of women "in the world." Where there is a difference, it can only be the formal one, that is, in religious life all must be performed in a spirit of obedience and of love for God.

Let us now examine how the essential elements of religious Orders relate to the feminine nature. The motive, principle, and end of the religious life is to make an absolute gift of self to God in a self-forgetting love, to end one's own life in order to make room for God's life. The more perfectly this is realized, the more richly will God's life fill the soul. Then, God's love is an overflowing love which wants nothing for itself but bestows itself freely; mercifully, it bends down to everyone who is in need, healing the sick and awakening the dead to life, protecting, cherishing, nourishing, teaching, and forming; it is a love which sorrows with the sorrowful and rejoices with the joyful; it serves each human being to attain the end destined for it by the Father. In one word, it is the love of the divine Heart. The deepest longing of woman's heart is to give herself lovingly, to belong to another, and to possess this other being completely. This longing is revealed in her outlook, personal and all-embracing, which appears to us as specifically feminine. But this surrender becomes a perverted self-abandon and a form of slavery when it is given to another person and not to God; at the same time, it is an unjustified demand which no human being can fulfill. Only God can welcome a person's total surrender in such a way that one does not lose one's soul in the process but wins it. And only God can bestow Himself upon a person so that He fulfills this being completely and loses nothing of Himself in so doing. That is why total surrender which is the principle of the religious life is simultaneously the only adequate fulfillment possible for woman's yearning.

Thus the divine life entering the being surrendered to God is love, ready to serve, compassionate, awaken and foster life; it corresponds thoroughly to what we have found to be the professional ethos required of woman.

What are the practical consequences of this? Must all women become religious in order to fulfill their vocation as women? Certainly not. But it certainly does mean that the fallen perverted feminine nature can be restored to its purity and led to the heights of the vocational ethos which this pure nature indicates only if it is completely surrendered to God. Whether she is a mother in the home, or occupies a place in the limelight of public life, or lives behind quiet cloister walls, she must be a *handmaid of the Lord* everywhere. So had the Mother of God been in all circumstances of her life, as the Temple virgin enclosed in that hallowed precinct, by her quiet work in Bethlehem and Nazareth, as guide to the apostles and the Christian community after the death of her son. Were each woman an image of the Mother of God, a *Spouse of Christ,* an apostle of the divine Heart, then would each fulfill her feminine vocation no matter what conditions she lived in and what worldly activity absorbed her life.

I was not assigned to show how the described ethos could be formed in practical professional life. But if I were to end here, the requirements I have presented could appear to be eccentric idealism, so fearfully different are they from the average life of contemporary women. It is necessary to add a few words about how this can actually be put into practice.

Let us begin by calmly comparing the actual life of women as it generally is today with our requirements. Many of the best women are almost overwhelmed by the double burden of family duties and professional life—or often simply of only gainful employment. Always on the go, they are harassed, nervous, and irritable. Where are they to get the needed inner peace and cheerfulness in order to offer stability, support, and guidance to others? Even when there is mutual love and recognition of achievements, there are small daily frictions between a woman and her husband and children; this results in uneasiness throughout the entire household and a slackening of relationships in the home. Along with this, there are many superficial and unstable women who chase after pleasure to fill their inner void, who marry and are divorced; often the home and children are abandoned either to themselves or to domestics, strangers who are no more conscientious than the mothers themselves. If it is necessary for them to seek gainful employment, they do so only as a means to an end, i.e., to make a living and to grasp life's pleasures to the nth degree; in their case, one can speak neither of profession or of ethos. They are like shifting quicksand. The breakdown of family life and the decline of morals are actually connected with the increase in number of such women and can only be checked by reducing their number; this can be done with the help of a qualified educational system for young girls. Finally, we would consider the group of women, by no means negligible, who choose a profession suitable to their ability and inclination. Among them may be found quite a few who discover, after their initial gratification, that their expectations are unfulfilled and they long to be elsewhere. Frequently, this is due to their having taken pains to fill their post "just like a man." They have neither searched for nor found the ways and means to make their feminine nature fruitful in professional life; and the denied, stifled nature asserts itself.

Even were we to look behind cloistered walls, we might discover that the average nun does not measure up to the ideal. Certainly in all times, there have been religious unsure of the full meaning of their vows or unable to maintain the total sacrifice required of their vocation after their first youthful ardor has declined; theirs is usually an agonizing existence, and the community is troubled by their presence. Moreover, there are difficulties first produced by modern living conditions: the twofold occupation of the nun who must meet contemporary requirements as a nurse, teacher, and social service worker while at the same time she must keep pace with the duties of her Order. Quite often, the right spiritual attitude is lost under the excessive load, in a way similar to that of the gainfully employed wife and mother.

Contrary to this sad image of the average woman, one can still find true heroines in all walks of life. They perform wonders on the job in families, professions, and the seclusion of the cloister. All of us are familiar with them from the church records and also from personal experience. There are the mothers who, radiating all warmth and light in the home, raise as many as nine children and impart to them and to their own children full blessings for their entire lives; and these women are magnanimous as well towards all strangers in need. There are the minor instructors and officials who support an entire family from their salary and look after domestic affairs before and after the professional work; yet, they can also find time and money for different church and charitable functions. There are the nuns who wrestle for endangered souls in nocturnal prayer, assuming voluntary penances for their sins. What is the source of their strength? How explain all their achievements which one might often declare to be impossible by nature? How account for that unruffled peace and cheerfulness even in the keenest nervous and emotional stress?

Only by the power of grace can nature be liberated from its dross, restored to its purity, and made free to receive divine life. And this divine life itself is the inner driving power from which acts of love come forth. Whoever wants to preserve this life continually within herself must nourish it constantly from the source whence it flows without end—from the holy sacraments, above all from the sacrament of love. To have divine love as its inner form, a woman's life must be a Eucharistic life. Only in daily, confidential relationship with the Lord in the tabernacle can one forget self, become free of all one's own wishes and pretentions, and have a heart open to all the needs and wants of others. Whoever seeks to consult with the Eucharistic God in all her concerns, whoever lets herself be purified by the sanctifying power coming from the sacrifice at the altar, offering herself to the Lord in this sacrifice, whoever receives the Lord in her soul's innermost depth in Holy Communion cannot but be drawn ever more deeply and powerfully into the flow of divine life, incorporated into the Mystical Body of Christ, her heart converted to the likeness of the divine heart.

Something else is closely related to this. When we entrust all the troubles of our earthly existence confidently to the divine heart, we are relieved of them. Then our soul is free to participate in the divine life. Then we walk by the side of the Savior on the path that He traveled on this earth during His earthly existence and still travels in His mystical afterlife. Indeed, with the eyes of faith, we penetrate into the secret depths of His hidden life within the pale of the godhead. On the other hand, this participation in divine life has a liberating power in itself; it lessens the weight of our earthly concerns and grants us a bit of eternity even in this finitude, a reflection of beatitude, a transformation into light. But the invitation to this transformation in God's hand is given to us by God Himself in the liturgy of the Church. Therefore, the life of an authentic Catholic woman is also a liturgical life. Whoever prays together with the Church in spirit and in truth knows that her whole life must be formed by this life of prayer.

Let us summarize. Every profession in which woman's soul comes into its own and which can be formed by woman's soul is an authentic woman's profession. The innermost formative principle of woman's soul is the love which flows from the divine heart. Woman's soul wins this formative principle through the most intimate union with the divine heart in a Eucharistic and liturgical life.

In closing, I would like to raise a question which comes to mind again and again: the convention program clearly designates the various kinds of professions (the doctor, the priest, etc.). What need was there for a special category of *women's professions?* Besides, why are there such frequent discussions on women's professions but hardly any on men's professions? Is not man like woman aware of the coexistence between individual and masculine tendencies and then eventually an opposition between them? Is it not also true of man that his nature is or should be a co-determining factor for the selection and formation of his vocation? Furthermore, do we not also find here the antithesis between nature made degenerate by the Fall and nature restored in purity?

I believe it would be very worthwhile if at some time these questions would be considered seriously and thoroughly. For a wholesome collaboration of the sexes in professional life will be possible only if both achieve a calm and objective awareness of their nature and draw practical conclusions from it. God created humanity as man and woman, and He created both according to His own image. Only the purely developed masculine *and* feminine nature can yield the highest attainable likeness to God. Only in this fashion can there be brought about the strongest interpenetration of all earthly and divine life.

Chapter II

The Separate Vocations of Man and Woman According to Nature and Grace

In everyday usage, the hackneyed word "vocation" retains little of its original connotation. When young people are about to graduate, one wonders what occupation they should pursue; the question whether women should enter the professional life or stay at home has been controversial for some time. Here the term designating vocation does not convey much more than gainful employment. The original meaning of the word survives only in particular allusions, i.e., when one says that a person has missed his vocation or when one speaks of a religious vocation. These idioms signify that a vocation is something to which a person must be *called*.

Yet, what does *to be called* mean? A call must have been sent *from* someone, *to* someone, *for something* in a *distinct manner*. We say that a scholar has been appointed to a professorial chair. The offer initiates at an institution through the respective school; it goes to a man who is apparently *called* because of ability and education for that to which he is being called, i.e., to work as scholar and teacher. The offer is made to him by way of an invitation in prescribed or customary linguistic forms. I have most certainly used a peculiar turn of expression here: "he is called to that to which he seems to be called." According to that, the appointment by a human institution evidently presupposes another call which these people believe recognized and therefore declared "called through ability and education." He himself and many others worked toward his formation, voluntarily and involuntarily; but it developed on the basis of his *ability* in the deepest sense of the word—all the gifts which he inherited. Thus his call, as well as his vocation—i.e., his works and creations to which he is destined—is prescribed in *human nature;* the course of life fructifies it and renders it recognizable to other people so that they are able to declare the *calling* in which he might happily find *his place* in life. But the *person's nature* and his *life's course* are no gift or trick of chance, but—seen with the eyes of faith—the work of God. And thus, finally, it is God Himself who calls. It is He who calls *each* human being to that which all humanity is called, it is He who calls each *individual* to that which he or she is called personally, and, over and above this, He calls *man and woman* as such to something specific as the title of this address indicates. What man and woman are called to does not appear to be easily recognizable, as it has been a controversial subject for some time. And yet there are any number of ways by which we receive this call: God Himself declares it in the words of the Old and New Testament; it is inscribed in the nature of man and woman; history elucidates this matter for us; finally, the needs of our time declare an urgent message. A diversely fibered texture is presented, but the design is not so complex that we may not isolate a few clear lines within it by viewing it clearly and objectively. So we may thus attempt to answer the question: to what are man and woman called?

I

The first passage of the *Bible* which concerns humanity assigns a common vocation to both man and woman. "'Let us make man in our image, after our likeness, and let them be masters of the fish of the sea and the birds of heaven and over the entire earth and all crawling animals that move upon the earth.'[1] And God created man in His own image, in the image of God He created him, He created them as male and female.[2]

And God blessed them and said: 'Be fruitful and multiply, fill the earth and conquer it, and be masters over the fish of the sea, the birds of heaven, and all creatures which move upon the earth.'"[3]

Thus, in the first account of the creation of man, the difference between male and female is immediately proclaimed. But mutually they are given the threefold vocation: they are to be the image of God, bring forth posterity, and be masters over the earth. It is not said here that this threefold vocation is to be effected in different ways by man and woman; at best, this is implied in the quotation cited on the separation of the sexes.

The second passage of Genesis, which deals more extensively with the creation of man, elucidates the question a bit further. It relates the creation of Adam, his placement in the "paradise of bliss" to cultivate and preserve it, and the manner in which the animals were brought to him and received their names from him.[4] "But no helpmate corresponding to him was found for Adam."[5] The Hebrew expression used in this passage is barely translatable[6] —*Eser kenegdo*—which literally means "a helper as if vis-à-vis to him." One can think here of a mirror in which man is able to look upon his own nature. The translators who speak of a "helpmate suitable to him" perceive it in this way. But one can also think of a counterpart, a *pendant,* so that, indeed, they do resemble each other, yet not entirely, but rather, that they complement each other as one hand does the other. "And the Lord God said 'It is not good that man should be alone. I will make him a helpmate who will suit him.'" And the Lord made Adam fall into slumber and took from him one of his ribs and formed a woman from it, and He led her to Adam. "Then Adam declared, 'This is now bone of my bone and flesh of my flesh. She is to be called woman, for she was taken from man.'[7] That is why a man leaves his father and mother and adheres to his wife and they both become *one* body.[8] Now they were both naked, Adam and his wife, but they felt no shame."[9]

A certain pre-eminence is indicated in that man was created first. Again, it is from the word of God that we are to understand why it would not have been good for man to be alone. God created man in His own image. But God is *three in one;* and just as the Son issues from the Father, and the Holy Spirit from the Father and the Son, so, too, the woman emanated from man and posterity from them both. And moreover, God is love. But there must be at least two persons for love to exist (as we are told by St. Gregory in his homily on the mission of the disciples who were dispatched two by two).

It is not a question here of a *sovereignty* of man over woman. She is named as *companion* and *helpmate,* and it is said of man that he will cling to her and that both are to become *one* flesh. This signifies that we are to consider the life of the initial human pair as the most intimate community of love, that their faculties were in perfect harmony as within one single being; likewise, before the Fall, all faculties in each individual were in perfect harmony, senses and spirit in right relation with no possibility of conflict. For this reason, they were also incapable of inordinate desire for one another. This is revealed in the words "They were naked and were not ashamed."

God's plan seems essentially altered after the Fall in respect to mankind and the human vocation. Eve had allowed herself to be ensnared by the tempter and had also enticed the man into sin. First Adam is called to account. He laid the blame on the woman: "The woman whom you gave me as companion—she gave me to eat from the tree and I ate."[10] At the same time, it sounds like a reproach to God. First Adam is now taken to task: his alibi is not accepted. ". . . Because you listened to the voice of your wife and ate from the tree of which I had forbidden you to eat, cursed be the soil because of your deed; you shall feed upon it with greatest toil all the days of your life.[11] It will bear thorns and thistles for you, and you shall eat the plants of the fields.[12] You shall eat bread by the sweat of your brow until you return to the earth from whence you were taken; for you are dust and unto dust shall you return."[13] Adam's disobedience is punished by the loss of his undisputed sovereignty over the earth and of the ready service of the lower creatures, by the harsh struggle with them over his daily bread, by the difficulty of his labor and its pitiful reward.

A different judgment is meted out to the woman: ". . . I will multiply the difficulties of your conceptions; you will give birth to children in suffering and be under the power of your husband and he shall rule over you."[14] We do not know in what way the blessing of fertility was to be fulfilled in humanity before the Fall. Woman's labor in childbirth and man's struggle for existence resulted from the Fall. The woman is punished further by subjugation to the man. That he will not be a good master can be seen in his attempt to shift responsibility for the sin from himself onto his wife. The serene community of love is ended. But something else has emerged of which they were not aware before; they recognize they are naked and they are ashamed. They themselves tried to hide their nakedness and God provided for them: "And the Lord God made robes from skins for Adam and his wife and so clothed them."[15] Concupiscence has awakened in them, and it has become necessary to guard them from it.

Thus there has been a change in the relationship of human beings to the earth, to their descendants and to one another. But all this is the result of a changed relation to God. The narration on the creation and Fall of man is full of mysteries which cannot be resolved here. But it is indeed not presumptuous to discuss a few questions which emerge and to try to answer them. Why was it forbidden to eat of the tree of knowledge? What kind of fruit was it that the woman ate and gave her husband to eat? And why did the tempter approach the woman first? Of course, man was evidently not without knowledge before the Fall—he who was created according to God's image, who gave names to all living creatures, and who was called to rule over the earth. Rather, a much more perfect knowledge can be attributed to him before than after the Fall. Therefore, it must have been a specific knowledge which is the point in question. The devil actually speaks of the knowledge of good and evil. Now, it is also not to be assumed that man lacked knowledge of good before the Fall. Adam and Eve had a more perfect knowledge of God, i.e., a more perfect knowledge of the highest good and, from that, of all particular good. But they were to be kept, no doubt, from that knowledge of evil which one gains in the doing of it.

The direct consequence of original sin gives a clue for what they may be held accountable: the consequence was that man and woman saw each other with different eyes than they had previously; they had lost innocence of interchange with one another. So the first sin may not only be considered as a purely formal one of disobedience to God. Rather it implied a definite act which had been forbidden and which the serpent presented enticingly to the woman and then the woman to the man. Indeed, the act committed could well have been a manner of union which was at variance with the original order. But that the tempter first tempted the woman may signify that he had easier access to her, not that the woman was more easily induced to evil (indeed, both Adam and Eve were still free of an inclination to evil), but because the nature of the temptation was in itself of greater significance for her. From the first it was intended that woman's life would be more strongly affected by procreation and the education of posterity. The difference of punishment for the man and woman is also indicative of this.

According to the biblical text, the loss of their own lives seems to be bound up with the expulsion from Paradise: the Lord pronounces the words to Adam with which He had threatened him from the first as punishment for disobedience: death. But preceding the expulsion, God utters a promise in the judgment meted out to the serpent: "I will set enmity between you and the woman, your offspring and hers; her descendants will tread on your head, and yours will lie wait-ing for their heel."[16] The terms "woman" and "offspring" designate the Mother of God and the Redeemer. This, how-ever, does not exclude the other meaning; the first woman, to whom Adam gave the name "mother of all living creatures," as well as all her successors had been given a particular duty to struggle against evil and to prepare for the spiritual restoration of life. "God has given me a son," said Eve, as she gave birth to her first child. That sounds as if she were aware of a bless-ing to be given to her in the person of her son. And later, the women of Israel also saw their vocation in this way: to bring forth offspring who were to see the day of salvation.

Thus a specific tie is established between the Fall and Redemption, and here and there the facts correspond remark-ably. As woman was the first to be tempted, so did God's message of grace come first to a woman, and each time woman's assent determined the destiny of humanity as a whole, In God's new kingdom, the role of the human couple has changed; it has become a relationship of mother and son. The Son of God is the Son of Man through his mother but not through a human father. God's son did not choose the usual way of human propagation to become the Son of Man. Can we not find here an indication that there is a flaw inherent in this fashion of procreation from the first sin, which can only be redeemed *by* the kingdom of grace? Also, does it not indicate the nobility of motherhood as the purest and most elevated union of human beings? The distinction of the fe-male sex is that a woman was *the* person who was permitted to help establish God's new kingdom; the distinction of the male sex is that redemption came through the Son of Man, the new Adam. And therein, man's rank of priority is ex-pressed again.

The Lord clearly declared that the new kingdom of God would bring a new order of relationship between the sexes, i.e., it would put an end to the relationships caused by the Fall and would restore the original order.[17] To the Pharisee's

question as to whether the husband is allowed to divorce his
wife, Jesus answered "Moses permitted you to do so because
of the hardness of your hearts. But from the beginning, this
was not so." And He rebuked them with the passage from
the account of creation: they will be two in one flesh. And
He sets the commandment of the New Covenant: "What God
has united let man not put asunder." But, moreover, He sets
up the ideal of virginity as something entirely new, as it is put
before us by the living example of the Virgin-Mother and the
Lord Himself.

   The letters of St. Paul contain the most detailed remarks
on the relationship between man and woman. The much discussed passage of 1 Corinthians reads: "However, what I want
you to understand is that Christ is the head of every man, but
man is the head of woman, and God is the head of Christ.
Any man who prays or prophesizes with his head covered
renders disrespect to his head.[18] But any woman who prays
or prophesizes with head uncovered shames her head; then it
is as if her hair were shaved off . . .[19] A man should not cover
his head, for it is the image and glory of God, but woman is
man's glory.[20] For man does not come from woman, but
woman from man.[21] For man was not created for the sake
of woman but woman for the sake of man . . .[22] Yet in the
Lord, man is neither independent of woman nor woman independent of man."[23] We should not be deemed disrespectful
to the Apostle if we suggest here that in this instruction to the
Corinthians, there is confusion as to the divine and human
aspects, the temporal and eternal. Coiffure and clothes are
matters of fashion, as even St. Paul says in the close of the
passage: "But anyone who may still be inclined to argue
knows that we do not have such a custom nor do the church-
es of God."[24] If this judgment regarding the dress to be
worn for public worship by the Corinthian women was binding for the community he had founded, that is not to say that
by the same token it is also binding for all times.

   What he says concerning the main relationship between

man and woman must be evaluated differently, for it is given as interpretation of the divine order in creation and redemption.

Man and woman are destined to live *one* life with one another like a single being. But the leadership in this community of life is proper to the man as the one who was created first. However, one has the impression that the original order and redemptive order are not rendered authentically by the interpretation of St. Paul; on the contrary, in the emphasis of man's sovereignty in the relationship, and absolutely in his postulation of man's role as mediator between the Redeemer and woman, the interpretation is still influenced by the order of fallen nature. Neither the account of creation nor the Gospel alludes to such an indirectness of relationship to God. But it is indeed found in Mosaic law and in Roman justice. Yet the Apostle himself knows another order which he speaks of in the same Letter to the Corinthians when he discusses marriage and virginity: "The unbelieving husband is sanctified by the believing wife . . ." and "Wife, how do you know that you will not bring your husband to salvation . . .?"[25] This is in accordance with the Gospel which teaches that every soul is won to life by Christ, and everyone who is justified by union with Christ, man or woman, is called to mediation.

The relationship of man and wife is handled even more fully in the Letter to the Ephesians.[26] "Wives should yield to their husbands as to the Lord, for the man is his wife's head just as Christ is the head of His Church, the savior of His body.[27] But just as the Church is resigned to Christ, so, too, should women be to their husbands in all things.[28] Husbands, love your wives even as Christ loved the Church and gave Himself up for her[29] in order to make her holy, purifying her in a bath of water by the word of life[30] in order to present His glorious Church without blemish or wrinkle or any such thing, but rather that she might be holy and immaculate.[31] So should men also love their wives as their own bodies. Whoever loves his wife loves himself.[32] For never has anyone hated his own flesh but rather preserves and attends to it as also Christ does the Church.[33]　For we are members of His body, of His flesh, and of His bones.[34]　For this reason, a man shall leave his mother and father and shall cling to his wife; and the two shall become one flesh.[35]　But this is a great mystery. I mean to say, of Christ and the Church.[36]　Nevertheless, each one of you should love his wife as himself; but the woman should stand in awe of her husband."[37]　This passage explains what the Christian concept of marriage should be. Although the Lord Himself has emphasized the indissolubility of marriage and the unity of the couple in one flesh, this unity is more closely defined here.

Just as in the single organism all limbs are ruled by the head, thereby maintaining the harmony of the entire being, so there must also be a head in the more extended organism; and in a sound organism there can be no contention concerning which is the head and which are the members and what are the functions of both. But it must not be forgotten that it is a matter of a symbolic relationship. Both the image of Christ and the Church remind us of this relationship. Christ is our head and His divine life overflows to us, His members, if we adhere to Him in love and we are subject to Him in obedience. The head is God Incarnate who has His autonomous existence beyond His Mystical Body. The members have their individual being as free and rational creatures, and the Mystical Body springs from the love of the head and a willing subordination of its members. The functions, which proceed from each member of the Mystical Body, are assigned to the member on the basis of the gifts of each, gifts of love and of spirituality; it is the wisdom of the head to utilize the members according to their gifts; but it is the divine power of the head to provide each individual member with gifts which can be of benefit to the entire organism. And it is the purpose of this entire body, the Mystical Body of Christ, that each individual member—who is indeed a whole human being with body and soul—attain to the fullness of salvation and sonship with God, and glorify in his own way the entire body, the communion of saints.

If the man is to be the leader, ("the head") of his wife—and we can add accordingly, likewise the head of the entire family—in the sense Christ is the head of the Church, so is it the duty of the man to conduct this microcosm of the great Mystical Body in such a way that each of its members may be able to develop his gifts perfectly and contribute to the salvation of the entire body, and that each may attain his own salvation. The husband *is not* Christ and does not have the power to bestow talents. But he does have the power to bring talents which are existent to development (or to suppress them), as a person most certainly can be helpful in developing the gifts of another. And it is wisdom on his part not to allow these gifts to atrophy but to permit them to be developed for the welfare of all. And since he himself is not perfect like Christ, but rather a creature with many gifts and many defects, his highest wisdom may be to permit the gifts of the other members to compensate for his defects, just as it could be the highest political wisdom of the sovereign to allow a judicious minister to rule. However, it is essential for the well-being of the organism that this should come about under the guidance of the head. If the body rebels against the head, the organism will suffer as much as if the head were to allow the body to atrophy.

Although the Letter to the Ephesians treats of the marriage union, the Apostle speaks even more emphatically concerning woman's place in the community in the First Letter to Timothy. She should be dressed simply and modestly and display her piety through good works.[38] "The woman must learn in silence, in total humility.[39] But I do not permit a woman to instruct, nor to exalt herself over the man; rather she should keep quiet.[40] For Adam was created first, then Eve;[41] and Adam was not seduced but the woman was seduced and thus initiated the transgression.[42] But she will attain salvation through childbearing, provided she perseveres in faith, love, and holy reticence."[43]

Here, even more strongly than in the Letter to the Corinthians, one has the impression that the original order and the redemptive order are subordinated by the order of fallen nature, and that the Apostle still expresses himself distinctly as a Jew in the spirit of the law. The evangelical concept of virginity appears to be forgotten completely. What is said here and what may have been feasible concerning certain improprieties in the Greek community is not to be considered as binding for the principal teaching on the relationship of the sexes. It contradicts too strongly the words and the whole custom of the Lord who had women among his closest companions, and who showed at every turn in His redemptive work that He was as concerned about the soul of woman as the soul of man. It even contradicts that passage of Paul himself which possibly expresses most purely the spirit of the gospel. "The law was our schoolmaster until Christ came to teach that we might be justified by faith. But now that faith has come, we are no longer under the tutelage of the law . . . There is neither Jew nor Greek, slave nor freeman; *there is neither male nor female.* For you are all one in Christ Jesus."[44]

Before we go on to discuss what the word of God holds for us regarding the nature of man and woman, as far as it is accessible to our understanding, we would like to summarize what has been said so far.

The vocation of man and woman is not exactly the same in the original order, the order of fallen nature, and the redemptive order. *Originally,* man and woman were both made responsible to preserve their own likeness to God, their lordship over the earth, and the reproduction of the human race. The pre-eminent position of the man, which seems to be implied by the fact that he was created first, is not explained in greater depth. After their Fall, the relationship between them is transformed from a pure partnership of love to a relationship of sovereignty and subordination and is distorted

by concupiscence. The difficult struggle for existence is allocated primarily to man and the hardship of childbirth to
woman. But a promise of redemption is present inasmuch as
the woman is charged with the battle against evil; the male
sex is to be exalted by the coming of the Son of God. The
redemption will restore the original order. *The pre-eminence
of man is disclosed by the Savior's coming to earth in the
form of man.* The feminine sex is ennobled by virtue of the
Savior's being born of a human mother; *a woman was the
gateway through which God found entrance to humankind.*
Adam as the human prototype indicates the future divine-
human king of creation; just so, every man in the kingdom of
God should imitate Christ, and in the marital partnership, he
is to imitate the loving care of Christ for His Church. A woman should honor the image of Christ in her husband by free
and loving subordination; she herself is to be the image of
God's mother; but that also means that she is to be Christ's
image.

II

If we try to describe the nature of man and woman as
we understand it normally, we find, on the one hand, a clear
explanation of what God's word tells us; on the other hand,
God's word is simply a guide to life. In this we again find
traces of the original order of creation, of the fall, and of
redemption.

Man was called by his original God-given vocation to be
master of the created world. Hence his body and soul are
equipped to fight and conquer it, to *understand* it and by
knowledge to make it his own, to *possess* and *enjoy* it, and,
finally, to make it in a sense his own *creation* through *purposeful activity.* But, of course, man's nature is limited, as
are all things created; his limitations have their origin in the
primitive condition caused by original sin; as a result, the

human being does not possess lordship over the earth as first intended. If the drive for knowledge is strong in him and if he uses all his strength to satisfy this drive, then, more and more, he will be forced to renounce the possession and enjoyment of the good things in life; and, in addition, his powers of creativity will be undermined. If his life's goal is possession and gratification, he will be less likely to attain pure, disinterested understanding and less likely to be capable of creative activity. But if he is content completely to transform a small realm by his own creative activity (as a farmer, artist, government worker, etc.), abstract knowledge and enjoyment in the material goods of life are of less importance. And we are constantly reminded that the more perfect the single achievement is, the more limited it is in scope. Perfection can only be achieved through a one-sidedness and the deterioration of the other qualities.

But, also, given man's fallen nature, this one-sided endeavor to achieve perfection easily becomes a decadent aspiration in itself; our desire for knowledge does not respect limits placed on it but rather seeks by force to go beyond these limits; human understanding may even fail to grasp that which is not essentially hidden from it because it refuses to submit itself to the law of things; rather, it seeks to master them in arbitrary fashion or permits the clarity of its spiritual vision to be clouded by desires and lusts. In the same way, the decay of man's dominion is seen when we consider his relationship to the natural riches of the earth: instead of reverential joy in the created world, instead of a desire to preserve and develop it, man seeks to exploit it greedily to the point of destruction or to senseless acquisition without understanding how to profit from it or how to enjoy it. Related to this is the debasement of creative art through the violent distortion and caricature of natural images.

The deterioration of kingship to brutal authority also holds true in the relationship of man to woman. According to the original order, she was entrusted to him as companion and helpmate. Consequently, if she is to stand by his side in lordship over the earth, she must be endowed with the same gifts—to understand, to enjoy, and to create. But, usually, she is less endowed with these gifts and consequently runs less danger of losing herself in one-sidedness. Thus she will be able to serve man in their mutual duties; she protects man from his natural one-sidedness by her own harmonious development. But the relationship of the sexes since the Fall has become a brutal relationship of master and slave. Consequently, women's natural gifts and their best possible development are no longer considered; rather, man uses her as a means to achieve his own ends in the exercise of his work or in pacifying his own lust. However, it can easily happen that the despot becomes a slave to his lust and thereby is a slave of the slave who must satisfy him.

The degenerate relations between man and woman are transmitted in their degenerate relations with their children. Originally, the care regarding procreation was charged to them jointly. Just as they are both directed to restore their differing predispositions, in that way also, and in a most intense manner, each must compensate the other for their inherent shortcomings as parents. On the one hand, the uncultivated nature of the child necessitates care, protection and guidance in the development of his faculties. Because of the close bodily tie between child and mother, because of woman's specific tendency to sympathize and to serve another life, as well as her more acute sense of how to develop the child's faculties, the principal share of the child's education is assigned to woman. On the other hand, she has need for man's protection in order to carry out her duties; yet, man's more intense drive and potential for achievements make him responsible for guiding the child to fulfill his particular potentialities, to "make good." And, finally, he is responsible by his duty as sovereign of all creation to care for the noblest of all creatures. Moreover, just as man and woman are made to complement each other, so, too, the successive generations are called upon also to fulfill the same function. Each generation, therefore, is called to achieve something new and individual; education should seriously consider the need to develop new and original elements in each new generation. Thus *fatherhood* appears as an original calling of man assigned to him along with his special vocation. On the one hand, the inclination to shirk his paternal duties is a sign of decadence; on the lowest level, this reveals itself in sexual intercourse simply for the sheer satisfaction of sexual desires without any concern for offspring; on a higher level, he may assume his material obligations well but perhaps he will disregard completely his duty to share in the child's formation. On the other hand, there is danger of a brutal exercise of the prerogatives of fatherhood which limits motherhood to the merely physical care and deprives it of its higher functions and which, moreover, may authoritatively repress the unique aspirations of the new offspring.

All of the defects in a man's nature which cause him to fail in his original vocation are rooted in a perverted relationship to God. Man can fulfill his most noble vocation which is to be the image of God only if he seeks to develop his powers by subordinating himself humbly to God's guidance. To be a finite image of divine wisdom, goodness, and power would mean that man would seek *to know* within the form and the limits ordained by God, *to enjoy* gratefully the glory of God as manifested in God's creatures, *to help perfect* creation in a free human act as God intended. Man's *non serviam* before God brings about in its turn his perverted relationship to all creatures.

We have the exact parallel in woman's nature. According to the intended original order, her place is by man's side to master the earth and to care for offspring. But her body and soul are fashioned less to fight and to conquer than to cherish, guard and preserve. Of the threefold attitude towards the world—to know it, to enjoy it, to form it creatively—it is the second which concerns her most directly: she seems more capable than man of feeling a more reverent joy in creatures; moreover, such joy requires a particular kind of perception of the good, different from rational perception in being an inherent spiritual function and a singularly feminine one. Evidently, this quality is related to woman's mission as a mother which involves an understanding of the total being and of specific values. It enables her to understand and foster organic development, the special, individual destiny of every living being. This awareness of the needs of the living being benefits not only her posterity but all creatures as well. It particularly benefits a man in making her a companion and helpmate appreciative of his aspirations. The complementary relationship of man and woman appears clearly in the original order of nature: man's primary vocation appears to be that of ruler and the paternal vocation secondary (not subordinate to his vocation as ruler but an integral part of it); woman's primary vocation is maternal: her role as ruler is secondary and included in a certain way in her maternal vocation.

A woman shares with man the powers to understand, enjoy, and act; but she also shares the same degenerate desire for the possession of things through violence, a desire which falsifies, distorts and destroys. However, the Fall affected man and woman differently; this becomes clear when examining the different meaning and orientation of the three functions (understanding, enjoyment and creativity) in the total personality and total life of man and woman. It has already been mentioned that, because of her predisposition, woman is better protected than man from one-sidedness and from dehumanization. On the other hand, *the* one-sidedness to which she is exposed is a particularly perilous one. Abstract thought and creative action are of less concern to her than the possession and enjoyment of the good life. Therefore, the danger exists that she will commit herself only to that and that alone. And now, in addition, her reverent joy in the things of this world may degenerate into greed, leading her, on the one hand, to the anxious, avaricious scraping together and hoarding of things for which she has no use; and, on the other hand, a lapse into a mindless, idle life of sensuality.

This leads in turn to a degenerate relationship with man: already threatened by man's need for domination, her free companionship by his side will be further undermined by her in yielding to her own desires. On the other hand, her anxiety to safeguard her property may lead her also to try to dominate man. And analogies can be seen in relation to the children. The woman who leads a life based solely on self-indulgence will attempt to shirk maternal duties just as a comparably oriented man will shirk his paternal duties. Of course, she may be prevented from this by an instinctive drive for children. The woman who hovers anxiously over her children as if they were her own possessions will try to bind them to her in every way, even by the greatest possible elimination of the father's rights. She will try to curtail their freedom of development; she will check their development and destroy their happiness instead of serving man, children, and all creatures in a reverential loving manner in order to foster their natural formation for the glory of God and thereby further their natural happiness.

The root of the evil lies again in her perverted relationship to God. Because woman rebelled against God at the time of the Fall and simultaneously assumed a superiority over man by seducing him, her punishment is subjugation to man's dominion. Because the sin which she encouraged him to commit was in all likelihood a sin of sensuality, woman is more intensely exposed to the danger of descent into stark carnality. And when this happens, she always becomes once again the evil seductress, whereas, paradoxically, God has specifically enjoined her to combat evil.

III

We have indicated how the nature and original vocation

of man and woman may be sought after and restored; only as God's children can this be attained. If we in addition do our share, our readoption as children of God is guaranteed by Christ's redemptive act. The Israelites of the Old Covenant did their part for redemption as they awaited the Messiah in true adherence to the Law. For women, this meant humble submission to man's sovereignty, a scrupulous vigilance to maintain their purity, a discipline of the senses more austere than that performed by men, a craving for posterity in whom they might envision their own salvation, and an authentic effort to raise their children in the fear of God. For each man this meant fidelity to the prescribed prayers and sacrificial worship, obedience to moral and social precepts, responsibility as head of the family for wife and children, esteem for woman as the mother of his children.

In the New Covenant, the human being fulfills his share of the work of redemption through the closest personal union with Christ: through *faith* which clings to Him as the way of salvation, as the truth which He reveals, and as the way to beatitude which He offers; through *hope* which awaits with absolute trust the life promised by Him; through *love* which looks for every possible way to approach Him. The human being seeks always to know Him more intimately through *contemplation* of His life and meditation on His word; he strives for the closest union with Him in the *Holy Eucharist;* he shares in His mystical, resurrected life through participation in the Church year and in its *liturgy.* Salvation admits of no differences between the sexes; rather, the salvation of each one and their relationship to one another both depend on the same close personal union with Christ.

The redemptive act did not restore corrupted nature with one stroke. Christ sowed the seed of salvation in humanity in order that it might grow not only in the inner and outer life of the Church, but that it might grow especially in each individual soul. We who are "on our way" in our pilgrimage to the heavenly Jerusalem experience in ourselves the conflict between corrupt nature and grace which, like a growing plant, can grow and bloom, triumphing over all pestilence. Everywhere about us, we see in the interaction of the sexes the direct fruits of original sin in most terrifying forms: an unleashed sexual life in which every trace of their high calling seems to be lost; a struggle between the sexes, one pitted against the other, as they fight for their rights and, in doing so, no longer appear to hear the voices of nature and of God. But we can see also how it can be different whenever the power of grace is operative.

In Christian marriage, the husband as head of the family community is concerned with its health: not only does he strive according to his powers to procure its livelihood and worldly "success," but also, he must contribute his share to its spiritual well-being.

This means that sometimes he will guide and lend a helping hand, at other times find it necessary to yield cautiously, and even occasionally to take preventative or opposing action. He will aid in the development of the talents and energies of his wife and children whenever he can and whenever need be. If he has to deal with weaker natures and limited abilities, if he observes a lack of courage and self-confidence, he will try to draw out the hidden talents. One of his duties is to strengthen the spirituality of his wife, not permitting her to lapse into a life of mere sensuality; this could be done by letting her participate in his own creative work or in independent activity of her own. Should she be deprived of both alternatives, should he try to confine her to a sphere too narrow for her talents, or should he relinquish her entirely to the merely sensual life, he would carry a great share of responsibility for the resulting consequences: responsibility for the atrophy of her higher life, for pathological disturbance, for an excessive dependence on husband and children, one which becomes a burden to them, and for the desolation of her life if one day she is left behind on her own. The analogy also holds true in relation to the children. On the other hand, it pertains to his duties as head of the family to make sure of the order and harmony of family life, to see to it that every member is made not only to care for his own individual development but also to consider the others and to practice the self-denial required in the performance of his household duties. And, finally, through concern for the well-ordered natural life of each individual and of the entire house, he must not neglect the family's spiritual life. In his small community, the husband should imitate Christ as head of the Church; he should consider his greatest mission to lead the entire family in the imitation of Christ and, according to his powers, to further all seeds of grace which are stirring in them. The more intimate his own union with the Lord, so much the more will he succeed.

The family burden which the husband bears in addition to his professional duties would seem all too heavy if his help-mate did not stand by his side; she is called in accordance with her nature to carry more than half of this load. She craves for an unhampered development of her personality just as much as she does to help another toward that same goal. And thus the husband will find that she can give him invaluable advice in guiding the lives of the children as well as of themselves; indeed, often he would fulfill his duties as leader best if he would yield to her and permit himself to be led by her. Part of her natural feminine concern for the right development of the beings surrounding her involves the creation of an ambi-ence, of order and beauty conducive to their development.

A quality unique to woman is her singular sensitivity to moral values and an abhorrence for all which is low and mean; this quality protects her against the dangers of seduction and of total surrender to sensuality. This is expressed by the mysterious prophecy, become legendary, that woman would be engaged in battle against the serpent; and this prophecy is fulfilled by the victory over evil won for all humanity through Mary, queen of all women. Allied closely to this sensitivity for moral values is her yearning for the divine and for her own personal union with the Lord, her readiness and desire to be completely fulfilled and guided by His love. That is why, in a rightly-ordered family life, the mission of moral and religious education is given chiefly to the wife. If her life is anchored completely in Jesus, then, also, she is best protected against the dangerous loss of moderation. This could happen by her being overly wrapped-up in those about her; or, on the contrary, it could happen by her being wrapped up only in herself and would cut the ground from under her feet, the ground on which she must stand if she is to be able to support and to help others. Her professional activity counterbalances the risk of submerging herself all too intimately in another's life and thereby sacrificing her own; however, an exclusive preoccupation with her professional activity would bring the opposite danger of infidelity toward her feminine vocation. Only those who surrender themselves completely into the Lord's hands can trust that they will avoid disaster between Scylla and Charybdis. Whatever is surrendered to Him is not lost but is saved, chastened, exalted and proportioned out in true measure.

We are led by these last comments to the question of the vocation practised outside of the home and of the relationship between man and woman in professional life. Obviously now, because of the development of the last decades and of recent years, we must consider as closed the historical epoch which made an absolute differentiation between the duties of the sexes, i.e., that woman should assume the domestic duties and man the struggle for a livelihood. Today, it is not at all too difficult for us to understand how this evolution took place. The victories of natural science and technology which progressively replaced human labor by mechanical means brought to women a great liberation and a desire to use their nascent powers in another way. In the transitional period, much unused power was senselessly squandered in empty dawdling; and, because of this, valuable human energy was wasted away. The necessary changes were brought about only after a series of difficult crises. These crises were partly caused through excessive passion, both on the part of the pioneers of the feminist movement and of their opponents, although they both often fought with humane arguments. In part, these crises were caused by the passive opposition of the inert multitude which tends to cling without objective scrutiny to the accustomed ways of the past. At last, post-war conditions in Germany brought revolutionary changes even in this domain; and the accompanying economic depression compelled even those who until then had had no thoughts of professional training to work for a living. Hence, the condition in which we find ourselves today is an abnormal one, and it does not constitute a suitable basis for fundamental analysis.

Above all, with regard to the previous explanation, we must ask: On the whole does woman's professional life outside of the home violate the order of nature and grace? I believe that one must answer "no" to this question. It seems to me that a common creativity in all areas was assigned in the original order, even if this was with a differing allocation of roles. The change in the original order which took place after the Fall does not signify its complete termination; thus nature also was not fully corrupted but preserved the same powers, only now weakened and exposed to error. The fact that *all* powers which the husband possesses are present in a feminine nature as well—even though they may generally appear in different degrees and relationships—is an indication they should be employed in corresponding activity. And wherever the circle of domestic duties is too narrow for the wife to attain the full formation of her powers, both nature and reason concur that she reach out beyond this circle. It appears to me, however, that there is a limit to such professional activities whenever it jeopardizes domestic life, i.e., the community of life and formation consisting of parents and children. It even seems to me a contradiction of the divine order when the professional activities of the husband escalate to a degree which cuts him off completely from family life. This is even more true of the wife. Any social condition is an unhealthy one which compels married women to seek gainful employment and makes it impossible for them to manage their home. And we should accept as normal that the married woman is restricted to domestic life at a time when her household duties exact her total energies.

After the Fall, woman was forced to care for the most primitive necessities of life, which resulted in a severe curtailment of her powers; in this respect, she has benefited from conditions brought about by cultural change. Moreover, the change in her destiny implied her subordination to man: the extent and type of her activity were made dependent on his will; and, because his judgment and will are not infallible, she is not guaranteed that his control over her will be regulated by right reason. Moreover, inasmuch as the harmony between the sexes was disordered by the Fall, the question of the subordination of woman involved a bitter conflict concerning the activities suitable to corrupted masculine as well as feminine nature.

The redemptive order restores the original relationship; the more redemption is personally adopted, the more it makes possible a harmonious collaboration and an agreement concerning the allotment of vocational roles. It caused a further basic change in the status of woman by asserting the ideal of virginity. This broke through the Old Testament norm which stipulates that woman effects her salvation only by bearing children. And in those particular cases where individual women like Deborah and Judith had been called divinely to extraordinary achievements for God's people, even the norm of the Old Covenant had been changed as well. Now a new way reveals that women can consecrate themselves exclusively to the service of God, and they can develop a manifold activity in His service. Even the same St. Paul whose writings so often strongly echo Old Testament views has pronounced clearly that, from his point of view, it is good for men as well as for women to marry but it may be better not to marry. And now and then, he emphasizes the praiseworthy achievement of women in the service of the first pastoral communities.[45]

Before considering men and women's common vocation in God's service, we would like to consider the problem of the distribution of vocations according to the natural order. Should certain positions be reserved for only men, others for only women, and perhaps a few open for both? I believe that this question also must be answered negatively. The strong individual differences existing within both sexes must be taken into account. Many women have masculine characteristics just as many men share feminine ones. Consequently, every so-called "masculine" occupation may be exercised by many women as well as many "feminine" occupations by certain men.

It seems right, therefore, that no legal barriers of any kind should exist. Rather, one can hope that a natural choice of vocation may be made thanks to an upbringing, education, and guidance in harmony with the individual's nature; unsuitable elements should be eliminated by strict objective requirements. The differences between masculine and feminine natures indicate clearly that a specific aptitude for certain professions is present in each. Thus, the choice of a profession will usually resolve itself.

Masculine vocations usually require bodily strength, the ability for predominantly abstract thought, and independent creativity: as an example, we might cite the hard physical labor required in industry, trade, and agriculture; or, to cite another example, the abstract thought required in technological fields such as mathematics and theoretical physics; and, finally, this can be seen even in the precision needed in clerical and administrative work of a mechanical nature and in certain branches of art. True feminine qualities are required wherever feeling, intuition, empathy, and adaptability come into play. Above all, this activity involves the *total person* in caring for, cultivating, helping, understanding, and in encouraging the gifts of the other. And since woman is mainly concerned with serving people and making provisions for them, she is able to function well in all educational and medical professions, in all social work, in the human sciences, in the arts which depict humanity, as well as in the business world and in public and parochial administration.

In times of extreme economic distress such as ours, it would not be feasible or possible to make distinctions between masculine and feminine professions; everyone must take any employment as soon as it is offered, whether or not it suits his or her specific individual talents. Today, almost on an average, people are in "vocations" to which they are not called by nature; one can almost consider it a stroke of luck when it is otherwise. Then there is nothing left but to make the most of the situation: the pertinent professional requirements must be satisfied but not at the cost of denying one's own nature by permitting it to atrophy; rather, it should contribute to the good of one's associates. (This may mean, for example, that the woman employed even in mechanical work will prove to be sympathetic and charitable to her colleagues; and the man caught in an unsuitable job nevertheless will exhibit inventive qualities in organizing his work.) Of course, this demands a high degree of personal maturity and an unconditional good will in doing one's best in any given situation. Such a perspective can hardly be attained without understanding that the circumstances of life are God-given, that one's work is service to God, and that the gifts which God gives must be developed to His glory in this work. This is valid not only for those vocations consecrated to God but for every vocation; and yet, of course, the vocation which is designated as being consecrated to God does stand out as being especially meaningful.

In common usage we say that priests and religious must be especially *called*, which means that a particular call must be sent to them by God. Is there any difference between the call sent to man and that to woman? Women just as men have been called to the religious state at all times. And when we consider the manifold ramifications of contemporary religious life, when we acknowledge that the extremely diverse works of charity in our times are practised also by the feminine Orders and congregations, we can see only one essential difference which still exists in reality: the actual priestly work is reserved for men. This introduces us now to the difficult and much debated question of *priesthood for women.*

If we consider the attitude of the Lord Himself, we understand that He accepted the free loving services of women for Himself and His Apostles and that women were among His disciples and most intimate confidants. Yet He did not grant them the priesthood, not even to His mother, Queen of Apostles, who was exalted above all humanity in human perfection and fullness of grace.

In the early Church, women played an active part in the various congregational charities, and their intense apostolate as confessors and martyrs had a profound effect. Virginal purity was celebrated in liturgy, and for women there was also a consecrated ecclesiastical office—the deaconate with its special ordination[46]—but the Church did not go so far as to admit them to the priesthood as well. And in later historical developments, women were displaced from these posts; also, it seems that under the influence of the Hebraic and Roman judicial concepts, there was a gradual decline in their canon law status. We are witnessing a decided change here in recent times: feminine energies are now strongly demanded as help in church charities and pastoral work. In recent militant movements, the women are demanding that their activities be recognized once more as an ordained church ministry, and it may well be that one day attention will be given to their demands. Whether this will be the first step then, finally, on the path leading to women in the priesthood is the question.

It seems to me that such an implementation by the

Church, until now unheard of, cannot be forbidden by
dogma. However, the practicality of such a recommendation
brings into play various arguments both pro and con. The
whole tradition speaks *against* it from the beginning. But in
my opinion, even more significant is the mysterious fact
emphasized earlier—that Christ came to earth as the *Son* of
Man. The first creature on earth fashioned in an unrivaled
sense as God's image was therefore a man; that seems to indicate to me that He wished to institute only men as His official
representatives on earth. Yet, He bound Himself so intimately
to *one* woman as to no other on earth: He formed her so
closely after His own image as no other human being before
or after; He gave her a place in the Church for all eternity
such as has been given to no other human being. And just so,
He has called women in all times to the most intimate union
with Him: they are to be emissaries of His love, proclaimers
of His will to kings and popes, and forerunners of His Kingdom in the hearts of men. To be the *Spouse of Christ* is the
most sublime vocation which has been given, and whoever
sees this way open before her will yearn for no other way.

It is the vocation of every Christian, not only of a few
elect, to belong to God in love's free surrender and to serve
Him. Whether man or woman, whether consecrated or not,
each one is called to the imitation of Christ. The further the
individual continues on this path, the more Christlike he will
become. Christ embodies the ideal of human perfection: in
Him all bias and defects are removed, and the masculine and
feminine virtues are united and their weaknesses redeemed;
therefore, His true followers will be progressively exalted over
their natural limitations. That is why we see in holy men a
womanly tenderness and a truly maternal solicitude for the
souls entrusted to them while in holy women there is manly
boldness, proficiency, and determination.

We are thus led through the imitation of Christ to the
development of our original human vocation which is to present God's image in ourselves: the *Lord* of creation, as one

protects, preserves and advances all creatures in one's own circle; the *Father*, as one begets and educates children for the kingdom of God through *spiritual* paternity and maternity. Transcendence over natural limitations is the highest effect of grace; however, this can never be attained by an arbitrary battle against nature and by denial of natural limitations but only through humble submission to the God-given order.

Chapter III

Spirituality of the Christian Woman

A discerning young girl recently asked me, "Why is it that at this time so much is being said, even by men, about the nature and vocation of women?" It is astonishing how this topic is constantly being taken up by various parties, and how differently it is being treated. Leading intellectuals are painting a shining ideal of feminine nature, and they are hoping that realization of this ideal will be the cure for all contemporary ailments and needs. At the same time, in the literature of the present and of the last decades, we see woman presented again and again as the demon of the abyss. A great responsibility is being laid upon us by both sides. We are being obliged to consider the significance of woman and her existence as a problem. We cannot evade the question as to what we are and what we should be. And it is not only the reflective intellect which faces us with this question; life itself has made our existence problematic.

An evolution which was sensed in advance by some, wanted and worked for by few, and one which surprised most people entirely, has torn women out of the well-enclosed realm of the home and out of a matter-of-course kind of life and has suddenly plunged them into the most manifold alien situations and undreamt of problems. We have been thrown into the river, and we must swim. But when our strength threatens to give out, we try to reach at least the shore for safety. We would like to think through the question of *whether* we should go on; and if we should go on, what we should do so that we will not drown. We would like

86

to scrutinize the direction of the current by taking into account, one against the other, its strength and our own powers and possibilities of movement.

It would now be feasible to take under consideration the following. We are trying to attain insight into the innermost recesses of our being; we see that it is not a completed being but rather a being in the state of becoming, and we are trying to achieve clarity relative to that process. Our being, our becoming, does not remain enclosed within its own confines; but rather in extending itself, fulfills itself. However, *all* of our being and becoming and acting in time is ordered from eternity, has a meaning for eternity, and only becomes clear to us if and insofar as we put it in the light of eternity.

I. WOMAN'S SOUL

Can we speak in general terms of *the* soul of woman? Every human soul is unique, no one soul is the same as any other. How can we then speak of the soul in general? But speculation concerning the soul usually considers the soul of *the* human being in general, not this one or that one. It establishes universal traits and laws; and, even when, as in *Differential Psychology,* it aims at differences, it is general types which it depicts rather than individual ones: the soul of the child, of the adolescent, of the adult, the soul of the worker, the artist, etc.; so it is with the soul of man and of woman. And to those who have reflected on the potentiality of science, the understanding of the individual appears ever more problematic than that of the general species.

But even if we intend to disregard individualities, is there then *one* type of woman? Is there something in common to be discovered in the prototype of woman as seen in Schiller's *Glocke* or Chamisso's *Frauenliebe und-leben,* and in the images which Zola, Strindberg and Wedekind paint for us? Can the complete multiplicity which we meet with in life be reduced to a single unity, and can this unity be distinguished from man's soul? This is not the place to provide philosophical proof that there is something in the range of the existent which we can denote as *species, woman's soul,* and that there is a specific cognitive function which is able to perceive it. Therefore, it will perhaps be more intelligible if we do not begin by outlining this general image of the *species* but rather sketch a series of types as different as possible one from the other, and then attempt to discover if we can find a general species in them. Since it is through poetry that the soul is most adequately described, I shall now analyze types taken from literary works to which I ascribe a particular symbolic value.

Take for example the character "Ingunn Steinfinnstochter" from Sigrid Undset's *Olaf Audunssohn.* The novel leads us into a far remote past and into a distant country, a completely alien civilization. Ingunn grows up free and unshackled in a medieval Nordic manor. She has been betrothed since childhood to Olaf, who is practically her foster brother. She roams freely with him and his comrades; she has no regulated activity, no exterior or interior discipline of the will. The children look to each other for support because they have no other. Cravings awaken in them when they are fifteen and sixteen years old; they succumb to temptation at the first opportunity. From that time on, Ingunn's entire life is one of insatiable longing. She and Olaf consider themselves insolubly bound to each other according to ecclesiastical law. But the family opposes the marriage, and they become separated for years. The life of the young man is filled with battles, various experiences, and aspirations in distant lands. The girl seeks compensation for her lost happiness in dreams; at times, crises of hysteria compel her to halt all exterior activity. She yields to a seducer although she yearns only for Olaf. However, realization of her fall breaks into this somber psychic existence like a supernatural light; and she rouses herself with astounding strength and severs the sinful relation-

ship. Olaf, returned home, is unwilling to break the sacred
bond which unites them simply because of her confessed
guilt. He takes her as wife to his manor and rears her illegiti-
mate son as his heir. But the desired happiness does not come
as yet. Ingunn is depressed through the consciousness of her
guilt, and she gives birth to one dead child after another. But
the more she considers herself to be a source of misfortune
for her husband, the more she clings to him; and the more
vehemently does she crave further proofs of his love. And
although she wastes away in this life, consuming his strength
as well, Olaf yields as he has always yielded to her. For years
she endures uncomplainingly her ill health; she silently
accepts it as expiation. Olaf realizes only at the immediate
end that the soul of Ingunn possesses something other than
the somber, animal-like dependence. He realizes that it
possesses a divine spark which lacked only support and a
conception of a higher world; this world had not attained
sufficient clarity to be of influence on her life. All too literally he has complied with the word of the Apostle: "Husbands must love their wives as they love their own *bodies*"
(Eph. 5:28). And because of this, two lives have been ruined.

As in other works of Sigrid Undset, the two worlds, or
actually prehistoric worlds, stand in firm opposition: the
gloomy, instinctive world of primordial chaos, and that of
God's spirit hovering over creation. The soul of Ingunn, this
child of nature, is like land untouched by the plough. There
are potent seeds of germinating power therein, and life in
them is stirred into tremulous motion through the ray of
light which comes from the other side of the clouds. But it
would be necessary that the gross clods be cultivated in order
for the light to penetrate to the seeds.

Ibsen's *Nora* is no child of nature; she has grown up
rather in the milieu of modern culture. Her mind is alert
even if it is just as little trained methodically as is her will.
She was the darling doll of her father, and now she is her husband's darling doll just as her children are her dolls. With

cutting criticism, she says this herself when her eyes have been opened. The spoiled child is faced with decisions for which she is in no way prepared. Her husband becomes severely ill, and means are lacking for the trip which can save him. She cannot ask her father for help because he is also ill. So she endorses a note herself with his name as co-signer. Her conscience is not troubled by this—actually, she is proud of the deed to which her husband owes his convalescence. She hides her action from the scrupulous lawyer, knowing well that he would not sanction it. But when the creditor is driven to extremes by his own need and threatens exposure, it is not fear of her husband's censure which causes her despairing decision to flee. She both fears and hopes that now the "miracle" will occur—her husband will take her guilt upon himself in his great love. But it happens quite differently. Robert Helmer has only condemnation for his wife; he considers that she is no longer worthy of raising his children. Nora recognizes herself and him for what they are in the disillusionment of this moment, that the hollowness of their life together does not deserve the name of *marriage*. And when the danger of social scandal is removed, when he graciously would like to forgive everything and re-establish their life again, she cannot accept his pardon. She knows that before she is able to try again to be wife and mother, she must first become a person. Certainly, Robert Helmer would also have to develop from the social figure into a human being in order that their joint life might become a marriage.

In Goethe's *Iphigenie,* a bizarre decree tore Iphigenie in early youth from the circle of her beloved family and led her to a strange, barbarian people. The hand of the gods delivered her from certain death for holy service in the quiet of the temple. The mysterious priestess is honored like a saint. But she is unhappy here. She yearns always for return to her home. She firmly declines the king's courtship in order not to cut herself off from this return. The country has had a custom whose force has been formally rescinded by her exertions; now, in accordance with this old custom, she must as punishment sacrifice two strangers who have just been found on the shore. They are Greeks, one of them her brother. Her longing to see one of her own once again is fulfilled. But he is defiled by matricide, agonized by remorse to the point of madness. He is destined for death at her hand. The old curse of her house, from which she appeared until now to be free, threatens to be fulfilled in her also. Faced with the choice whether to save her brother, his friend, and herself through lies and deceit or to abandon all of them to ruin, she first believes that she must choose the "lesser evil." But her pure soul is not able to bear untruthfulness and breach of trust; she defends herself against these as does a healthy nature against germs of fatal disease. Trusting in the veracity of the gods and the nobility of the king, she reveals her plan of flight to him and receives as reward the lives of those endangered and her return home. Her brother is already healed through her prayer. Now she will carry joy and reconciliation with the gods into the ancient noble house.

Before we proceed to look for a common *species* in all three different types of women, it might be useful to discuss briefly the relation of these types to reality. Are we not dealing here with pure creatures of poetic imagination? With what right, then, are we able to use them to gain insight into real psychic existence? For a solution of this difficulty, we will first try to clarify what the poetic spirit has intended to convey in each of these types.

Hardly anyone could conceive of Sigrid Undset's work as "l'art pour l'art." Her creativity is reckless confession. Indeed, one has the impression that she is compelled to express that which presses upon her as brutal reality. And I believe that whoever gazes into life as sincerely and soberly as she did will not be able to deny that the types she represents are real, even if they are chosen with a certain bias. There is obviously a method in this one-sidedness: she wishes to emphasize the animal-instinct to better reveal the inadequacies of a mendacious idealism or an exaggerated intellectualism in dealing with earthy reality.

The figure of *Nora* was created by a man who wishes to adopt entirely the woman's perspective, a man who has made the cause of woman and the feminist movement his own. His heroine is chosen from this point of view—but she is precisely *chosen* and depicted with keenest analysis; she is not invented arbitrarily nor constructed rationalistically. The strength and consequence of her thought and action may be surprising in contrast to what has previously transpired; she may be unusual, yet her action is not an improbable or a completely impossible one.

The classical lineaments, the simple grandeur and exalted simplicity of Goethe's most noble female character may appear at first glance to the modern person as most nearly removed from reality. And idealism is certainly under consideration here; but again, this is no construction of fantasy but rather an idealized image which is envisioned, experienced, and empathized from life itself. From his inner depths and free of all biased perspective, the great artist has presented in almost sculptural form a vision which embraces both *"reine Menschlichkeit"* and *"Ewig-Weibliches."*[1] And we are gripped, as only total purity and eternal truth can grip us.

So much for the "reality" of these types. Do these three women have anything in common? They come from different worlds in the writings themselves; also, they are the creation of very different writers. No traditional discipline shaped the soul of Ingunn, a child of nature; Nora, the doll of *The Doll's House,* inhibited by artificial social conventions, asserts nevertheless her healthy instinct to cast off these fetters in order to take her life into her own hands and refashion it freely. Iphigenie, the priestess in the sacred temple, has surpassed nature through union with the godhead and has entered into supernatural clarity. These three women share one common characteristic: a longing to give love and to receive love, and in this respect a yearning to be raised above a narrow, day-to-day existence into the realm of a higher being.

Ingunn's dream is to live at Olaf's side in a manor and to have many children. In her torpor, she is unable to imagine any other pattern of existence and consciously to choose another. And when the exterior union with her spouse finally comes as the only fulfillment, it is the physical side of the relationship to which she clings with all her life energy. In so doing, she does not find the longed-for happiness; but she knows no other way to find it or even to look for it, and she remains with what she does have.

Nora's *real* life, concealed behind her "doll's" existence of which she is at first scarcely aware, consists in waiting for the *miraculous,* which is nothing else but the end of her puppet existence, the breaking forth of great love which will reveal the true being of her spouse and of herself. And as there is no response from her husband, as she becomes aware that nothing exists behind his mask of social convention, she is determined to make the effort alone to break through to her true being, to its very core.

With Iphigenie, it is no longer a question of the breakthrough to true being; she *has* already achieved true being, in having reached the highest level of human perfection; she has only to put it to the test and to allow it to have its effect. She longs that the level of being she has reached will serve as an instrument of that redeeming love which is her true destiny.

Do these examples suitably illustrate the essence of woman's soul? We could, of course, provide here just as many types of women as you like; however, I believe, just as long as they are types of *women,* we will always find fundamentally the compulsion to become what the soul should be, the drive to allow the latent humanity, set in her precisely in its individual stamp, to ripen to the greatest possible perfect development. The deepest feminine yearning is to achieve a loving union which, in its development, validates this maturation and simultaneously stimulates and furthers the desire for perfection in others; this yearning can express itself in the

most diverse forms, and some of these forms may appear distorted, even degenerate. As we shall show, such yearning is
an essential aspect of the eternal destiny of woman. It is not
simply a human longing but is specifically feminine and opposed to the specifically masculine nature.

Man's essential desires reveal themselves in action, work,
and objective achievements. He is less concerned with problems of being, whether his own or of others. Certainly being
and doing cannot be wholly separated. The human soul is
not a complete, static, unchanging, monolithic existence. It
is being in the state of becoming and in the process of becoming; the soul must bring to fruition those predispositions with
which it was endowed when coming into the world; however,
it can develop them only through activation. Thus woman
can achieve perfect development of her personality only by
activating her spiritual powers. So do men, even without
envisaging it as a goal, work in the same way when they
endeavor to perform anything objectively. In both instances
the structure of the soul is fundamentally the same. The soul
is housed in a body on whose vigor and health its own vigor
and health depend—even if not exclusively nor simply. On
the other hand, the body receives its nature *as* body—life,
motion, form, gestalt, and spiritual significance—through the
soul. The world of the spirit is founded on sensuousness
which is spiritual as much as physical: the intellect, knowing
its activity to be rational, reveals a world; the will intervenes
creatively and formatively in this world; the emotion receives
this world inwardly and puts it to the test. But the extent
and relationship of these powers vary from one individual to
another, and particularly from man to woman.

I would also like to believe that even the relationship of
soul and body is not completely similar in man and woman;
with woman, the soul's union with the body is naturally more
intimately emphasized. (I would like to underline the term
"naturally," for there is—as I have at one time intimated—the
possibility of an extensive emancipation of the soul from the

body, which now, oddly enough, seems to be more easily accomplished normally in the case of woman.) Woman's soul is present and lives more intensely in all parts of the body, and it is inwardly affected by that which happens to the body; whereas, with men, the body has more pronouncedly the character of an instrument which serves them in their work and which is accompanied by a certain detachment. This is closely related to the vocation of motherhood. The task of assimilating in oneself a living being which is evolving and growing, of containing and nourishing it, signifies a definite end in itself. Moreover, the mysterious process of the formation of a new creature in the maternal organism represents such an intimate unity of the physical and spiritual that one is well able to understand that this unity imposes itself on the entire nature of woman. But a certain danger is involved here. If the correct, natural order is to exist between soul and body (i.e., the order as it corresponds to unfallen nature), then the necessary nourishment, care, and exercise must be provided for the healthy organism's smooth function. As soon as *more* physical satisfaction is given to the body, and it corresponds to its *corrupted nature* to demand more, then it results in a decline of spiritual existence. Instead of controlling and spiritualizing the body, the soul is controlled by it; and the body loses accordingly in its character as a human body. The more intimate the relationship of the soul and body is, just so will the danger of the spiritual decline be greater. (On the other hand, certainly, there is also the greater possibility here that the soul will spiritualize the body.)

Now, after considering the relationship of soul and body, let us turn to the interrelationship of the spiritual faculties. We see that they are in a state of interdependence—one cannot exist without the other. Intellectual cognition of reality is the necessary point of departure for emotional response. The incitements of the emotions are the mainsprings of the will; on the other hand, the concern of the will is to regulate intellectual activity and emotional life. But the faculties are in no manner equally dispensed and developed. Man's endeavor is exerted to be effective in cognitive and creative action. The strength of woman lies in the emotional life. This is in accord with her attitude toward personal being itself. For the soul perceives its own being in the stirrings of the emotions. Through the emotions, it comes to know what it is and how it is; it also grasps through them the relationship of another being to itself, and then, consequently, the significance of the inherent value of exterior things; of unfamiliar people and impersonal things. The emotions, the essential organ for comprehension of the existent in its totality and in its pecularity, occupy the center of her being. They condition that struggle to develop herself to a wholeness and to help others to a corresponding development, which we have found earlier to be characteristic of woman's soul. Therein, she is better protected by nature against a one-sided activation and development of her faculties than man is. On the other hand, she is less qualified for outstanding achievements in an objective field, achievements which are always purchased by a one-sided concentration of all spiritual faculties; and this characteristic struggle for development also exposes her more intensely to the danger of fragmentation. Then, too, *the* one-sidedness, to which by nature she inclines, is particularly dangerous: unilateral emotional development.

We have attributed much importance to emotion in the total "organismus" of spiritual being. It has an essential cognitive function: it is the central pivot by which reception of the existent is transmuted into personal opinion and action. But it cannot execute its function without the co-operation of intellect and will, nor can it attain cognitive performance without the preparation of the intellect. Intellect is the light which illuminates its path, and without this light, emotion changes back and forth. In fact, if emotion prevails over the intellect, it is able to obscure the light and distort the picture of the entire world just as of individual things and events and drive the will into erroneous practice.

Emotional stirrings need the control of reason and the direction of the will. The will does not reach any absolute power for invoking or suppressing emotional reactions, but it does adhere to its freedom to permit or to restrict the development of mounting agitations. Where discipline of mind and will are lacking, emotional life becomes a compulsion without secure direction. And because it always needs some stimulation for its activity, it becomes addicted to sensuality, lacking the guidance of the higher spiritual faculties. Thus given the intimate union of body and soul, it results in the decline of spiritual life to that of the sensuous-animalistic one.

Consequently, only if its faculties are correspondingly trained will the feminine soul be able to mature to that state conformable to its true nature. The concrete feminine types which we have cited represent to us not only diverse natural predispositions but also diverse formative levels of the soul of woman. We have seen in Ingunn a woman's soul which was nearly like unformed matter but which still permitted intuitions of its capacities. Another, Nora, through the influences of chance and social conventions, had found a certain formation but not that proper to her. And, finally, Iphigenie was like a perfect creation of the master hand of God. This presents us with the task of investigating what the formative powers are through which woman's soul can be led to the nature for which it is intended and can be protected from the degeneration with which it is threatened.

II. WOMAN'S FORMATION

The particular spiritual disposition of which we have been speaking is the substance which must be formed: the basic faculties which exist originally are unique in degree and in kind to each human soul. It is not inanimate material which must be entirely developed or formed in an exterior way, as is clay by the artist's hand or stone by the weather's elemental forces; it is rather a living formative root which possesses within itself the driving power *(inner form)*[2] toward development in a particular direction; the seed must grow and ripen into the perfect gestalt, perfect creation. Thus envisaged, formation of the spirit is a developmental process similar to that of the plant. However, the plant's organic growth and development do not come about wholly from within: there are also exterior influences which work together to determine its formation, such as climate, soil, etc.; just so, in the soul's formation, exterior factors as well as interior ones, play a role. We have seen that the soul can be developed only through activation of its faculties; and the faculties depend on material to be activated (and, indeed, on material which is suitable to them): the senses, through impressions which they receive and process, the intellect through mental performance, the will through achievements which are characteristic to it, the emotions through the variety of feelings, moods, and attitudes. Definite motives which place the faculties into motion are needed for all of this.

Simple contact with other people and with one's surroundings is often sufficient to stimulate certain responses. Ordinary daily existence conditions the formation of the spirit. However, instruction and guidance are needed for other responses, especially those involving the higher faculties. Allowance should be made for spontaneity as well as planned *work* and instruction. Formation requires the creation of *educational subject matters* which will place duties before intellect and will, stir the emotions, and fulfill the soul. But here we enter into the realm of values—the good, the beautiful, the noble, the sacred—the specific values which are unique to each soul and to its individual quality.

Cognitive work and achievements of the will are *free actions;* so, too, surrender to or rejection of original, involuntary, self-governing emotional stimulations is a matter of freedom. Thus, the human being awakened to freedom is not simply delivered to exterior formative influences; but, on the contrary, he can yield himself to them or reject them as he searches for or avoids possible formative influences. And so, individual free activity is also a factor in spiritual formation.

All of the exterior educational factors—everyday existence, planned as well as free, self-developmental work—are bound in their efficacy to the first factor, the natural predisposition; they cannot endow the person with qualities which are not in him by nature. All human education can only provide subject matter and render it "palatable"; it can lead the way and "demonstrate" in order to stimulate activity, but it cannot force acceptance or imitation. Nature sets the limits of personal formative work. Nature and the subject's freedom of will impose limits on spiritual formation. But there is *one* Educator for whom these limits do not exist: *God,* who has given nature, can transform it in a manner which turns it from its natural course of development (just as He can intervene by His miracles in the normal course of external natural occurrences). And even though He has excluded also a mechanically necessary rule of the human will by His gift of freedom, He can bring the will's *interior* inclination toward a decision to execute that which is presented to it.

Thus we have attained a certain insight into the nature of education: the process of shaping the natural spiritual predisposition. In customary usage, the term "education" also signifies the result of these processes—the gestalt which the soul assumes thereby, perhaps also the soul thus formed, and even the spiritual matters which it receives.

In trying to formulate a proper educational program for women, the stress is often laid on questions of method. Whoever is concerned with the spiritual formation of woman must first of all be aware of the material with which he is dealing, that is, the predisposition of the human being whom he is supposed to educate. He must especially understand the unique quality of feminine spirituality and the individual nature of his pupils. He must also be aware of earlier influences, such as home environment, which have already affected and still affect his students. He must know whether they are in harmony or not with his own aims and purposes or whether, if they are not, an effort should be made to eliminate them. The educator must be fully conscious of the *objectives* he has set for himself and for others, which, of course, depend on his total vision of the world. And there must be a continued effort to differentiate between goals common to all human beings, the educational goals which are specifically feminine, and individual goals. These cannot be set up arbitrarily but are determined by God Himself. Holy Scripture counsels us on the destiny of the human being in general and that of woman in particular. Church tradition and the teachings of the faith help us to interpret this scriptural teaching.[3] The parable of the talents refers to the unique gift given to each individual; the Apostle's word describes the multiplicity of gifts afforded in the Mystical Body of Christ. The individual must discover his own unique gift.

God has given each human being a threefold destiny: to grow into the likeness of God through the development of his faculties, to procreate descendants, and to hold dominion over the earth. In addition, it is promised that a life of faith and personal union with the Redeemer will be rewarded by eternal contemplation of God. These destinies, natural and supernatural, are identical for both man and woman. But in the realm of duties, differences determined by sex exist. Lordship over the earth is the primary occupation of man: for this, the woman is placed at his side as helpmate. The primary calling of woman is the procreation and raising of children; for this, the man is given to her as protector. Thus it is suitable that the same gifts occur in both, but in different proportions and relation. In the case of the man, gifts for struggle, conquest, and dominion are especially necessary: bodily force for taking possession of that exterior to him, intellect for a cognitive type of penetration of the world, the powers of will and action for works of creative nature. With the woman there are capabilities of caring, protecting, and promoting that which is becoming and growing. She has the gift thereby to live in an intimately bound physical compass and to collect her forces in silence; on the other hand, she is created to endure pain, to adapt and abnegate herself. She is psychically directed to the concrete, the individual, and the personal: she has the ability to grasp the concrete in its individuality and to adapt herself to it, and she has the longing to help this peculiarity to its development. An equipment equal to the man's is included in the adaptive ability, as well as the possibility of performing the same work as he does, either in common with him or in his place.

In the Old Testament, those testimonies from the Fall on, i.e., those which reckon with *fallen* nature, marriage and maternity are presented with a certain exclusiveness as the destiny of woman. These are even the means for fulfilling her supernatural goal: she is to bear children and raise them in faith in the Redeemer so that one day she will behold her salvation in them. (This interpretation is also voiced from time to time in the Pauline epistles.)

Next to this, the New Testament places the ideal of virginity. In place of the marriage bond, there is offered the most intimate, personal communion with the Savior, the development of all faculties in His service, and spiritual maternity—i.e., the winning of souls and their formation for God. One should not interpret this differentiation of vocation as if in one case it were only the natural goal being considered, and, in the other case, only the supernatural one. The woman who fulfills her natural destiny as wife and mother also has her duties for God's kingdom—initially, the propagation of human beings destined for this kingdom, but then, also works for the salvation of souls; only for her, this lies first within the family circle. On the other hand, even in the life which is wholly consecrated to God, there is also need for the development of natural forces, except that now they can be more exclusively dedicated to problems pertaining to the kingdom of God and can thereby even benefit for a wider circle of people. These works for God's kingdom are not foreign to feminine nature but, on the contrary, are its highest fulfillment and also the highest conceivable enhancement of the human being. This is true as long as the action of personal relationship is born out of love for God and neighbor, works through love of God and neighbor, and leads to love of God and neighbor.

Thus the education of the Christian woman has a dual goal: to lead her to that which makes her capable of either fulfilling her duties as wife and mother in the natural and supernatural sense or of consecrating all her powers to the kingdom of God in a God-dedicated virginity. (Marriage and the religious life should not be set up as alternatives. Signs indicate that our time needs people who will lead a God-dedicated life "in the world"; this is certainly not to say, however, that conventual life is "outmoded.")

What can we do to aim towards this goal? We have already indicated that woman was created for this purpose; in *fallen* nature, however, there are drives working at the same time in opposition to it. So it will be a question of supplying the educational subject matters which are necessary and conducive to the soul's pure development and qualified to impede unwholesome drives. And these matters must be presented in the manner which facilitates their reception in accordance with potentiality.

The emotions have been seen as the center of woman's soul. For that reason, emotional formation will have to be centrally placed in woman's formation. Emotion exists in sentiments such as joy and sorrow, moods such as cheerfulness and gloom, attitudes such as enthusiasm and indignation, and dispositions such as love and hate. Such emotional responses demonstrate the conflict of the individual with the world and also with himself. It is only the person who is deeply involved with life whose emotions are stirred. Whoever is aiming to arouse emotion must bring it into contact with something which will hasten this involvement. Above

all, these are human destinies and human actions as history
and literature present them to the young—naturally, this will
be contemporary events as well. It is beauty in all its ramifications and the rest of the aesthetic categories. It is truth
which prompts the searching human spirit into endless pursuit. It is everything which works in this world with the
mysterious force and pull of another world. The subjects
which are especially affective in emotional training are religion, history, German, and possibly other languages if the
student succeeds in overcoming the external linguistic difficulties and is able to penetrate to the spiritual content.

But, generally speaking, it is not enough only to stir the
emotions. An evaluating factor exists in all emotional response. What the emotions have grasped are viewed as being
either positively or negatively significant, either for the concerned individual himself or, independent of him, viewed in
the significance of the *object in itself.* It is thereby possible
for the emotional responses themselves to be judged as being
"right" or "wrong," "appropriate" or "inappropriate." It is a
matter of awakening joyful emotion for *authentic* beauty and
goodness and disgust for that which is base and vulgar. It is
important to guide the young person to perceive beauty and
goodness, but this is not sufficient. Often the child is first a-
wakened to the value of things by his awareness of the adult's
responses—above all, that of the teacher—enthusiasm inspires
enthusiasm. The guidance of attitudes is simultaneously a
method of training the ability to discriminate. One cannot
introduce him only to the good and the beautiful: life will
also bring him into contact with ugliness, and by then the
child should have already learned to differentiate between the
positive and the negative, the noble and the base, and to learn
to adapt himself in suitable ways. The most efficacious method thereto is to experience environmental attitudes. The attitude of the developing individual towards the world depends
greatly on environmental influences which are both arbitrary
and instinctive. And thus it is of extraordinary significance

that the child's education be placed in the hands of people who themselves have received proper emotional formation.

However, this most essential, even indispensable, method of emotional formation through value judgments is accompanied by a certain danger as well: feelings and emotional attitudes are "contagious"; they are easily picked up by one person from another. These attitudes are, indeed, but pure predispositions in the affected soul. In the first place, the mind is not open to the values presented; and these sentiments, moreover, are neither momentarily or generally vital. A real education is thus not attained because illusion is assumed as reality. Hence there is need for education relevant to the authenticity of sentiments, the differentiation of appearance from reality both in the environment and in one's own soul. This is not possible without sufficient intellectual training. Intellect and emotion must cooperate in a particular way in order to transmute the purely emotional attitudes into one cognizant of values. (It is not our concern here to demonstrate this method of cooperation.) Whoever knows exactly *why* something is good or beautiful will not simply assume the attitudes of another. And then the exercise of this intellectual critique develops the ability to distinguish between spiritual truth and falsehood. Emotional reactions invoke action. The authentic art lover will gladly sacrifice comfort for the sake of artistic enjoyment. Those who truly love their neighbor will not be unsympathetic and apathetic to their neighbor's need. Words should inspire action; otherwise, words are mere rhetoric camouflaging nothingness, concealing merely empty or illusory feelings and opinions.

In earlier decades, the subjects which trained the emotions constituted the principal aim of the education of young women. Such formation corresponded to feminine nature. But there was a neglect of the indispensable complement, the practical training and activation of the intellect. This kind of education produced a type of woman who lives on illusion, a woman who either denies realistic duties or surrenders herself helplessly to fluctuating sentiments and moods, who constantly seeks excitement. Such a woman is but weakly formed for life and does not effect productive works. The modern school seeks to remedy such deficiencies. It has introduced more subjects designed to train the mind—mathematics, natural sciences, and the classics. In order that the thematic content be grasped by the intellect, mere memorization is de-emphasized and spontaneity is encouraged. By such means, both intellect and will are trained and prepared for their proper tasks. Modern education also stresses community life and practical participation in it by such means as school clubs, walking tours, celebrations, and team activities. Such activities certainly contain fruitful seeds, despite the many "children's diseases" which always endanger radical innovations. The great danger is that the reform may not take sufficiently into account the unique nature of woman and the type of education it needs, while being only too narrowly confined to the model of educational institutions for males. The changing demands of practical life make this danger obvious.

Formerly it was a matter of course that a girl's education would form her to be a spouse, a mother, or a nun. For centuries, hardly any other feminine vocation was known. Girls were expected to be initiated into domestic activity and religious practices either in family or convent life, and thereby prepared for their later vocation. The nineteenth-century Industrial Revolution revolutionized average domestic life so that it ceased to be a realm sufficient to engage all of woman's potentialities. At the same time, the diminishing life of faith excluded convent life as a serious consideration for most people. In passive natures, this climate has led to an immersion into an overly sensual life or empty dreams and flirtations. In strongly active natures, there has resulted a turning away from the house towards professional activity. So the feminist movement came into being. Vocations other than domestic had been exercised for centuries almost exclusively by men. It was natural, therefore, that these vocations assumed a masculine stamp and that training for them was adapted to the masculine nature. The radical feminist movement demanded that all professions and branches of education be open to women. In the face of severe opposition, the movement was able to advance only very gradually until, almost suddenly, it obtained nearly all its demands after the revolution. In the beginning of the movement, the women who entered into professional life were predominantly those whose individual aptitude and inclination went in this direction; and they were able, comparatively speaking, to acclimate themselves easily. The economic crisis of recent years has forced against their will many women into professional life.[4] Various conflicts have thus emerged, but valuable experiences have also been made. And we have reached the point where we may ask questions which, according to right reason, should have been cleared up before the movement began. Are there specifically feminine professions? What are they? Do women require education different from that given to men? If so, how should such education be organized?

Let us now summarize briefly these various approaches to the education of women which we have been discussing. The nature and destiny of woman require an education which can inspire works of effective love. Thus, emotional training is the most important factor required in the formation of woman; however, such authentic formation is related to intellectual clarity and energy as well as to practical competence. This education forms a proper disposition of the soul in accordance with objective values, and it enables a practical execution of this disposition. To place supernatural values above all earthly ones complies with an objective hierarchy of values. The initiation of this attitude presents as well an analogy with the future vocation of forming human beings for the kingdom of God. That is why the essence of all feminine education (as of education in general) must be religious education, one which can forcefully convey the truths of the faith in a manner which appeals to the emotions and inspires actions. Such formation is designed to exercise simultaneously the practical activities by the life of faith. The individual will be concerned with these activities through his entire life: the development of the life of faith and of prayer with the Church through the liturgy, as well as with creating a new personal relationship to the Lord, especially through an understanding of the Holy Eucharist and a truly Eucharistic life. Of course, such religious education can only be imparted by those personalities who are themselves filled with the spirit of faith and whose lives are fashioned by it.

Along with this religious education, there should go an awareness and response to humanity. Subjects which can contribute to such awareness are history, literature, biology, psychology, and pedagogy; of course, these subjects should be presented in a simplified form to meet the student's potential. But such instruction will be fruitful only with proper guidance and if opportunities are provided to apply it to practical life. Necessary for intellectual development are the predominantly formal educational subjects—mathematics, the natural sciences, linguistics, and grammar. But they should not be overstressed at the expense of the student's capacity or the more essential elements of feminine education.

Instructional methods should be free and flexible in order to take into account not only the specifically gifted but also to provide opportunity for all to study theoretical subjects and cultivate technical and artistic talents. The individual's later choice of a profession must be kept in mind. Obviously, in doing all this, the teachers themselves must be thoroughly trained in their respective fields. And, of course, for women to be shaped in accordance with their authentic nature and destiny, they must be educated by authentic women.

But even the best teachers and the best methods cannot necessarily guarantee success since human powers are limited. However, formal education is only *one* part of the integral educational process. Formal education must reckon with the capacities of the student and with the outside influences to which the student is subjected; but it has neither the possibility to identify all these factors nor to deal effectively with them. Moreover, formal education ends long before the total educational process is completed. The instructor may even consider the education successful if the pupil has been prepared to continue her education independently in the initiated direction. But the circumstances of daily life often intervene and make it possible for the purely natural drives to prevail.

Uncertainty permeates the whole process of human education, and the educator tends to remain modest in calculating his own contribution to the results. Yet he must not yield to skepticism or despair. The educator should be convinced that his efforts are important, even though he cannot always measure the results of his efforts, even though sometimes he can never be aware of them at all. He must never forget that, above all, the primary and most essential Educator is not the human being but God Himself. He gives nature as He does life's circumstances under which it comes to development; He also has the power to transform nature from within and to intervene with His works where human powers fail. If religious education succeeds in breaking down resistance to divine instruction, then one can be certain about everything else. We should also be convinced that, in the divine economy of salvation, no sincere effort remains fruitless even when human eyes can perceive nothing but failures.

III. FEMININE VOCATIONS

What formation does woman's soul yearn for? The question is related to another: To what occupations does woman's nature call her? It is not our concern here to compile statistical data to demonstrate the vocations in which contemporary woman is engaged. (She is engaged in nearly all of them.) Rather, our intent is to discover woman's genuine inclinations. In doing so, statistics are of little help. A presentation of numbers involved in particular vocations does grade the inclinations and talents concerned; even so, it can inform only clumsily regarding the success of the various activities. Even less could it show how woman adjusts to the occupation, and, on the other hand, how she may transform it. We must here limit ourselves to that which nature and destiny demand in true feminine vocations. But it is necessary to cite concrete examples. Therefore, we shall attempt to show how woman can function in marriage, in religious life, and in various professions in conformity with her nature.

According to Genesis, woman was placed by man's side so that he would not be alone but would have a helpmate who suits him; she will primarily fulfill her vocation as spouse in making his concerns her own. Normally, we understand "his concerns" to mean his profession. The woman's participation in her husband's profession can be performed in various ways. In the first place, it will be her duty to shape their home life so that it does not hinder, but rather furthers, his professional work. If his work is in the home, she must see to it that disturbances are kept as far away from him as possible; if his work is away from the home, she must be sure that the home affords appropriate relaxation and recovery when he returns to it. There can be immediate participation in the performance of direct help; indeed, this happens frequently in modern marriages between people of similar or related professional training, or at least with those of congenial interests. In former times this was the case to a large extent, generally in country life but also frequently in business enterprise (especially in those on a small scale), in doctor's households, and also very prominently in those of Protestant pastors.

"Man's concerns," however, does not only refer to the purely objective content of his work but also to the procurement of his family's livelihood—the "battle for existence." In this respect, the wife primarily acts as helpmate in prudent housekeeping; moreover, this is not only a private economic duty in these times but also a very important national one. But possibly more nowadays than in former times, both husband and wife will work. Therein arises the difficult problem of the double vocation: there is danger that her work outside of the home will so take over that finally it can make it impossible for her to be the heart of the family and the soul of the home, which must always remain her essential duty.

But the woman who "suits" man as helpmate does not only participate in his work; she complements him, counteracting the dangers of his specifically masculine nature. It is her business to ensure to the best of her ability that he is not totally absorbed in his professional work, that he does not permit his humanity to become stunted, and that he does not neglect his family duties as father. She will be better able to do so the more she herself is mature as a personality; and it is vital here that she does not lose herself in association with her husband but, on the contrary, cultivates her own gifts and powers.

Her mission as mother relates closely to her mission as spouse, only here she must primarily care for the children and bring them to development. She must guide and then gradually withdraw to attain, in face of the mature human being, the role of a companion. This demands, on the one hand, an even more refined gift of sympathy because it is necessary to comprehend the dispositions and faculties of which the young people themselves are as yet unaware; she has to feel her way towards that which wishes to become, but which as yet does not exist. On the other hand, the possibility of influence is greater. The youthful soul is still in the formative stage and declares itself more easily and openly because it does not offer resistance to extraneous influences. However, all this increases the mother's responsibility.

In order to develop to the highest level the humanity specific to husband and children, woman requires the attitude of selfless service. She cannot consider others as her property nor as means for her own purposes; on the contrary, she must consider others as gifts entrusted to her, and she can only do so when she also sees them as God's creatures towards whom she has a holy duty to fulfill. Surely, the development of their God-given nature is a holy task. Of even higher degree is their spiritual development, and we have seen that it is woman's supernatural vocation to enkindle, in the hearts of husband and children, the sparks of love for God or, once enkindled, to fan them into greater brightness. This will come about only if she considers and prepares herself as God's instrument. How this can be will be considered at a later time.

It would not be difficult to mention women in the most diverse professions who have achieved excellence, but this would not prove that their occupations were specifically feminine ones. Not every woman is a pure embodiment of feminine nature. Individualities are not simply variations of feminine nature but are often approximations of masculine nature and qualify, thereby, for an occupation not regarded as specifically feminine. If the care and development of human life and humanity are women's specific duty, so the specifically feminine vocations will be those in which such efforts are possible outside of marriage as well. I do not wish to enter here into the question of domestic service because here it is not a question of specifically feminine work, and in many respects it produces tasks other than those which the woman of the house must fulfill. It is more important to clarify the significance of occupations outside of the household, occupations which were denied women for some time and have only become available for women gradually through the struggles of the feminist movement.

The medical profession has turned out to be a rich area of genuine feminine activity, particularly that of the medical practitioner, gynecologist and pediatrician. There have been severe objections to the admission of women into this profession: a young lady may encounter many things in her medical studies which would otherwise be kept away from her; a serious objection has been that the studies make extraordinary demands of bodily strength and nervous energy, and professional practice even more. Indeed, professional practice requires a particular physical and spiritual constitution, as well as the professional zeal necessary for the assumption of the difficulties unique to that profession. Such misgivings are dispelled when these stipulations are respected. Of course, one will always be grateful to encounter the untroubled, innocent beauty which moves us, and which is completely unaware of the seamy side of human nature. Today it is hardly possible, but in former times how many women who were so protected in their innocence until marriage were suddenly robbed of all their ideals, in the cruelest manner, in marriage itself! In this respect, could one not say that the matter-of-fact and objective, scientific approach is still one of the most accepted methods, if not the absolutely best one, to become acquainted with natural data? Since most women are obliged to come to grips with these data, should not individual women who have the calling and opportunity make all sacrifices in order to fulfill this calling and stand by their sisters' side?

Experience indicates that this has happened in large degree. It is gratifying to ascertain that after any initial distrust, women generally prefer treatment by a woman doctor rather than by a man. I believe that this is conditioned not only by the patient's modesty but even more so by the specifically feminine manner of empathy which has beneficial effects. The human being, especially the invalid, needs sympathy in his total condition. The widespread method of modern specialization does not satisfy this need in treating a limb or organ while disregarding the rest of the person, even though the specific treatment is pertinent. (Also, in many cases, specialization is not the best method because most illnesses are illnesses of the total human being even if they are manifested in only one organ; the patient needs treatment in his individual peculiarity as a whole organism.) Counteracting this abstract procedure, the specifically feminine attitude is oriented towards the concrete and whole person. The woman doctor has only to exercise courage in following her natural inspiration and liberating herself whenever necessary from methods learned and practiced according to rule. (Of course, it must not be denied that it often happens as well with masculine specialists, although not generally—in earlier times the house doctor typified this total approach.) It is not only a question of summoning up the patience to listen to much which is absolutely irrelevant to the subject. The intent must be to understand correctly the whole human situation, the spiritual need which is often greater than the corporal one, and perhaps to intervene helpfully not only by medical means but also as a mother or a sister.

So conceived, the medical profession is a truly charitable one and belongs together with other social professions. These professions have been developed for the most part only in recent years, and they are specifically feminine vocations as rightfully as the housewife's. In all such vocations, it is a matter of actions which are truly maternal in the care of a large "family": parishioners, the poor or sick of a rural parish or of a municipal precinct, the inmates of a prison, endangered or neglected youth. There is always the potentiality, and basically the necessity, of understanding and helping the whole person whether one initially encounters these human beings to care for them in bodily sickness or to assist them financially, or to give them legal counsel. Demands here on the power of love are even greater than in one's own family: the natural bond is lacking, the number of people in need is greater, and preponderantly there are people who repel rather than attract by their disposition and frame of mind.

In this type of work more than others, it will be shown that normal psychic power does not suffice in carrying out the tasks noted above. It must be sustained by Christ's power and love. And where it is so supported it will never stop at mere attendance to natural humanity; but, on the contrary,

it will always aim at the same time towards the supernatural
goal of winning these human beings for God.

Chapter IV

Fundamental Principles of Women's Education[1]

Our entire educational system has been in a state of crisis for decades. Continuous calls for reform are being made everywhere. Although some important guidelines have emerged from the confusion of diverse efforts, one feels as though in the midst of preparatory experiments rather than a peaceful, efficient evolution.

Women's education is part of this general crisis, and it also has its own unique problems. A final solution will be possible only in conjunction with a reform of the entire German educational system. Today, even if we try to consider women's education separately, we must do so in considering it in its relation to the problem as a whole. Women's education, although a special case, involves, in fact, the entire range of educational reform.

I. CONCEPT OF EDUCATION[2]

Should we look for the cause of the crisis which has shaken the old system, we would do well to search for it in the *concept of education* basic to that system, a concept which we today consider as having failed. The "old system" is essentially a child of the Enlightenment. (I am thinking here of the elementary and high schools and the teachers' colleges. Humanistic secondary schools, universities, seminaries for priests, and other vocational schools have evolved from

115

another foundation, but they show—due to practical inter-lockings—distinct marks of the influence of the rest of the school system.)

The former ideal of education was that of *encyclopedic knowledge:* the presumed concept of the mind was that of the *tabula rasa* onto which as many impressions as possible were to be registered through intellectual perceptions and memorizations. The system which emerged from this concept has occasioned ever increasing criticism through its evident defects and, finally, there is an all-out attack on it. Today, it is like a house that is being torn down—here and there one still sees part of a brick wall, a bow window, rubbish heaped up in between; in the midst of this, here and there a new segment rises. I wonder if it is possible to remove all this and to erect a new edifice on solid ground in accordance with a uniform plan? The tendency for this is here: for years, we have been witnessing the struggle for a new concept of education. Yet this concept is fundamentally a very old one.

I will try briefly to outline the goal of all these efforts. *Education* is not an external possession of learning but rather the *gestalt*[3] *which the human personality assumes under the influence of manifold external forces,* i.e., the process of this formation. The material which is to be formed is, on the one hand, the inherited physical-psychic disposition; on the other hand, it is the formative materials constantly being integrated. The body draws from the physical world; the psyche from its intellectual environment—from the world of people and from the values which nourish it.

The first fundamental formation happens within the soul. Just as *an inner form resides* in the seed of plants, an invisible force making a fir tree shoot up here and a beech there, there is in this way an inner mold set in human beings which urges the evolution into a certain direction and works towards a certain *gestalt* in blind singleness of purpose, that of the personality which is mature, fully developed, and uniquely individual.

Other forces accompany this first one, some from without and some from within. The small child with its physical-psychic disposition and its innate singleness of purpose is delivered into the hands of human sculptors. The fulfillment of his goal depends on whether or not they furnish the necessary formative materials for his body and soul. It is characteristic of the psychical *organs* that they only fructify by being activated on adequate material: i.e., the senses through observation, discernment, comparison of colors and shapes, tones and noises; reason through thought and understanding; will through achievements of will (decision, resolution, renunciation, etc.); emotions through emotional responses, etc. Adequate external tasks contribute accordingly to the cultivation of these faculties.

There are many predispositions which would block the development prescribed by inner determination if permitted to grow uncurbed. The forming hand which curtails such sprouting wild seedlings serves the inner formation.

Along with these interventions, there are active environmental factors. Actual *formative material* is received not merely by the senses and intellect but is integrated by the "heart and soul" as well. But if it actually becomes transformed into the soul, then it ceases to be mere material: it works itself, forming, developing; it helps the soul to reach its intended gestalt.

The external formative powers are conditioned by yet another inner formative force. The small child is put into the hands of human educators, but the maturating person awakening to spiritual freedom is given into his own hand. He himself can work for his growth through the faculty of *free will:* he can discover and develop his faculties; he can open himself up to the formative influences or cut himself off from them. He, too, is bound by the material given to him and the primary formative principle acting within: nobody can make of himself something which he is not by nature.

In contrast to all powers already named, there is only

one formative power which is not bound to the limits of nature, but, on the contrary, can transform the inner form further and from within: that is the *power of grace*.

We recognize that education is more complex and mysterious and less subject to arbitrary will than the Enlightenment conceived; and because the Enlightenment did not deal with the essential factors of formation, its system of education had to suffer shipwreck.

II. WOMEN'S NATURE AND VOCATION

All formal educational work must recognize given nature. Hence the slogan of the school reformers: "Everything depends on the child!" Because this given nature is an individual one, they insist it needs "Individual Education!" Because the faculties develop only through application, they call for "Student autonomy!"—"Spontaneity!" If we want to lay the foundation for a sound, enduring educational system for women, we must therefore ask ourselves:

1. What is *woman's nature* and the *educational goal* prescribed for that nature: what inner formative powers do we have to count upon?

2. How can formal education help the inner process?

In consideration of the first question, I would like to limit myself to the nature of woman.[4] Extensive individual differences shall not be denied; in many instances, women indicate predominantly masculine traits. Each woman has the expectancy for a particular vocation by dint of individual predispositions and gifts; this vocation is irrespective of her feminine one. Consideration of individuality is a requirement for general education; what matters above all in our context is to lay the *specific* basis for woman's education.

Woman's nature is determined by her original vocation of *spouse and mother*. One depends on the other. The body of woman is fashioned "to be one flesh" with another and to nurse new human life in itself. A well-disciplined body is an accommodating instrument for the mind which animates it; at the same time, it is a source of power and a habitat for the mind. Just so, woman's soul is designed to be subordinate to man in obedience and support; it is also fashioned to be a shelter in which other souls may unfold. Both spiritual companionship and spiritual motherliness are not limited to the physical spouse and mother relationships, but they extend to all people with whom woman comes into contact.

The soul of woman must therefore be *expansive* and open to all human beings; it must be *quiet* so that no small weak flame will be extinguished by stormy winds; *warm* so as not to benumb fragile buds; *clear*, so that no vermin will settle in dark corners and recesses; *self-contained*, so that no invasions from without can peril the inner life; *empty of itself*, in order that extraneous life may have room in it; finally, *mistress of itself* and also of its body, so that the entire person is readily at the disposal of every call.

That is an ideal image of the gestalt of the feminine soul. The soul of the first woman was formed for this purpose, and so, too, was the soul of the Mother of God. In all other women since the Fall, there is an embryo of such development, but it needs particular cultivation if it is not to be suffocated among weeds rankly shooting up around it.

Woman's soul should be *expansive;* nothing human should be alien to it. Evidently, it has a natural predisposition to such an end: on average, its principal interest is directed to people and human relations. But, if one leaves the natural instinct to itself, this is expressed in a manner apart from its objective. Often the interest is chiefly mere curiosity, mere desire to get to know people and their circumstances; sometimes it is real avidity to penetrate alien areas. If this instinct is simply indulged in, then nothing is won either for the soul itself or for other souls. It goes out of itself, so to speak, and remains standing outside of itself. It loses itself, without giving anything to others. This is unfruitful, indeed, even detrimental. Woman's soul will profit only if it goes abroad to *search* and to bring home the hidden *treasure* which rests in every human soul, and which can enrich not only her soul but also others; and it will profit only if it searches and bears home the well-known or hidden *burden* which is laid on every human soul. Only the one who stands with wholesome awe before human souls will search in such a manner, one who knows that human souls are the kingdom of God, who knows that one may approach them only if one is *sent* to them. But whoever is sent will find that which she is seeking, and whoever is so sought will be found and saved. Then the soul does not remain standing on the outside but, on the contrary, carries its booty home; and its expanses *must* widen in order to be able to take in what it carries.

The soul has to be *quiet*, for the life which it must protect is timid and speaks only faintly; if the soul itself is in tumult, it will not hear this life which will soon be completely silenced and will disappear from the soul. I wonder whether one can say that the feminine soul is fashioned by nature for this? At first sight, the contrary seems to be true. Women's souls are in commotion so much and so strongly; commotion itself makes much noise; and, in addition, the soul is urged to express its agitation. Nevertheless, the faculty for this quiet must be there; otherwise, it could not be so profoundly practiced as it is, after all, by many women: those women in whom one takes refuge in order to find peace, and who have ears for the softest and most imperceptible little voices.

Woman succeeds if the other requirements are filled: if the soul is *empty of self* and is *self-contained.* Indeed, when the inherent agitated self is completely gone, then there is room and quiet to make oneself perceptible to others. But no one can render himself so by nature alone, neither man nor woman. "O Lord God, take me away from myself and give me completely to you alone," the ancient German prayer says. We can do nothing ourselves; God must do it. To speak to Him thus is easier by nature for woman than for man because a natural desire lives in her to give herself completely to someone. When she has once realized that no one other than God is capable of *receiving* her *completely* for Himself and that it is sinful theft toward God to give oneself completely to one other than Him, then the surrender is no longer difficult and she becomes free of herself. Then it is also self-evident to her to enclose herself in her castle, whereas, before, she was given to the storms which penetrated her from without again and again; and previously she had also gone into the world in order to seek something abroad which might be able to still her hunger. Now she has all that she needs; she reaches out when she is sent, and opens up only to that which may find admission to her. She is *mistress* of this castle as the handmaid of her Lord, and she is ready as handmaid for all whom the Lord desires her to serve. But, above all, this means that she is ready for him who was given to her as *visible* sovereign—for her spouse or, also, for those having authority over her in one way or other.

The soul of woman is no doubt *warm* by nature, but its natural warmth is too seldom constant. It consumes itself and fails when it may be most needed; or it is augmented by a flying spark to the fire which destroys when it should only gently warm. But here again, that can only be helped when, instead of the worldly fire, the heavenly one is known. When the heavenly fire, the divine love, has consumed all impure matters, then it burns in the soul as a quiet flame which not only warms but also illuminates; then all is bright, pure, and *clear*. Indeed, clarity also does not manifest itself as given by nature. On the contrary, the soul of woman appears dull and dark, opaque to herself and to others. Only the divine light renders it clear and bright.

Thus, everything points to this conclusion: woman can become what she should be in conformity with her primary vocation only when formation through grace accompanies the natural inner formation. Because of this, religious education must be the core of all women's education.

III. THE WORK OF FORMAL EDUCATION

We see that the possibility exists of the inner formative functions needing the help of exterior ones; indeed, that is the hypothesis of all education. Formal education enhances the development of the given physical and intellectual *organs,* and it produces suitable educational material. Both work extensively together. Trained functions are needed for the reception of the materials; on the other hand, these functions can only be trained by material. The treatment of the body belongs naturally in an integral theory of women's education. I leave it to the experts to deduce the natural educational work provided by anatomy and physiology; I wish only to investigate education in respect to the soul. What materials does the soul need for its development? It must receive something into itself in order to grow. And, as we have seen, only that which the soul receives *internally* can become an integral part of it so that we can speak of growth and formation; that which is received by senses and intellect remains an exterior possession.[5] We call *qualities* the objects which have something in themselves which make them fit for reception into the interior of the soul; we call this something itself *value.*

An especially strong natural desire for such spiritually nourishing values lives within the soul of woman. She is predisposed to love the beautiful, inspired by the morally exalted; but, above all, she is open to the highest earthly values, the inexpressible ones which remain in the essence of the souls themselves. It was thus undoubtedly legitimate when *emotionally formative* subjects—literature, art, history—occupied an extensive place in the education of girls until a few years ago. I quite believe that, in the former period, at least the more gifted girls of the often derided *"Höheren Töchterschule"*[6] profited by a good share of effectual education.

Yet the fact that emotionally formative material is generally received is of less importance; such material must become assimilated in the right way, thereby cooperating in formation. There is a law which rules this formation—the law of *reason.* The respective place in the soul to be reasonably yielded to values and qualities corresponds to the structure of the external world and to its gradation of these values and qualities. In order that the soul be rightly formed and not *mal*formed, it must be able to compare and discriminate, weigh and measure. It may not be impregnated with an equivocal enthusiasm; it may not be filled with fanaticism; and it must attain fine perception and sharp judgment.

A well-developed intellect pertains to that end. Even if abstract intellectual activity is on average less suited to women, the intellect is nevertheless the key to the kingdom of the mind; it is the eye of the mind, and through it light penetrates into the darkness of the soul. In her Graz address on *Woman's Mission,* Oda Schneider said that it suffices for women to live and not to ask a protracted "what" and "to what purpose." But in that lies the strong danger of error, of loss of purpose and aim. The significance of masculine control was elucidated in that address. But that should not mean the relinquishing of one's own judgment in favor of dependence. The intellect, which for all that is surely *there,* may and must be moved to action. It cannot, by any means, become lucid and acute enough. But, of course, the development of intellect may not be increased at the expense of the refinement of emotion. That would mean turning the means into the end. The main point is not to admit into the curriculum *everything* recommendable as purely intellectual training. It would be advisable, on the contrary, if the trouble were taken to achieve a maximum result with a minimum expense so that the greatest possible opportunity remains for material improvements.

Moreover, one must remember that there is not only a theoretical but also a practical intelligence which is faced in daily life by the most diverse tasks. It is, first of all, of extraordinary importance for later life to train this faculty; and it is formed through exercise in concrete tasks, not in theoretical problems. It suits the nature of woman better because she is indeed more oriented to the concrete than to the abstract. And along with it should go schooling of the will from which achievements are constantly asked: choice, judgment, renunciation, sacrifice, etc. And training of the practical intellect is also essential for the cultivation of proper emotions. Only where conviction and intention are successfully translated into action can it be shown whether an enthusiasm is legitimate, whether higher things are actually preferred over lower things. Finally, human nature is geared not only toward receiving but also toward acting by giving shape to the external world.

For that reason, an essential part of the educational process is the activation of one's practical and creative capacities. And practical abilities in life are required of the majority of women. Only if we have allowed them to already *act* during the time of schooling will we rear practical, able, energetic, determined, self-sacrificing women.

Several basic points of reference for an *educational plan* now emerge as exacted by the nature and vocation of woman. One would have to be entirely free of the notion that schooling should give a compendium of all the areas of knowledge of our time. On the contrary, one should endeavor to form people who are intelligent and capable enough to familiarize themselves with any area of knowledge which will become important for them. That is why the subject matter within the so-called *exact sciences* should be intensively limited, as well as the time allotted to foreign languages for children with little linguistic talent. The mind must be given adequate opportunity to exercise itself. To that end, abstract activity cannot be lacking. For that purpose, depending on talent, one should refer preferably to the classics or to mathematics. Practical exercises of mind should be placed in any case next to abstract, intellectual exercises.

Teaching girls to know and understand the world and people, and learn how to associate with them, should be considered the essential duty of the school. It has become impressively clear to us that a right relation to our fellow-creatures is only possible within the framework of a right relation to the Creator.

Thus we come back to the concept that religious education is the most important component of education. The most urgent duty is to open the child's path to God. Thus we can also say that to be formed religiously one must have *living faith*. To have living faith means to know God, to love Him, to serve Him.

Whoever knows God (in the measure in which knowledge of God is possible through natural and supernatural light) cannot do other than love Him; whoever loves Him cannot do other than serve Him. Thus, matters of mind and heart, achievement and act of will are living faith. He who knows how to awaken faith trains all faculties. But one can only awaken it when one also summons up all the faculties. This cannot be done through tedious intellectual instruction, but it also cannot be done through fanatic instruction which "appeals to the emotions"; on the contrary, this can be done only through a religious instruction which leads from the fullness of one's own religious life to the depths of the God-head, an instruction which is able to present God in His kindness; such instruction enkindles love and exacts proof through deed, and it may so challenge because one achieves this by oneself. Wherever the soul is enkindled, that soul itself longs for action; and it eagerly grasps the forms of practical life for which God and Holy Church have provided: participation in the Holy Sacrifice of the Mass, a participation which consummates the holy sacrifice *as* an offering in union with the Eucharistic Lord, festive praise of God, and all works of love in which Christ is served in the members of His Mystical Body. The entire abundance of the supernatural world of the spirit is opened to the soul thereby, and an inexhaustible abundance of formative material which enters into it is thus able to build up and transform it.

IV. CHALLENGES OF THE PRESENT–
ROADS TO PRACTICAL REALIZATION

How can we organize an educational institution in which people live with God and humanity, in which they work for God and humanity? Such an organization must be based on an understanding of the nature and vocation of woman as I have presented them.

But I believe that this must be considered from an entirely different perspective. *What does our age demand of women?* First of all, it requires most of them to earn their own living. It is reasonable to expect that those who manage a household conduct it in a rational way and assist the common condition of the economy, which summons them to contribute (as wives and mothers) to the moral recovery of the people. It desires that they pave the way for heaven. That means, it requires women who have a knowledge of life, prudence, and practical ability; women who are morally steadfast, women whose lives are imperturably rooted in God. How can all this be brought about if the foundation for this purpose is not laid in youth?

There is no lack of initiatives in this direction. The officials have adopted largely the methodical foundations of the reform pedagogy: they require *educational instruction* and "Selbsttätigkeit."[7] A start has been made with the new teaching arrangement for the elementary schools in Bavaria in order to convert the corresponding teaching plan: in Prussia in recent years, concern has been shown in the secondary schools for a greater freedom of movement by teacher and student. But all in all, it must be said that there are difficult hindrances such as the overloaded curriculum and the extended system of examination and qualification. I believe that a general reform of the educational system can be realized only in conjunction with a systematic regulation of the vocational system. And such a control appears to me as an urgent need of the present time, one even more urgent than educational reform; today large numbers of people are undecided about their choice of a vocation and have nowhere to go for counseling concerning a choice of vocation, and hardly anyone is able to give advice. We are warned that many vocations are overcrowded. Besides, there are so many theoretical requirements involved even in training for essentially practical vocations that many persons who have practical skills are excluded from them.

As a first step in finding a remedy for this state of affairs, general occupational statistics are needed: this would ascertain simultaneously how great the demand is for each vocation and would thereby control the inexcusable rumor of overcrowding. Vocational training should then be developed in accordance with actual requirements of the vocation; it should be uninfluenced by completely irrelevant viewpoints— for example, the desire of the officials to restrict the number of candidates through the most difficult terms of admission, or a certain vanity of some vocational classes which strive to maintain equality in the training process even if the real requirements indicate other paths.

It would be more suitable, then, to prepare systematically for this vocational school system in youth institutions inasmuch as such institutions could observe and differentiate the students according to their individual gifts; the vocational aptitude would be allowed to stand out early and would thereby lay the basis for appropriate vocational guidance and choice. A choice of educational matter could ensue, with regard to the future vocation showing early indications.

At these educational centers, great freedom and versatility in the work naturally would be required. What I have in mind is a kind of Montessori system which would be followed from earliest infancy up to the threshold of the vocational school.

The core curriculum in girls' schools should be the sort of general education dictated by woman's nature and vocation: a basic religious education suitable for each age level; at the same time, training in household skills, drawing up a budget, care of children and adolescents, and political-social issues. All this should be not purely theoretical but theoretical and practical at the same time, and, of course, not through laboratory experiments but through actual solutions of real, if smaller and more modest, tasks. Affiliated to this would be the purely intellectual fields; here division would enter according to individual aptitude and inclination, and the transfer into the vocational school would be prepared.

The transfer from a general educational institution into a vocational school appears to me as normal and desirable. In the first place, vocational preparation will be an economic necessity for a long time. Secondly, it appears to me to lie in the interest of personality formation. Individual abilities and energies of the mature person strive toward practical effect and capable performance. Only in the fewest number of cases is there still place in family life for such basic formation. In addition, it is a social requirement. The vocation is the place where the individual is incorporated into the community or into the function which he has to fulfill in the organism of community. The singular mission of the working woman is to fuse her feminine calling with her vocational calling and, by means of that fusion, to give a feminine quality to her vocational calling.

Naturally, such a school transformation cannot be enacted so easily. First of all, suitable teaching forces may be lacking. Secondly, any teething troubles in a new system might appear epidemically in the whole country, and that could be so disastrous that one would look back with nostalgia to the "good old times" and give up the healthy principles.

All reform measures must first of all be tested on a small scale; indeed, some have in fact been tested by inspired reformers in private or public experimental schools before they were officially recommended or ordered for general realization.

So it would appear as a desirable beginning for a reform

of women's education if a few resolute Catholic women might be discovered in order to build such a school, women who are firmly rooted in the faith, cultivated in basic pedagogy; but, above all, women who are familiar with all modern work methods. Also, of course, pertaining to this would be a circle of parents who are courageous and trustful enough to entrust their children to this school, and a circle of sponsors to finance it. Provisionally I would desire from the officials only that they create the scope of the new concept of education through reduction of subject matter and freedom of action of teachers' powers. Moreover, I would wish that the system of examination and qualification should undergo a basic revision and there be a new arrangement of the entire vocational system.

In this exposition, I have knowingly and deliberately placed *women's* education as such at the center. It has been emphasized well enough that women just as men are *individuals* whose individuality must be taken into consideration in educational work. However, in order to avoid a misunderstanding, it is perhaps not superfluous to emphasize that women and men are given a common goal of education as *human beings:* "You are to be perfect as your Father in heaven is perfect." This educational goal stands in visible gestalt before our eyes in the person of Jesus Christ. To become His likeness is everyone's goal. To be formed to this through Christ Himself is the path for us all as members bound to Him as head. But the basic material is diverse. God created humanity as man and woman, and He gave to each his and her particular duty in the organism of humanity. Masculine and feminine nature degenerated through the Fall. They can be freed from this slag in the furnace of the divine molder. And whoever relinquishes himself unconditionally to this formation, not only will nature in its purity be restored in him but he will grow beyond nature and become an *other Christ* in whom the barriers have dropped and the positive values of masculine and feminine nature are united. But all natural work has to proceed from the natural foundation.

St. Lioba, January 12, 1932[8]

In the talk which I gave in November 1930 in Berndorf concerning the foundations of women's education, I tried to draw the picture of woman's soul as it would correspond to the eternal vocation of woman, and I termed its attributes as *expansive, quiet, empty of self, warm,* and *clear.* Now I am asked to say something regarding how one might come to possess these qualities.

I believe that it is not a matter of a multiplicity of attributes which we can tackle and acquire individually; it is rather a single total condition of the soul, a condition which is envisaged here in these attributes from various aspects. We are not able to attain this condition by willing it, it must be effected through grace. What we can and must do is open ourselves to grace; that means to renounce our own will completely and to give it captive to the divine will, to lay our whole soul, ready for reception and formation, into God's hands.

Becoming empty and still are closely connected. The soul is replenished by nature in so many ways that one thing always replaces another, and the soul is in constant agitation, often in tumult and uproar.

The duties and cares of the day ahead crowd about us when we awake in the morning (if they have not already dispelled our night's rest). Now arises the uneasy question: How can all this be accommodated in one day? When will I do this, when that? How shall I start on this and that? Thus agitated, we would like to run around and rush forth. We must then take the reins in hand and say, "Take it easy! Not any of this may touch me now. My first morning's hour belongs to the Lord. I will tackle the day's work which He charges me with, and He will give me the power to accomplish it."

So I will go to the altar of God. Here it is not a question of my minute, petty affairs, but of the great offering of reconciliation. I may participate in that, purify myself and be made happy, and lay myself with all my doings and troubles along with the sacrifice on the altar. And when the Lord comes to me then in Holy Communion, then I may ask Him, "Lord, what do you want of me?" (St. Teresa). And after quiet dialogue, I will go to that which I see as my next duty.

I will still be joyful when I enter into my day's work after this morning's celebration: my soul will be empty of that which could assail and burden it, but it will be filled with holy joy, courage, and energy.

Because my soul has left itself and entered into the divine life, it has become great and expansive. Love burns in it like a composed flame which the Lord has enkindled, and which urges my soul to render love and to inflame love in others: *"flammescat igne caritas, accendat ardor proximos."*[9] And it sees clearly the next part of the path before it; it does not see very far, but it knows that when it has arrived at that place where the horizon now intersects, a new vista will then be opened.

Now begins the day's work, perhaps the teaching profession—four or five hours, one after the other. That means giving our concentration there. We cannot achieve in each hour what we want, perhaps in none. We must contend with our own fatigue, unforeseen interruptions, shortcomings of the children, diverse vexations, indignities, anxieties. Or perhaps it is office work: give and take with disagreeable supervisors and colleagues, unfulfilled demands, unjust reproaches, human meanness, perhaps also distress of the most distinct kind.

It is the noon hour. We come home exhausted, shattered. New vexations possibly await there. Now where is the soul's morning freshness? The soul would like to seethe and storm again: indignation, chagrin, regret. And there is still so much to do until evening. Should we not go immediately to it? No, not before calm sets in at least for a moment. Each one must know, or get to know, where and how she can find peace. The best way, when it is possible, is to shed all cares again for a short time before the tabernacle. Whoever cannot do that, whoever also possibly requires bodily rest, should take a breathing space in her own room. And when no outer rest whatever is attainable, when there is no place in which to retreat, if pressing duties prohibit a quiet hour, then at least she must for a moment seal off herself inwardly against all other things and take refuge in the Lord. He is indeed there and can give us in a single moment what we need.

Thus the remainder of the day will continue, perhaps in great fatigue and laboriousness, but in peace. And when night comes, and retrospect shows that everything was patchwork and much which one had planned left undone, when so many things rouse shame and regret, then take all as it is, lay it in God's hands, and offer it up to Him. In this way we will be able to rest in Him, actually to rest, and to begin the new day like a new life.

This is only a small indication how the day could take shape in order to make room for God's grace. Each individual will know best how this can be used in her particular circumstances. It could be further indicated how Sunday must be a great door through which celestial life can enter into everyday life, and strength for the work of the entire week, and how the great feasts, holidays, and the seasons of Lent, lived through in the spirit of the Church, permit the soul to mature the more from year to year to the eternal Sabbath rest.

It will be an essential duty of each individual to consider how she must shape her plan for daily and yearly living, according to her bent and to her respective circumstances of life, in order to make ready the way for the Lord. The exterior allotment must be different for each one, and it must also adjust resiliently to the change of circumstances in the course of time. But the psychic situation varies with individuals and with each individual in different times. As to the means which are suitable for bringing about union with the eternal, keeping it alive or also enlivening it anew—such as contemplation, spiritual reading, participation in the liturgy, popular services, etc.—these are not fruitful for each person and at all times. For example, contemplation cannot be practiced by all and always in the same way.

It is important to each case to find out the most efficacious way and to make it useful for oneself. It would be good to listen to expert advice in order to know what one lacks, and this is especially so before one takes on variations from a tested arrangement.

Chapter V

Problems of Women's Education

I. INTRODUCTION

A. The Problems as Viewed from the Present Position of Woman

At the onset of the feminist movement, a fierce battle was waged over the question of the education of women; this seems to have died down in the course of the last decade. However, the question is being debated again today very hotly. Therefore, the problem can be approached best by a consideration of the present position of the woman. Here a difficulty immediately arises. Actually, can we speak of the situation of *the* woman?[1] We will have to question later if there is a general *species* "woman." But in any case, we are speaking of the *position of woman* as a general concept. However, within this concept there is such a great diversity of types and individuals that we can hardly speak of a situation common to all of them. Putting aside for the moment a general consideration of individuals, we must admit that the situation of woman differs according to generation, status, and Weltanschauung; and these differences must not be overlooked.

1. WOMAN'S ATTITUDE TO THE PREDOMINANT QUESTIONS OF OUR TIME

We can try to characterize the spiritual and intellectual

134

attitudes of woman by considering her views about the weighty questions of our times: her outlook on marriage and motherhood, on her vocation, on national as well as on world politics, and, finally, on questions of eternity.

a. Marriage and Motherhood

The Berlin Academy for Women's Social and Pedagogical Work has published a highly credible work on *Family Life Today*.[2] It contains 183 descriptions of families in north, central, and south Germany from large cities, provincial towns, and rural areas. Social strata are not represented. The study is mostly concerned with the families of laborers, white-collar workers, and minor civil servants. The selection was unbiased. Rather, the respective groups were chosen according to external criteria such as the occupants of a particular house or block, the families of children attending the same class in a school, etc. In addition to purely external criteria like the number of children, the ages of the family members, their occupations, their source of income, etc., the given analysis had a well-defined purpose to distinguish the families which had a close relationship from those which were weak or broken. Although most families lived in very cramped conditions, although the wife and the grown children frequently worked outside of the home, most of them nevertheless had close family ties. The children were mindful of parental authority; the parents were doing their utmost faithfully to assure the care and education of their children; in many cases, every member of the family contributed to support according to his means. And wherever such a close relationship existed, it was mostly the woman's merit which kept the family together; at times she struggled with admirable, often heroic, effort against the most trying circumstances to prevent a family breakdown. Conversely, wherever family ties weakened, it could be attributed usually to the woman's failure.

In the light of these findings, it would appear that the current opinion concerning the breakdown of married and family life may be exaggerated since so many families which are to some extent entirely patriarchal still exist. However, on a closer examination, one must revise this appraisal. In the recorded case histories, the women were mostly about 35-50 years old. The picture would be essentially different if we should include married people who are between 20 and 30 years of age. Surely in the group we would find more child-less marriages, divorces, and unmarried unions. What will happen in the next generation we are entirely unable to fore-see. Moreover, studies of the upper and lowest social strata might change the picture somewhat. And, finally, we must assume that changes will take place now from year to year. Yet we may state safely that there are still extensive circles in German society which cling to the ideal of marriage and motherhood and to the ideal of family life as a saving and protecting support for its members. I would even like to believe from private observation that in the young generation there is a deep marital joy and a desire for married and do-mestic life which is more pronounced than in the preceding generation. This is partly connected with the attitude toward professional life concerning which there is still more to be said. But it is also connected partly with the increased signif-icance attributed to eroticism and sexuality which hold such a predominant position in scholarly writing as well as in belles lettres, in public discussion, and in daily life that even children are confronted with them at every turn.

Modern youth has proclaimed its sexual rights. If young people are still influenced by older traditions or if they are aware through their own philosophical convictions that mar-riage is holy, then a purposeful striving for the establishment of families must follow. If these ideals are abandoned, it results in the practice of free unions or absolutely promiscu-ous intercourse. The latter has increased in frightening pro-

portion in all circles from year to year. This is partly a manifestation of the universally growing uninhibited drives; partly,
it is an exact consequence of the negative theories aired in
public discussion on marriage which a more traditional morality cannot withstand.

A solid bulwark against these, in fact, progressively
effective theories can only be a clear and incontestably proven
concept of marriage. We have such a clear and incontestable
substantiation solely in Catholic dogma which views marriage
as a sacrament and the begetting and upbringing of progeny
as its essential purpose. In his encyclical on marriage, our
Holy Father (Pius XI) has clearly and distinctly proclaimed
to the entire world the meaning of this Catholic concept
which opposes all undermining tendencies of the present
time. But the concept of marriage on a Catholic foundation
must be further elaborated. The discussion concerning sexual
problems, involving the psychology, pedagogy, and pathology
of sex has spread so extensively and has already made such a
powerful, practical impact on the upbringing and education
of the young, in health care, and the way of life, that it is
necessary to come to an understanding of all these trends on
the basis of Catholic thought. We must do so critically, i.e.,
not negatively but in a thorough and serious analysis of what
is acceptable and unacceptable for us. For, in fact, we can
learn a great deal from modern research methods. The traditional Catholic handling of these questions or, indeed, the
traditional disregard for them could and should be revised if
it is to meet the challenging questions of the time.

The setup of a genuinely Catholic broad-minded approach
to marriage and sexuality and the educational principles to be
derived from this should therefore be considered as an urgent
problem in contemporary education. This means the education of all youth, including young girls. At the same time, it
would be of the greatest significance for our nation as a whole
because such an achievement, which can come only from the
Catholic perspective, would offer firm support in a positive

sense to conservative, traditional circles outside of the Church.

b. *Vocation*

Now let us consider woman's attitude regarding her vocation; we are using this word in its usual sense, not in the strictly proper linguistic usage which sets vocation apart from the *natural destiny* of woman instead of including it. We must also note here the conspicuous difference existing between generations and social classes. It is also common custom that in the fourth estate[3] the woman must work; this has been so as long as the estate exists which has been about 100 years (actually this has been basically true in the lowest social strata from the earliest times of antiquity). The necessities of life compelled women to work on the land, in the factory, or in the homes of strangers. This was taken for granted by them as a necessary evil and accepted without much brooding or resistance. It was the Reformation which actually first recognized the value of family life in its rejection of virginity as an ideal. It was at this time that the employment of women in the middle and highest strata was something unrecognized and disapproved of, with the exception of just a few vocational fields; and this was true until a few decades ago.

Economic conditions accounted for the waste of much of women's abilities in domesticity until a radical change took place. At the end of the eighteenth and in the beginning of the nineteenth centuries, philosophical thought used to attribute growing value to *individual personality*. Finally, an enhanced *social responsibility* developed in the second half of the nineteenth century and in our time. This led to the pioneering struggles of the feminists for educational and professional opportunities which would provide scope for diverse gifts and abilities. The girls who today take their "Abitur"[4] and go on to the universities more often than not know nothing as to what had to be done until the German universi-

ties finally opened their doors to women in 1901 after countless meetings, memoranda, and petitions to the *Reichstag* and
state governments. Women who are now between 40 and 60
usually obtained employment only after long struggles, not
only with their families but with the public at large. Whether
or not they were able to find gratification in their jobs or not,
there is no doubt they are at one with their profession. Today the situation is different. In every class of society, girls
as well as women are usually obliged to work through necessity. If they are able to afford the education, girls from good
middle-class and aristocratic families often choose an academic profession to make a living, since they consider such a
profession suitable to their rank even though they may lack
the ability and inclination for it. Even though we were to
disregard such adverse factors as economic necessity, the
overcrowding of the profession with the accompanying difficulty of obtaining a position, these girls certainly would find
little gratification in their vocation.

In addition, other factors have brought about what might
be called a crisis today in the feminist movement and generally in women's professional life. In the beginning, the anti-
feminists wanted to bar women from all occupations outside
of the home; they denied them every opportunity for education and professional work open to *men.* On the other hand,
many radical leaders demanded the complete equality of all
educational and professional opportunities, denying completely the concept of a particular feminine nature. Today,
reading material that was written 30 years ago, one is frequently amazed by its lack of objectivity, indeed by the
naïveté of its arguments. The feminist revolution nearly
obtained its ends without first having prepared the way for
them sufficiently. The difficulties were thus demonstrated;
but, in spite of this, it also brought positive results. Many a
woman was at odds with her profession, which explains a
certain fatigue. But on the whole, we have today such an
extensive system of feminine vocational training and of pro-

fessional life that we can scarcely imagine a retrenchment, although there are those who advocate it.

Only, we must realize that we are at the beginning of a great cultural upheaval; at this early stage we must expect to suffer what we might call "childhood diseases" and make every effort to overcome them. There is still essentially basic work to be done. We virtually have to go back to the very nature of man and of woman in order to initiate vocational training and direct the choice of vocation suitable to each; in this way there can be an integration of the sexes into the whole social structure in accordance with their nature. Thus we have come to the fundamental problem of the education of young women: i.e., the question about *essential feminine nature.* This question brings up other problems. Is feminine nature suited to particular professions? What vocational training does this nature require?

c. Relation of Woman to National Life and to International Politics

Now more than ever before, their professional life brings most women into contact with public life. They often hold responsible positions as delegates and civil servants in ministerial, provincial, and civic agencies. But the women who practice a social or pedagogical profession are also given a deep insight into the context of national life, into the state of national health and morality. In their position they can exert a beneficial influence on others, warding off what is harmful and receiving thereby an enhanced sense of responsibility for the public at large. Finally, those secure in domestic life who had concern only about their own personal affairs and those of the immediate family and circle of acquaintances also were stirred by the years of misery. To begin with, the war intervened so vigorously in the lives of almost all families that wives and mothers, sisters and daughters must needs be inspired to an active participation in their country's destiny. And although a certain lack of concern and a selfish carelessness about public conditions sprang up again in the postwar years of inflation, this was again ended by the continuing economic crisis now in a more advanced and extreme state than before.

Today, most Germans are forced to become aware of the connections between their vocational work, salary, household budget, the individual and family economic conditions with general economics and internal and foreign affairs of state. Now at least each person begins to realize that he is *co-sufferer* as a member of the vast national body. But the thinking person must also realize that in addition he is a *jointly responsible* member of the whole nation. Women's franchise has been perceived now many times as a serious option to *duty*. Also, those who are not interested in political affairs today must remind themselves that the whole political situation depends on how they use their political rights; and it depends on the political situation whether their husband and children will have work and bread, whether they will find opportunities to develop and utilize their intellectual gifts, whether they will be allowed to practice their faith and live.

We must still go one step further. It became increasingly clear after the post-war years that there is a connection between success and adversity in both private and national life; just so are the individual nations and states connected one with the other. The people of Europe who struggled in a life and death combat during the World War were plunged into misery together; and all the hard facts of life furthered the recognition that a recovery is possible only through joint effort. No one can be sure, however, that the effort to reach such an accord will be able to prevail in the face of strong resistance. It is obvious that this is a matter of immediate concern to women. If it is their vocation to protect life, to keep the family together, they cannot remain indifferent to whether or not federal and national life will be able to assure prosperity for the family and a future for youth. The important international petition of February 6, 1932 in Geneva showed that many women today regard the issue of peace and international agreement as their concern.

Thus, in the course of the last few years, woman's sphere of action has been extended from the home to the world. This development necessitates a common program to prepare girls for effective thinking on public questions. But other questions arose: whether the practice of a vocation and involvement in public life is a danger to the status of the family, whether and how this danger could and should be prepared for by a common educational program for girls.

d. Attitude to Eternal Questions

Our time in which all established values of existence are undergoing constant change is also a time of bitter disagreement about fundamental spiritual problems. Certainly there are still today obtuse and indifferent spirits who ignore these questions. But we must recognize that in comparison to preceding decades their number has become negligible. On the one hand, we have a horrible and satanic hatred of God which has perhaps never been known before; for the persecution of Christians during the early centuries was not directed against the faith itself but against a new form of faith which threatened the old forms. But, on the other hand, we can observe today individual souls who have an ardent yearning and desire for God, and even those who were conventional in all forms of faith seek a deepened and animated spirituality. It is indeed well-known that women especially are religiously receptive, and, consequently, it is natural that they become involved in this movement. Vocational training and professional life have detached many women from their families. For many this resulted in their breaking away from the religious traditions of their home; many lost their childhood faith and never sought to replace it; but this experience brought many to a personal conviction of faith through a profound conversion.

Mature feminine nature is characteristically consistent and whole. With these characteristics, there arises from a sound and inwardly sustained conviction of faith a yearning conformable to nature to live *completely* in the faith; and that means to place oneself completely in the service of the Lord. Today there is new lifeblood in the religious orders. First of all, many new orders have sprung up, and the old ones have attracted novices in greater numbers. In addition, there are certain religious cooperative societies which testify anew to the many different congregations whose special objective is charitable work. Then, too, everywhere in the old orders there is a struggle for spiritual renewal and enrichment. But it does seem to me that it is characteristic of our times that the drive to serve God with complete undivided devotion is *not* necessarily confined to traditional religious life. More and more intensely we are developing an *army of Christ* clothed in the garments of the world: there are those women who live in inner solidarity with the Lord, shaping their entire output from this relationship whether they work in solitude in the home or in a so-called "worldly" profession; then there are women who, without exterior manifestation, have united with others of like mind in order to follow a regulated life. They have all found a firm basis on which to build their discussion of the burning contemporary questions which I have previously indicated. The mission of religious education for girls is to guide them to such a confirmed stand.

2. ATTITUDE TOWARD WOMAN

a. Public Opinion

Still another aspect of the entire problem before us

today must now be clarified. In order to characterize woman's position it is not sufficient to discuss *her* attitude towards contemporary questions. We must attempt to clarify the response to her position, i.e., what is the attitude of the forces which shape life concerning woman's nature and destiny? First of all, I want to consider *public opinion.* The opinions and judgments of individuals are determined extensively by what *they* think and *they* say. But these opinions and judgments wield the strongest kind of practical influence. Until a few decades ago, public opinion concurred that *woman belongs in the home* and is of no value for anything else; consequently, it was at the cost of a weary and difficult struggle that woman's too narrow sphere of activity could be expanded. It is very difficult to know what is meant by *they.* Of course, opinions and judgments originate from individuals. But we cannot explain this simply by saying that certain prominent people coin these opinions and judgments which are gradually accepted by wider circles. The mind of the individual is formed by the modes of the time; that is also true of prominent people so that they incline to a certain mentality even if it is in a sense other than that of the masses.

We are unable to discuss these problems at this time. The actual question which concerns us now is what we think about woman in contemporary society. Here as elsewhere we find vacillation or either a duality or much divisiveness. There is still a multitude of thoughtless people satisfied with hackneyed expressions concerning the *weaker sex* or even the *fair sex.* They are incapable of speaking about this weaker sex without a sympathetic or often a cynical smile as well. They do this without ever reflecting more profoundly on the nature of the working woman or trying to become familiar with already existing feminine achievements. Sporadically, there are Romanticists who idealize women, painting them in delicate colors against a gold background, who would like to shield woman as much as they could from the hard facts of life. Curiously, this romantic view is connected to that brutal attitude which considers woman merely from the biological point of view; indeed, this is the attitude which characterizes the political group now in power. Gains won during the last decades are being wiped out because of this romanticist ideology, the use of women to bear babies of Aryan stock,[5] and the present economic situation. The woman is being confined to housework and to family. In doing so, the spiritual nature of woman is as little considered as the principles of her historical development. Not only is violence being done to the spirit by a biological misinterpretation and by today's economic trends but, also, by the materialistic and fundamental point of view of opposing groups.

Through the bait of radical equalization with men, the feminine following can also be recruited by a politics which views woman as an important factor not only in economics but in the class struggle. But the callous disregard of woman's nature and destiny is running into very strong opposition, especially among young women.

In addition to these widely expressed opinions, there is one characteristic feature of our time which cannot be ignored. There are a great number of men and women seriously attempting to penetrate woman's unique nature and characteristic value; they are using the methods of philosophy and theology, physiology and psychology, sociology and the history of civilization. Certainly, even here there is a diversity of opinion. On the one hand, there is a tendency to see the differences of the sexes as something that has come into existence historically; by studying externally conditioned relationships, they try to understand what can be done by altering these relationships; they see that both sexes share a common human nature. On the other hand, there is the conviction of an essential differentiation of human nature. However, in comparison to earlier discussions of this topic, woman's difference is no longer considered as inferiority but rather as a characteristic value; for that reason tendencies to deny woman's uniqueness completely have diminished.

b. The State

We pass now from the indefinite *they* to entirely concrete factors to inquire about the government's attitude to
woman. Here we have to report a violent upheaval. Until
about 30 years ago, the governmental aid for girls' education
was insignificant in comparison to that devoted to the education of boys. Moreover, the elementary, the lower grade, and
secondary schools for girls were maintained predominantly
by private and municipal funds, although sometimes with
federal subsidies as well. In addition, teachers' colleges for
women have been supported since the second half of the
nineteenth century after the beginning feminist movement
had demanded such action, and they were motivated by the
shortage of teachers at that time. Today we have a widely
ramified system of general educational institutions and vocational schools; although all questions are still not satisfactorily
resolved, we should be amazed at what has been created within a short space of time. Nevertheless, this entire system is
threatened by the present economic and political situation.

Around the turn of the century, women were minors
legally and politically; they were analogous to children and
the mentally retarded. The 1919 constitution of the Reich
made them equal, thus granting them full rights as citizens.
Given active suffrage, they became a factor of political power
which could be ignored no longer. This eligibility opened
responsible federal positions to them. On average, the practical experience gained by the feminine delegates and civil
servants in higher positions was not the same as that of men.
Doubtlessly, there are among them, just as among their masculine colleagues, people who are suited more or less to their
post by talent and character. But I believe that one can say
that those administrators with longer periods of experience
are hardly inclined to do without the cooperation of women
because there are many tasks for which women are simply
indispensable. This situation implies an obligation on our

part to ensure systematic training for such administrative work in order that it may not be taken on by dilettantes. We need basic political and social preparation for civic responsibilities; however, this is true not only for women but for the entire German nation which entered into a democratic form of government while still immature and unfitted for it. And we need special methods to prepare for government service in posts open to women. All this would come about if we had years of peaceful development before us. Naturally, we cannot foresee how conditions could be formed after a forcible break with the organic development.

c. The Church

What is the Church's position on woman? Here we must differentiate between the attitude expressed in dogma, in canon law, and by the hierarchy of the Church and that taken by Our Lord Himself. We do not have a precisely defined dogma *ex cathedra* on the vocation of woman and her place in the Church; but we do have traditional doctrine which voices the authoritative teaching on the natural vocation of woman. This teaching is contained in our Holy Father's encyclical on marriage previously mentioned wherein he declares that woman's primary and most essential duty is to be the heart of the family as wife and mother; the woman is warned about undertaking other duties if they would endanger the stability of family life.

In present canon law, equality between man and woman is doubtlessly out of the question inasmuch as she is excluded from all liturgical functions. As V. Borsinger has established in her dissertation on the legal status of women in the Church,[6] their present position has deteriorated in comparison to the early years when women had official duties as consecrated deaconesses. The fact that a gradual change took place indicates the possibility of development in an opposite direc-

tion. And in the contemporary Church we may expect that
increasingly women will be called to Church duties—in Caritas,
in pastoral work, and in teaching. But usually, laws are
juridicial expressions of already existing modes of life. How
far such a development can go cannot be predicted. I have
stated on another occasion[7] that I personally do not believe
that future development includes the possibility of priesthood
for women.

In our time the increasing employment of women for
Church duties reveals that the views of the hierarchy have
changed in regard to their nature and function. Naturally, we
have here again differences between generations. But this
does not mean in any way that it is only the elderly who are
constantly unable to liberate themselves from opinions based
on prevailing circumstances and contemporary outdated ideas.
In the first volume of the handbook on the feminist movement in which G. Bäumer outlines the history of the German
feminist movement, she states as an obvious fact that, according to the Church's views, a Catholic feminist movement is
not possible. Obviously, she interpreted certain remarks of
priests concerning woman's vocation as binding dogma of the
Church. No doubt there have been utterances in the patriarchal vein stating that woman's activity outside of the home is
out of the question and that man's tutelage of woman is
necessary in all domains. Although there are still advocates
of this opinion, it is by no means universally true. And, on
the other hand, we must emphasize that straightforward, far-
sighted theologians were part of the very first group who set
out to examine impartially the claims of the liberal feminist
movement; they evaluated its compatibility with the entire
Catholic philosophy of life; and, in doing so, many of them
like Joseph Mausbach became the pioneers of the Catholic
Women's Movement. The imperturbability of the Church
resides in her ability to harmonize the unconditional preservation of eternal truths with an unmatchable elasticity of
adjustment to the circumstances and challenges of changing

times.

Thus we can see today that ecclesiastical circles are seeking to fructify the diversity of feminine powers and abilities in the service of the Church which forms a part of the effort to permeate with the spirit of the Church all aspects of everyday life. The call to Catholic action was issued to both men and women. It is clear that the preservation and reconstruction of families is not possible without the active and conscious participation of women. They are indispensable for the upbringing of young people, both within the family and out of it, carrying out works of love in community groups as in parishes. They are called to carry the spirit of faith and love to souls in the most diverse spheres of activity and to help form with this spirit private as well as public life. This is the Catholic interpretation on the question of woman's vocation; and today when liberalism has collapsed and with it the intellectual foundations of the old interdenominational women's movement, we have in this Catholic concept the firm rampart for our defense against those powerful contemporary currents which aim at sweeping away everything which women have struggled for during the last decades.

Catholic women have a strong support in the Church; it needs their strength. The Church needs us. That means the *Lord* needs us; not that He could not manage without us but He has granted us grace, forming us as members of His Mystical Body and employing us as His living members. Did the Lord at any time make a distinction between men and women? Perhaps when He delegated the priesthood to His apostles but not to the women serving Him. (That is exactly why I maintain that the exclusion of women from the priesthood is not simply a question of temporal contingency.) But in His love He knew and knows now no distinction. His means of grace are equally at the command of all Christians, and He has showered His grace in prodigious abundance directly on women. And it seems that today He is calling women in ever greater numbers for specific duties in His Church.

From this arises a problem concerning girls' education: Is there a preparation for such vocations and for their performance? Doubtlessly, one would be at first inclined to say that such preparation is an individual matter and cannot be carried out in the present setup. Again, it may be something mysterious and unpredictable for which there is no preparation possible. Finally, the Lord usually has His own ways of fashioning His instruments Himself. But let us remember that the formation which the Lord Himself undertakes must be considered as an educational problem. So then, wherever the divine calling occurs, it can be obeyed or not obeyed. Nature, freedom, and grace collaborate. And so there also arises here problems and tasks for work in formation of the person. Finally, if vocation is also something personal, it is very probable that the specific nature of the individual must be considered. But then, we also have to deal now with the special problem of girls' education.

3. PROBLEMS IN THE EDUCATION OF YOUNG GIRLS

I would like to review now some of the problems brought up in our inquiry into the present position of woman.

The basic concept must be the *nature of woman,* for this is the *foundation* on which the entire educational system for girls must be built. But this nature is not uniform but varies according to types and individuals. We will have to investigate whether or not these different types share a uniform and unchangeable core which can be regarded as characterizing woman as a species (the historical types as well as the contemporary ones). If, indeed, there is such a core, we must inquire into the relationship of the species to the types. We must try to discover the factors determining the formation of types. We must seek clarity regarding how and in what ways they can be practically influenced.

Actually, the goal of feminine education is already

determined by the nature of woman. It may be that the educational process has an inwardly defined purpose which limits external goals. Several goals have already emerged from the proceeding discussion: woman as wife and mother; woman employed outside the home, as a responsible member of the nation as a whole and of the family of nations; and woman in the Lord's service. We will have to search out how extensively these roles are advanced or at least permitted by woman's nature; we will have to see whether or not all of them or some of them are *common goals of all* training for girls or if they correspond to varying types and lead to the use of varying educational methods; whether the goal of girls' education is totally circumscribed or whether other aspects are to be considered, namely the broadly human aspect and that of personality formation.

The basic nature of woman and the educational goal to be achieved imply the following questions: *who* is to perform the educational work, which *course* is to be followed, and with what *methods* are the goal or goals to be attained.

B. Solutions Attempted during the Last Decades

The foregoing analysis has provided us with a practical view of the problems involved.[8] But at the same time, it should make clear that the present situation is the outcome of an historical development and represents a point of transition. For a long while battles have been waged over a solution to these problems; and we cannot simply disregard earlier attempts, even though the problems have been changing and hence prompting ever new solutions.

During recent years, an abundant literature inquiring into the uniqueness of woman has become available. But it still remains to be seen how much of this is serious methodical inquiry and how much is dilettantish. Because we must

soon embark upon this question at great length, I should like
to say straight off that there are few fields in which both oral
and written discussion evidence so much naive self-confidence
and so little concern for methods as this one. And so it seems
to me that serious, scientific treatment of the topic has only
just begun.

Therefore, in establishing the educational goals suitable
for the feminine nature, scientific, positive inquiry has played
a very small part; rather, these have been determined by a
traditional or sentimental basis or through arbitrarily designed, predetermined attitudes. In addition, other factors
have influenced the objective, most of all general ideological
points of view and economics.

The first positive goal proposed for restructuring the
educational system for girls and a vigorous attempt at its
realization emerged from the feminist movement. However,
if we want to understand this new goal and the struggles
involved in carrying it out, we must first ask against what
these struggles were directed in the first place. And now we
have touched the crux of the matter: the struggle was directed
against an educational system for girls which was exclusively
conducted by men and whose purpose and methods were
determined by men. This system was accepted by society as
an unalterable fact. And yet, this state of affairs came about
historically: it did not originate at some time in remote antiquity but rather came about in modern times; this male-
dominated system had taken root in Germany, but by no
means was it so throughout the world. Also, it did not take
hold in all of Germany. Ever since the beginning of Christian
culture, the monastic schools in German territory were cared
for and also often conducted by nuns.

The first decades of the feminist movement were not
denominational and especially not Catholic. It reacted to
conditions prevailing at the time. The Reformation had
closed the convents and repudiated the ideal of virginity.
Thus it followed that the activities of women were restricted

to family and home, and their value was measured in terms of marriage and maternity alone. The Reformation deprived women of many rich fields of activity and robbed them of appropriate educational institutions. To be sure, Luther did demand that the civil authorities make proper provision for girls: after all, the Bible was to be read by women also; and there were to be *women teachers* for these schools, just as there had been in the urban elementary schools of the preceding centuries. But there was a lack of women teachers. On the whole, nothing higher than elementary education was considered necessary for girls.

All educational systems declined after the great war (1618-1648). Schools revived in the eighteenth century under the influence of the Enlightenment, and at this time the lack of trained feminine teachers was again evident. Public high schools for girls gradually came into existence in the nineteenth century, but they were under the jurisdiction of men. And the standard concepts for their organization seem about unbelievable today. I will give as evidence a citation frequently found in the writings of the feminist movement, a passage from the memorandum of the *First General Meeting of the Headmasters and Teachers of High Schools for Girls* (1872):

> It is necessary to make available to women the same opportunities for intellectual culture as are available to men. This should be done so that the German husband may not suffer boredom at home by the shortsightedness and narrow-mindedness of his wife, and so that he may not become inhibited in his devotion to higher interests, and so that his wife may stand by his side and share his interests with understanding and warmth of feeling.

Another typical passage can be found in Paul de Lagarde's declaration of the Prussian Conservative Party's program (Göttingen 1884, p. 25):

> Every woman actually learns only from the man

whom she loves, and she learns what the beloved
man wants her to learn as is pleasing to him through
his love and how much he wants her to learn.   Normally, a girl acquires her formation in marriage; however, something can be made of sisters, daughters,
and nurses through their brothers, fathers, and older
men if they serve these men with warm hearts.

Indeed, in the grains of truth found in these documents,
one still hears an echo of those Biblical texts concerning
woman's vocation as man's *helper* from which these ideas
may be derived.   But apart from this, the woman described
here appears as a grotesque, petty, middle-class, half-witted
carricature of the Old Testament view.   For how can we
recognize the image of the *mulier fortis* (Prov. 31:10-31),
which the liturgy holds up to us on the feastdays of holy
women, in this description of an *ornament of the domestic
hearth* which was supposed to be the ideal of girls' education
in the nineteenth century!   The curricula for *high school girls*
was dictated by this mentality.

Schools were established for girls to procure that indefinite something called *general education:* this meant some
knowledge of languages, a lively interest in literature and history, and anything else that would otherwise warm the heart
and inspire ideals.   But no consideration was given to the
actual theoretical or practical ability of the student, to the
formation of her personal judgment, and to independent
activity.   A number of courageous, resolute women waged a
single-minded campaign against this system.   The memoirs of
Helene Lange, *Lebenserinnerungen*,[9] convey a strong and vital
impression of the motives behind this struggle.   Impelled by
an innate authentic hunger for intellectual nourishment, she
finds her way along untrodden paths and wins for herself a
share in the cultural life which young men take as a matter of
course.   The memoirs give us an insight into the pressing
needs of that time: among them, preserving *women of the
lower classes* from exploitation,[10] of opening up new branch-

es of industry for the *women of the upper classes,*[11] of changing opinion so that "Work might be considered a responsibility and honor for the female sex";[12] of liberating powers that
have lain fallow for so long a time. Thereby the motives
were, on the one hand, to bring the women to maturity and
to form independent personalities in the idealistic sense of
humanism, and, on the other hand, to make them capable of
fruitful collaboration in national and cultural life. Radical
feminists[13] supported their views by insisting that both sexes
shared the same nature and the same rights. Helene Lange
throughout her life insisted that the dissimilarity of the sexes
must be emphasized in order that the feminine nature be
freely developed and properly formed. Only then might this
nature achieve its own cultural fulfillment, an achievement
indeed necessary in our time as a suitable compensation for
the obvious defects of our *masculine* Western culture; then
feminine nature might be capable of authentic human formation and an activity of helping love. That was the goal she
strove for; so also did her followers the General Society of
German Teachers founded in 1890 in Friedrichroda. The
methods proposed for this were, first, an intensified participation of women in girls' education on the principle that authentic women can be formed only by women; secondly, the
provision of adequate preparatory training needed by teachers for instruction in the middle and serior classes and for
school management.

Step by step they forced their way forward. In 1887, a
petition was submitted to the Prussian Diet and to the Ministry of Education citing the above mentioned demands. Included with this petition was Helene Lange's *Yellow Pamphlet
(die Gelbe Broschure).* The failure of the petition stirred
private initiative: in 1889 the establishment of science courses
whose aim was to impart solely a heightened education without certification; then came the opening of courses which led
to the university entrance examination, and in 1892 the first
six Abiturients passed the examination. There are records of

successive concessions on the part of government: the Prussian Girls' School Reform of 1894 provided for senior teachers with academic qualifications and for head mistresses; admission to the universities in 1901; in 1906 a conference called by Althoff concerning girls' education. The Reform of 1908 brought about reformed secondary schools: the seventh class of traditional high school was to be followed by six more years; at the same time there was to be an additional three years on top of the traditional ten school years, and this was permitted against the wishes of the women as the *fourth* way of entry to the university; (and in) 1908 the admittance to regular matriculation.

Thus the path was opened up for women to enter professions, although until 1919 there were still severe limitations in their admission to the bar examinations and in the practice of professions.

At the same time, efforts were also made to promote formation of the domestic and maternal vocations and also for the opening up of social and governmental jobs. There were efforts as well to ensure preparatory training for the professions in nursing, social services, the arts, and technology: the *Women's Schools* which built upon the *Lyzeum* with an additional one or two years (1917); the three-year *Women's Secondary School* has been in existence since 1926. But according to the directives of 1925, the feminine nature and the particular cultural vocations of women should be considered in the schools which lead to the university; these must objectively satisfy the same requirements as the boys' schools do. The years 1923 until 1931 brought into Prussia a general regulation of secondary education. Whereas the women's schools and women's secondary schools continue the girls' educational work on a secondary level with certain limitations also of the work of middle schools, the works of the grade schools is carried on in *girls' vocational schools*. They are also indebted for their maintenance to private initiative. Luise Otto-Peters founded the first secular continuation school for girls, an initiative which was subsequently followed by other cities.

It was only by the Reich Constitution of 1919 that general school attendance for girls up to eighteen years was authorized in various counties.[14]   This authorization had a manifold purpose: particular consideration was to be paid to the specifically feminine functions in an otherwise continuing general education, also to social and civic life, and to training for particular professions and education for their corresponding ethos.

On the basis of this first survey, it is not possible for us to examine the methods to be used in achieving our goals and to verify to what degree we could achieve them. Just so, for the time being, we cannot investigate the new channels of vocational training which have assumed importance through the opening up of new jobs for women (for instance, women's schools for welfare workers); and we must dispense with an inquiry of the new regulation concerning preparatory work for certain professions which have been open to women for a longer time (for instance, teachers of gymnastics and technology); finally, we cannot follow in other states developments which have taken place chiefly in Prussia.

On the other hand, it is essential to consider the relationship of the Catholic Women's Movement and our work for the education of women to that of the interdenominational movement. I already mentioned[15] that a Catholic feminist movement was thought to be impossible when the interdenominational movement went into action. The concept which assumes that everything in the Church is irrevocably set for all times appears to me to be a false one. It would be naive to disregard that the Church has a history; the Church is a human institution and like all things human, was destined to change and to evolve; likewise, its development takes place often in the form of struggles. Most of the definitions of dogma are conclusive results of preceding intellectual conflicts lasting for decades and even centuries. The same is true of ecclesiastical law, liturgical forms—especially all objective forms reflecting our spiritual life.

The Church as the kingdom of God in this world should reflect changes in human thought. Only by accepting each age as it is and treating it according to its singular nature can the Church bring eternal truth and life to temporality. The conditions of life for Catholic women have changed just as for others, and new living conditions had to be created for them also. Heretofore, these changes were not necessarily dictated; rather, there was a widespread practice of primarily watching the play of natural forces. If it were true that a Catholic feminist movement was by no means disqualified on principle, one must still ask, on the other hand, whether the movement was and is necessary. We are raising the question here only in regard to girls' education. And here we have seen that Catholic Germany did have educational institutions where girls were formed by women for marriage and mother-hood, but they were not educated for that *exclusively*. Other paths were always open. And in view of the ultimate and highest goal, the most superior of all special goals was to fashion God's creatures for God, to develop them for the glory and honor of God. This preserved the Catholic educa-tional system from the bourgeois narrowness prevalent in girls' education during the Enlightenment. It also placed women on those heights of freedom presented to them by German Idealism and aspired to by prominent women outside of the Church.

Nevertheless, a Catholic Women's Movement began sev-eral decades after the interdenominational movement; it was organized as the *Catholic Women's League* and the *Associa-tion of Catholic Women Teachers*. This is not to be taken as a mere imitation[16] or counter-movement. After the schism, the lives of Catholic women and the education of Catholic girls had been influenced by what was happening outside of the Church, a development which also occurred throughout German cultural life. In the eighteenth and beginning of the nineteenth centuries, Rationalism and Positivism had affected philosophy and theology; it is only since the last few decades that the struggle against this influence was again established through the modern revival of the old established treasury of Catholic thought.   In the same way, Catholic pedagogy up until our time has been influenced again and again by these non-Catholic psychological and pedagogical currents, and it is in no way certain whether or to what extent the ultimate principles of Catholic pedagogy are in harmony with them. In addition, we must consider the influence of the state which is spreading more and more extensively. Catholic educational institutions are no longer free to choose their goal. The school curriculum and teaching procedures are prescribed by the state and are subject to state control. Teachers must satisfy state requirements.

Thus masculine and non-Catholic influences have become the leading influences to a large extent, not only because of the government's position but also from what is happening in the institutions themselves: it is necessary to work with secular assistants as long as we do not have enough of our own adequately trained personnel; and our own employees are trained at universities which cannot guarantee a structure of Catholic education for girls. Thus the need arose for more liberal organizations in order to gain influence for a specifically *Catholic* and *feminine* approach to girls' education.

The goals of the Catholic Women's Movement have much in common with the non-Catholic movement and are indebted to it for valuable preparatory work: the opening up of educational opportunities and gainful employment in the economic field for women; the establishment of jobs in the legal, political and social fields; also in the value placed on marriage and motherhood, the Catholic movement is still in agreement with the moderate elements of the middle-class feminist movement. But it should never be forgotten that the latter developed on a foundation foreign to us, that of German Idealism, of philosophical and political Liberalism. The

Catholic Women's Movement must rest on its own foundation, the foundation of faith and a Catholic world view which is well thought out in all its consequences. Reflection is a duty which can be realized only gradually, step by step. For a thorough discussion of all envisioned goals and endeavors to follow from the respectively won principles, we must also consider the concepts from the outside which influence us.

Yet, it must be emphasized that Catholic women as *Catholics* are not alone in their endeavors. Through all time the education of youth has been a matter of concern for the Church, and always that care included feminine youth as well. Every noble missionary activity, that of St. Boniface as well as those of the present, works with feminine personnel in the education of feminine youth. And whenever faith is threatened by hostile forces, we see that the educational work of women dedicated to God plays a significant role in resisting them. St. Dominic began his fight against heresy in Southern France, establishing first of all his missionary work in Prouille. There pious women supported the work of the wandering preaching friars by their prayers; occasionally, they opened up their homes to them; also, they sought to imbue the daughters of the nobility with Dominican spirituality in order to counteract the corresponding efforts of Albigensian women. Similarly, the educational order of Mary Ward originated as an instrument of the Counter-Reformation, and it was supported effectively by the congenial Society of Jesus. And in the last decades, far-sighted priests and prelates have often stimulated the orders charged with schools and education to equip their members with all the methods of modern academic and pedagogical education in order to satisfy governmental requirements.

The *Collegium Marianum* was thus founded in Münster in 1899 in order to make an academic education available to the religious of teaching orders. The study group of conventual educational institutions in Bavaria was established for the same purpose. In the years before the war, the school reform movement outside of the Church set in. At the same time, the organization of Catholic schools developed to bring together *all* groups interested in the schools and to prepare for the forthcoming struggle over them. The Catholic Women's Movement has a support in all these efforts inasmuch as they share the common goal of an authentic Catholic education for girls. However, they should not simply leave this work to others but must cooperate with all their strength with them because the education of girls, which requires theoretical foundation as well as practical applications, is specifically a feminine responsibility.

II. THE NATURE OF WOMAN: IT'S RELATION TO THE CONTENT OF EDUCATION

A. Its Significance in the Process of Formation and Education

By the term *education,* we mean that formation experienced by a person designated for development. Such formation is either an inner instinctive process or a planned program carried out either independently or directed by others. It is thus evident that it is basic to understand the *object* which is being formed. If we limit *education* here to a planned program, there is a fundamental practical requirement to understand the nature of the person for whom this work is designed.

When we stand in front of the class, we see at first glance that no child is exactly like another. And not only do we notice external differences, but we perceive together *with* them inner ones as well. (We cannot explore here what these inner differences signify nor *which* external differences are particularly important in discerning them.) We see they are so many different human beings, so many unique *individuals.* After having known them awhile, we shall perceive that they also constitute groups, groups united by common characteristics and separated from each other by typically different characteristics. Now it appears that each individual also represents a *type,* and, in addition to the types represented within one age group, a comparison of students from different classes reveals types characteristic of their age groups. (In addition, we have the *class type* which is to be differentiated completely from the age group.)

For the time being, we must defer the question of what causes these types, several of which can coexist in one individual. Should we compare a class of girls to a class of boys, we would again find typical differences. And, in addition, the question is whether we are dealing with types in the same sense as those *within* the girls' or boys' class respectively or whether we have discovered a universal type common to both.

I have spoken before[17] of the species "woman."[18]   By *species* we understand a permanent category which does not change. Thomistic philosophy designates it by the term *form,* meaning an *inner* form which determines structure. The type is not unchanging in the same sense as the species. An individual can develop from one type to another. For instance, this happens in the process when the individual advances from childhood to adolescence and then to adulthood. Hence, this progress is prescribed within the individual by an inner form. Also, a child can change type if transferred from one class into another (i.e., among other children) or displaced from one family into another. Such changes are attributed to the influence of environment. But such influences are limited by inner form. And types can vary within the limits of inner form or species.

It is quite clear that species is the core of all questions concerning *woman.* If such a "species" exists, then it cannot be modified by environmental, economic, cultural or professional factors. If we question the concept of species, if *man* and *woman* are to be considered as types as we have defined them, then the transformation of one type to another is possible under certain conditions. This is not *as* absurd as it may appear at first glance. At one time this view was considered valid on the basis that although physical differences were unchanging, the psychological differences were capable of infinite variation. But certain facts, such as the existence of hybrid and transitory forms, can be quoted to dispute the immutability of physical differences.

However, this question of species as a principle affecting women's problems is related to philosophical principles. In order to answer the question properly, we must understand the relationship between gender, species, type, and individual, i.e., we must be clear about the basic problems of formal ontology; in this I perceive what Aristotle means by his concept of *First Philosophy*. The material disciplines involving their specific subjects must needs investigate what is clarified in formal universality by this fundamental philosophy. The inquiry into the essence of woman has its logical place in a *philosophical anthropology*. Anthropology clarifies the meaning of sexual differences and proves the substance of the species; moreover, it is proper to this work to prove the place of the species in the structure of the individual human being, the relationship of the types to the species and to the individual, and the relationship of types to conditions in which they develop.

As a basis for practical educational work, we must be clear about the claims and limits set by the species, the types and individuals actually encountered in a given case, and the ways they are to be influenced. This concrete, basic perception of the practical work in girls' education may be possessed without the total theoretical preparatory work having been achieved generally or by a teacher personally. But it should be evident that an educational program based on faulty theories must also lead to faulty practice.

B. Methods of Analysis

How, then, should we begin to lay the theoretical foundation of girls' education? From the abundant literature on women's problems, where can we get a standard for selecting the components for such a solid foundation? We must ask ourselves what methods there are at our disposal to attain this knowledge; and if we should try to evaluate an existing inquiry, we must then ascertain what its purpose was, what method was used, whether its goals could be attained by this method, and whether it was, in fact, attained.

1. METHODS RELATING TO THE NATURAL SCIENCES (EXPERIMENTAL-PSYCHOLOGICAL)

There is a purely scientific method of dealing with woman's unique nature. This is the procedure of anatomy and physiology which describe and explain experientially the structure and functions of the feminine body. So also does that branch of psychology called scientific or experimental psychology: with the help of observation and experiment, it examines psychic data pertaining to the largest possible number of cases; and it seeks to derive universal laws of psychic characteristics from them. At the beginning of the twentieth century, sexual psychology also advanced in this manner. Individual psychic performances and their recognizable attributes of a number of persons from both sexes were investigated: such as the acuteness of the senses, the capacity to learn and to retain learning, the aptitude for different disciplines, the kinds of tendencies manifested (for instance, in such things as favorite games and activities), pecularities of imagination, emotion, and will, etc.[19]

All of these scientific investigations assume the differences between the sexes as a universal fact; they strive to establish as exactly as possible the details of this difference. They describe the uniqueness of each through *traits* which are present *on average* or whose frequency, perhaps also whose degree of occurrence, can be quantified. However, they do not succeed in giving an overall picture of uniqueness; and, moreover, they are unable to determine whether it is to be considered as a variable type or as a fixed species.

2. METHOD RELATING TO THE LIBERAL ARTS

Psychology underwent a great change by the turn of the century: behavioristic psychology was repressed more and more in favor of another kind known as *cognitive, structural,* and also *humanistic* psychology. Here several lines of thought would need to be differentiated. Common to them all is the *psychic* life conceived as a *uniform whole* which can neither be separated into its component parts nor reassembled into them. (In the beginning of scientific psychology, one was apt to hear of "psychology without the soul"; at the least, it was left undecided whether or not an authentic unity existed among individual, psychic facts. This scepticism regarding the existence of the soul has yet in no way been surmounted in humanistic psychology.)

Structural psychology, in particular the branch termed as *psychology of the individual,* maintains the conviction that individual factors—actions, achievements, even characteristics —cannot be understood apart from the total psychic context from which they originate, in which they progress, and whose development they themselves can determine. Thus this branch of psychology must be aware of, understand, and explain this total context in order to comprehend its individual factors.

This new method has been established in answer to the needs of the humanities (history, literature, etc.) and for the diagnosis and therapy of psychical abnormalities. In both instances, it is a matter of grasping definite individual personalities; hence, the description of the entire individual psychic context plays an important role in this new method. Its material is supplied by personal experiences, educational and psychiatric practice, diaries, and memoirs. However, such analysis could not be satisfied with simply the description of the individual. First, every description of an individual must also deal with the concept of his type because the individual as such cannot be understood abstractly. Secondly, definite types are brought into relief by the evidence under study; the structural context is neither simply universal (the same with all beings, without any differentiation), nor is it simply individual (singular to each one, without being common to all). Third, the types are of practical importance for the methods used in education and medicine; hence the feminine type or a diversity of feminine types is respectively encountered here.

The psychology of the individual cannot be content with making one momentary cross-section at a time through the psychic life but must rather strive for the most attainable grasp of its total progress within a given time; hence it also escapes the danger of taking the types as it finds them in each case to be something inflexible and permanent. The changing behavior of the type according to the change of outer circumstances is most evident. Moreover, the outlook which views personality as a totality is impelled to accept the psyche in its psychosomatic oneness. Since the human being is always a being in the world and since his psychic characteristics are always defined by it, it is necessary that psychology embrace anthropological, sociological, and cosmological considerations.[20] As Rudolf Allers rightly emphasizes, the educator must strive to investigate how far the changeability of types extends since this factor determines the possibility of his influence. He may not stop too soon before a supposedly *unalterable predisposition,* but rather he must try to comprehend every attitude as a reaction to outer circumstances and that in other circumstances, this attitude might be different. That which lies beyond the limitation of this method and which proves to be virtually unable to be influenced, Allers suggests be considered as an irrational residue, "X." If this were applied to our problem, it would mean that the existence of a species is not to be denied but that its nature is incomprehensible. Consequently, the part played by the species in the development of types and in the respective behavior of persons would also be unknowable. Therefore, there would be no available basis to uphold practical pedagogical procedure.

It seems to me that it may be admitting to defeat too soon to hold that this *ignorabimus*[21] is mainly true not only of individual psychology but also of knowledge itself. It certainly appears that the limits of empirical psychology have been reached here. Like every positive science, and by that I mean a science of natural data based on natural experience, this psychology can only signify that a thing is conditioned in one way or another under this or that circumstance and that it may act, or possibly must act, in one way or another. These sciences do not at all reach the inner form, the ontological structure of the cosmos, from which world events arise and progress in the manner ascertained by the positive sciences.

3. PHILOSOPHICAL METHOD

However, the problems of philosophy begin where the work of positive sciences leave off. For philosophy the "X" of an unknowable *natural predisposition* could not suffice. I would like to affirm that philosophy is able to make a three-fold analysis of this "X" (separable only by abstraction, not in reality): the "species" of humanity,[22] the species of woman, and individuality.

We are now faced with the important question of *philosophical method*. Within our context it is impossible to develop this method in its entire scope and to derive a method based on the primary causes. I can only specify the ways which could lead, according to my conviction, to the solution of the problems raised.[23]

With the phenomenological school, i.e., the school of Edmund Husserl, I share the view that the philosophical method differs in principle from that of the positive sciences: it commands its own function of cognition, and it is exactly this function which makes possible the foundation necessary for the other sciences; this foundation, which the various sciences are not able to achieve themselves, delimits the scope of their subject-matter and shows the means and method suitable for each of them. Phenomenology has designated this peculiar function of cognition as intuition or *Wesensanschauung*. These terms have given rise to many misunderstandings because their meanings bear the charge of history. By this function of cognition, I mean the perceptual achievement which confers on a concrete subject its universal structure; for instance, it enables us to say what a material thing is in its entirety—a plant, an animal, a person—or what the meaning is of these terms. What I am calling *intuition* here relates very closely to what traditional philosophy signifies as *abstraction*. A thorough phenomenological analysis of intuition and abstraction could perhaps demonstrate that there is really no sense in arguing about which of the two is the true philosophical method.

This is obviously related to the formulation of our question. It is possible to present the meaning of the terms "essence of woman" or "species of woman" only if a function of cognition exists capable of grasping such a universal slant. On the whole, most of the writers on these questions began their work without considering the question of method inasmuch as they were not confined within the framework of a positive science. They wrote out of *feeling* or *instinct*. That is not to say that this entire literature may be worthless. It has the value of all disciplines formed by prescientific experience and hypotheses: the value of material which must be critically processed. To be sure, everyone knows women from experience and believes he knows what a woman is from that experience. But should he generalize on the basis of that experience, we could not be certain whether or not it is a true generalization or whether or not that which may be actually observed in this or that case may in no way be true of others. But even beyond that, a criticism of the individual experience is necessary. Has even the individual woman been rightly understood? All experiences are prone to the dangers of error and delusion which are perhaps more numerous and more serious here than elsewhere. What guarantee do we have that such hazards have been avoided? Or it may be that an ideal image of woman is being presented to us by which particular women are to be measured as *authentic* women. Then again, we must inquire into the origin of this ideal image and of what value it is as a contribution to understanding.

In any case, there is one significant factor which must be singled out from all these considerations: the self-evident *claim* of being able to make universal statements. Without justifying it to himself, a person takes it for granted that he is grasping something of a universal nature through his own experiences. From this arises the philosopher's task of identifying this universal function of cognition which is operative in experience, of organizing it into a system, and by this means raising it to the rank of a scientific method.[24]

4. THEOLOGICAL METHOD

With this we now come to the remaining method for discussion concerning the treatment of our question, the *theological* method. It is of fundamental importance to us to know what Catholic doctrine affirms regarding the essence or nature of woman. To be informed we will first of all refer to doctrine in the narrowest sense, that which we are obligated to believe, i.e., to definitions of dogma. We will not gain very much here. We shall then extend the area of inquiry to interpretation of doctrine, i.e., we will cite the writings of the Doctors and Fathers of the Church as well as contemporary statements concerning dogma. Of course, in the latter we shall find more plentiful material; however, this material possibly invites criticism.

For instance, when St. Thomas says[25] "Vir est principum mulieris et finis" (Man is the source and end of woman), we musk ask what meaning this sentence has and from what source it was taken. In this instance, it is not difficult to specify the source. It is the Bible and, indeed, it is the account of creation; some passages from the Letters of St. Paul come to mind as well.[26] To determine the meaning of this sentence from St. Thomas, it would first be necessary to know from the context of the Thomistic world of thought what he means by designating one thing as the principle and end of another. It would then be necessary to refer to all scriptural passages from which a definition of the end of woman could be drawn (and likewise, anything concerning her *subordination* to man); and what appears here as principle and end would have to be compared to that sentence of St. Thomas.[27] Should there be a conformity, one would have to ask what inference might be drawn concerning the *nature* of woman from the definition of woman's end and the relationship of order between her and man. For it is clear that, if woman were created for a predestined purpose, her nature must needs be suited to that purpose. The types which we are familiar with from experience could be compared to the concept of nature yielded by this indirect method of cognition. If deviations were found, we should have to ask how such a falling-off from nature is possible and how this is to be explained. But, moreover, should we attain a concept of woman's *essence* entirely by philosophy, we would have to compare this directly perceived essence to the concept of nature made accessible by theological considerations. Should there prove to be inconsistencies, this could be due to error in either perspective. However, it may also be that the terms *nature* and *essence* are not completely identical in meaning. This is an ontological problem which we will not investigate at this time.[28]

Finally, with the discussion of theological didactic concepts, we are faced with still another method of theological analysis, one to which dogma refers, namely, ascertaining what the Bible itself says. I have made a small beginning in the essay "The Separate Vocations of Man and Woman According to Nature and Grace"[29] in which I tried to compile and explain several passages which seemed important to me. But it would be an important and meritorious task at some time to work through the Bible in its entirety from this aspect.

C. Potential of the Individual Methods for an Understanding of the Content of Women's Education

We have now established a whole range of different methods which have attempted or could attempt to discover woman's unique nature. It would now be feasible to summarize once more the potential contribution of each method to our problem according to the means of cognition utilized.

To expound on *species* is proper to the cognitive function of *philosophy* which alone can achieve a valid explanation. To even begin to explain how I think this problem can be solved, I must integrate it as I see it into the totality of philosophic problems.

As I have already stated in a previous passage, I regard Ontology, i.e., a science of the basic forms of Being *(Sein)* and of beings *(Seienden),* as the fundamental discipline. It is able to demonstrate that there is a radical division within being: *pure Being* holds nothing of non-being in itself, has neither beginning nor end, and holds in itself all which can be; *finite being* has as its allocation both beginning and end. We call the one uncreated Being, the other created being; the Creator corresponds to the former and creatures to the latter. (These terms are borrowed from the language of theology, but the reality thus signified can be shown by purely philosophical methods.)

Creatures are arranged into grades depending on how

they more or less approximate pure Being, for all created being is an analogy to divine Being. However, the *analogia entis* is different for each grade; each one corresponds to another kind of Being and a different basic form of beings: material, organic, animal, and rational Being.

Inasmuch as all lower grades are contained in man's structure of being, he occupies a place peculiar to him in this graded structure. His body is a *material body,* but not *only* that. Rather, at the same time, it is an *organism* which is formed and activated from within. Again, man is not *only* an organism but rather an *organism with a soul* who, in the sensitive manner peculiar to him, is open to himself and his environment. And, finally, he is a *spiritual* being who is consciously cognizant of himself and others and can act freely to develop himself and others. All this belongs to the *human species,* and whatever does not evidence this structure of being cannot be termed a *human being.* However, this species appears differentiated in individuals: notwithstanding his specific human nature, every person has his own unrepeatable singularity. Philosophy can also demonstrate that *individuality,* in the sense of uniqueness, is proper to the human species. To comprehend respective individuals is not the concern of philosophy; rather, we utilize a specific experiential function in our daily contact with people. Another, simple differentiation cuts across this differentiation of humanity into a limitless multiplicity of individuals: *sexual* differentiation.[30]

I would now like to point out several significant questions regarding the education of girls. Does the difference between man and woman involve the whole structure of the person or only the body and those psychic functions necessarily related to physical organs? Can the mind be considered unaffected by this difference? This view is upheld not only by women but also by many theologians.[31] Should this latter view be valid, education would then strive towards development of the intellect without consideration to sexual difference. If, on the other hand, the difference does involve the person's entire structure, then educational work must consider the specific structure of the masculine and feminine mind. Furthermore, if the nature of each individual contains both masculine and feminine elements and if only one of these elements is predominant in each person, would not individuals of both *species* then be needed to represent perfectly the human species as a whole? Could it not be fully represented by one individual? This question is also of practical significance because, depending on the answer, education must be geared to either overcoming limitations of the specifically masculine and feminine natures or to developing their potential strengths.

In order to answer this question, we would need to refer to the entire context of *genetic* problems; this has hardly been done so far. It would be feasible to examine at some time the specific existential mode exclusive to the human being: the species does not come about in ready-made form at the beginning of existence; rather, the individual develops progressively in a process dependent on time. This process is not unequivocably predetermined but depends rather on several variable factors, among others, on man's freedom which enables him to work towards his own formation and that of others. The possibility of a diversity of types is rooted in this human characteristic which encourages the formation of the species in changing circumstances. There are also further questions to be considered: the generation of new individuals; the transmission of the species through successive generations; and their modification in a variety of types as sexual evolution advances. In considering these questions, philosophy is not concerned with specific changes either in a particular individual's existence or in the factual course of history but rather with their potentiality for change. The connection of genetic problems to that of the development of the species can be expressed in a further question: Is the concrete development of the species as a whole perhaps possible only in the entire succession of generations in their sexual and individual differentiation?

The concern of philosophy is to investigate the necessary and potential characteristics of being through its specific function of cognition. *Theology* seeks to establish woman's unique nature according to divine revelation. Its direct concern is not to investigate the problem itself but rather to assemble and explain historical records. Generally, Scripture does not deal with natural necessities and potentialities but rather reveals facts and gives practical instructions. For instance, philosophy asks whether the world was created in time or whether we may consider it as existing through eternity. But the account of creation tells us *that* it did begin in time and how it began. The Scriptures do not ask whether the sexual differentiation is necessary or accidental but says "God created man according to His image. He created them as man and woman." Here we find the expression of the facts of oneness and of differentiation. However this is a terse statement which requires explanation. What is meant by God's image in man? We find the answer in the complete history and doctrine of salvation, and it is summarized briefly in the words of Our Lord: "Be ye perfect as your heavenly Father is perfect." I will not at this time discuss the nature of this ideal of perfection. I would simply suggest that in the words "Be ye" the image of God is established as a duty, vocation, or destiny of mankind—i.e., of man and of woman. From this theology concludes that what is customarily signified as *woman's natural vocation*—wife and mother—cannot be considered as her only vocation.[32]

It is true that this *natural vocation* is also discussed in Scripture, in the passage justifying the creation of woman: "It is not good that the man should be alone," and also in the call to motherhood, "Be fruitful and multiply."

Moreover, the New Testament holds up the ideal of virginity. And, with all due respect to the sanctity of marriage, it is a matter of faith that the state of virginity takes precedence over the married state.[33] Thus, from the point of view of the Catholic faith as well, it is impossible to consider marriage and motherhood as woman's exclusive vocation.

I cannot delve any further into this explanation of what could be learned from the theological perspective, especially from the Bible, on the problem of the sexes. Revelation does not, by any means, provide us with all the knowledge that we can and would like to assimilate; rather, it leaves us much latitude for rational inquiry. Yet we find here positive facts and norms resting on a firm foundation, and many errors in theory and practice could be averted if this scriptural source were thoroughly utilized. Rightly understood and employed, the theological and philosophical approaches are not in competition; rather, they complete and influence each other (*Credo ut intelligam. Fides quaerens intellectum*).[34] The philosophizing mind is challenged to make the realities of faith as intelligible as possible. On the other hand, these realities protect the mind from error, and they answer certain questions concerning matters of faith which reason must leave undecided.

This is true also of the *positive sciences* occupied with identifying natural data. Physiology can inform us of the actual physical capacity of girls for work: it can set guiding principles for what we can expect from them at different age levels and for suitable physical activities to promote good health, strength, adroitness, etc. Elementary psychology can give us valuable information on their actual strength of memory, intelligence, etc. Nevertheless, we can judge established data only by accepting other considerations and findings. It must be clear under what circumstances the duties are fulfilled, for instance, what practice and preparation preceded them. It is necessary that individual psychology and sociology supplement these findings: consideration must be given to the whole unique nature of the persons whose achievements have been identified and also to the milieu from which they come. Individual psychology indicates types with which we have to deal and tries to make them intelligible to us by showing the context of motives in which all individual modes of behavior are involved.

Thus Else Croner[35] outlines five types of the young girl: she defines her unique nature by contrasting it on the one hand to that of the child and mature woman, and, on the other hand, to that of the young man: the *maternal* type's outlook regarding children emerges distinctly in play, favorite pastimes, and desires; the *erotic* type shows a predominantly male directed mentality and recognizable marks of high sexuality; the *romantic* type longs for experiences and is impelled to surrender unconditionally to a leader, this possibly without any sexual impact; the *level-headed* type emerges in life's practical duties and adapts easily to surrounding circumstances; lastly, the *intellectual* type is predominantly involved with objective interests and is perhaps capable of creative achievements. Those of us involved in teaching girls will surely recall students representing one or another of these types, as well as those of mixed types, and still others belonging to types we have not mentioned.

Such a delineation of types has a practical value for the teacher and educator. Sometimes this value is apparent in a keener awareness of the human nature before her although, in order to be fair to them as individuals, she must guard herself against classifying them schematically in a fixed system of types. Moreover, the delineation warns us that we have to deal with a diversity of types, that not all are amenable to all things nor can they be formed to all things, that different goals, ways and means are necessary. On the other hand, the types are not to be regarded as naturally given facts which are rigid and unchangeable. A transition from one type to another is frequently demonstrated when individuals are observed over a longer span of time; changing influences must be considered, such as different teachers or decisive changes of environment (this could be a transition from family to boarding school or from school to an occupation). Valuable material regarding the adaptability of types is yielded by experience in the treatment of abnormal youth or even those who are difficult to educate. Moreover, an historical outlook perceives that different types predominate in different times and different circumstances, and that new types occur and old ones disappear. The factor of adaptability necessitates a consideration of value and purpose. Which types *deserve* to be preserved? Which types need a specific educational program in order to change them? And which types can be set up as models, i.e., types into which we can try and ought to try to change the existing ones?

D. A Sketch of the Subjects to be Educated

These extended considerations of method may lead us towards an understanding of the subjects to be educated. I will attempt to give an anticipatory short outline of the human material with which we have to deal in girls' education. This is done in a provisional manner because we have indeed found an abundance of unsolved problems embedded in all the methods. I can only sketch in a few strokes the concept that I presently have. Further studies would lead to an enrichment of it and probably to modifications as well.

I am convinced that the species *humanity* embraces the double species *man* and *woman;* that the essence of the complete *human* being is characterized by this duality; and that the entire structure of the essence demonstrates the specific character. There is a difference, not only in body structure and in particular physiological functions, but also in the entire corporeal life. The relationship of soul and body is different in man and woman; the relationship of soul to body differs in their psychic life as well as that of the spiritual faculties to each other. The feminine species expresses a unity and wholeness of the total psychosomatic personality and a harmonious development of faculties. The masculine species strives to enhance individual abilities in order that they may attain their highest achievements.

This differentiation of the species as presented by philosophy corresponds to the destiny of the sexes as shown to us by theology. Man and woman are destined "to rule over the earth," that means, to know the things of this world, to delight in it, and to develop it in creative action. But these cultural achievements were allocated to man as his first duty; woman was placed at his side as helpmate. Man and woman are destined to beget and to raise up posterity. However, woman is bound more intensely to a child both physically and spiritually, and the entire arrangement of her life is committed to this union; she finds in this her first duty. Man is placed by her side as helper and protector. Her peculiar characteristic of discernment suits her duty as companion and mother; her strength lies in her intuitive grasp of the concrete and the living, especially of the personal. She has the gift of adapting herself to the inner life of others, to their goal orientation and working methods. Feelings are central to her as the faculty which grasps concrete being in its unique nature and specific value; and it is through feeling that she expresses her attitude. She desires to bring humanity in its specific and individual character in herself and in others to the most perfect development possible. The erotic attitude (not the sexual) dominates her entire life whose purest unfolding is in the service of love. To reveal God's image in themselves is the mission assigned to man and woman; it belongs to the criteria of finite being imparted to them that they must also do this in specific ways. *One* difference has been suggested already: woman strives towards the divine perfection more by the harmonious development of all her faculties; man through a more intense development of particular ones. However, there can also be demonstrated differences in the relations of man and woman to the attributes of God's nature and to the divine Persons.

The species humanity, as well as the species femininity, is revealed differently in different individuals. First of all, they represent the species more or less perfectly; then, they illustrate more or less one or another of its characteristics. Man and woman have the same basic human traits, although this or that trait predominates not only in the sexes but also in respective individuals. Therefore, women may closely approximate the masculine type and conversely. This may be connected to their individual vocation. If on the whole, marriage and motherhood are the primary vocations for the feminine sex, it is not necessarily true for each individual. Women may be called to singular cultural achievements, and their talents may be adapted to these achievements.

This brings us to *feminine types* classed *according to their natural abilities.* Given the finiteness of human nature, the impulse to cultural creativity expresses itself in a multiplicity of vocations. And since human nature is finite, man constantly longs for perfection to which all human beings are called; this longing expresses itself in a special vocation such as religious orders. The religious life, including the state of virginity, suits those women who renounce marriage and motherhood as well as other close ties to people. However, the highest form of love for God, which forms the lives of such women, enables them to achieve the fundamental personal attitude and to bring about the reign of eros. Each individual has his place and task in the one great development of humanity. Humanity is to be understood as one great individual; it is possible to understand salvation history only by this interpretation. Each person is a member of this whole, and the essential structure of the whole is shown in every member; but, at the same time, each has his own character as a member which he must develop if the whole is to attain development. The species *humanity* is realized perfectly only in the course of world history in which the great individual, humanity, becomes concrete. And the species *man* and *woman* are also fully realized only in the total course of historical development. Whoever is active in educational work is given the human material which he must help form in order that it may become part of *the* membership to which it is called.

The types and individuals are not determined only by their character as members of humanity as a whole. We cannot understand the human material before us and the duties it places upon us if we do not consider the reality of original sin. Everything referred to as *sickness, abnormality, problem children within the school system* spring ultimately from this source. Just as the nature of fallen man differs from that of the integral man, so is the nature of man and of woman tainted by *formes* [sic] *peccati.*[36] All human educational work has the duty of cooperating in the restoration of man's integral nature.

Fallen man is characterized by two basic principles: the rebellion of the spirit against God's dominion; the rebellion of the lower faculties against the higher—the senses versus the spirit's control, the will versus the intellect. There results from the first a changed relationship to the other creatures which man wants to exploit for himself instead of preserving for God. The lower creatures react by revolting against man, and this brings about hostility. The rebellion of the senses and of the spirit results in their both going astray as seen in deceit, error, and practical mistakes, with all ensuing harm to body and soul. All this is true of man and woman. The specific degeneracy of man is seen in his brutal despotism over creatures—especially over woman, and in his enslavement to his work up to the point of the atrophy of his humanity. The specific degeneracy of woman is seen in her servile dependence on man and in the decline of her spiritual life into a predominantly sensual one. This is evident in several different types of women. It is most apparent in the type which E. Croner calls *erotic* but which might be better termed as sexual. The degeneracy appears in this type of woman's fascination with sexual matters: her interest and imagination are already preoccupied with such matters in early years, in any case by the beginning of puberty; her whole demeanor changes in the presence of the opposite sex; her violent and uninhibited sexual drives makes her an easy prey to seduction and finally to prostitution. With the *romantic type* of woman, however, all this seems to be transmuted into the spiritual and the ideal: here we find the tendency to daydream and rhapsodize; her inner life with phantasy heroes in a phantasy world paralyzes her capacity for judgment and fitness for the real world. Then we have the type of the *rebellious slave* in the emancipated woman: she denies not only her servitude to man but also the God-willed subordination to him; she is set against men by her hostile attitude, but even this attitude of hostility betrays the tie existing between them. Still other types could be described. This form of degeneracy obviously is less evident in the level-headed, practical type and in the objective-intellectual type previously mentioned. But possibly, it could also be shown that this merit expresses a weakness, i.e., an inferior manifestation of woman's integral nature.

The types and individuals to be considered as variants of pure human nature give us positive standards for our educational work; the degenerate types require measures leading to their transformation. The human beings which we have before us are not irretrievably imprisoned within those types which they presently embody. If today the sexual type appears to be more prevalent than it perhaps was twenty years ago, this can certainly be attributed to environmental influences which direct even children to this subject and cause tendencies to become manifest which otherwise would not have emerged at all. If at one time the romantic type was more prevalent, this can be attributed certainly to the whole kind of existence led by girls and women: their isolation from real life and the type of education available to them. And we should mention the importance of the influence of an adolescent literature created by women who were themselves of the romantic type, as well as the ideal of women held by romantic men. If the level-headed, practical type is coming forward decidedly today, it is doubtlessly due to the harsh demands of real life.

III. THE GOAL OF EDUCATION

In reviewing woman's present position, we encountered the demands made by our *times* on girls' education.[37] Our consideration of the human material subject to educational work shows that this itself seems to be determined by a goal.[38] Rationally, we cannot try to consider the material and the goal as set apart one from the other; rather, we must evaluate them in terms of each other and achieve a uniform orientation of the goal, although possibly, it may not be a simple one.

Now, no goal is attainable which is not shown to be necessary to or, at least, as possible for the material; thus the demands of the time must be measured by those of eternity, which means the eternal order of beings. In the first place, therefore, we must treat the goal or goals prescribed by the nature and destiny of woman.

A. The Goal Determined By the Eternal Order

1. THE NOTION OF A PERFECTED HUMANITY

We saw a threefold goal prescribed by the nature of woman: the development of her humanity, her womanhood, and her individuality. These are not separate goals just as the nature of a particular human individual is not divided into three parts but is *one:* it is human nature of a specifically feminine and individual character. Only in abstract thought are we obliged to consider separately what is separable in concept.

Where do we get the idea of a perfected humanity? The function of ethics is to propose goals and demands to tell us what our obligations are. If we had to construct ethics here as a philosophical discipline, we would have to ask and explain critically how far an autonomous ethics would be able to develop the concept of perfected humanity; we would consider an autonomous ethics to be one not based on faith. If, on the contrary, on the basis of faith we proceed to clarify the goal which must be accepted as the norm for our educational work, we thus find that the truths of faith are part of our theoretical foundation. We shall start with the goal of man as presented to us by faith; we shall cite philosophical considerations only insofar as they are qualified to penetrate the intellectual content of faith or to supplement what this content leaves undecided.

Pius XI's encyclical *Rappresentanti* on the Christian education of youth, indicates as

> the authentic and immediate goal of Christian education . . . cooperation with God's grace in the formation of the true and perfect Christian; that means in the formation of Christ Himself in the person reborn through baptism . . . The real Christian, the fruit of Christian upbringing, is consequently the supernatural person who thinks, judges, and acts always and consistently according to right reason, enlightened by the supernatural light of Christ's example and teachings; or, to say it in today's language, the true and perfect man of character. For true character is not represented by just any optional conduct of life showing consistency and perseverance according to purely subjective principles, but rather by perseverance in obeying the eternal principles of justice . . . On the other hand, perfect justice can exist only where God is given what belongs to Him, as is done by the true Christian.[39]

We shall refrain from discussing here what is already said in these words about the forces working toward the goal— God's grace and human cooperation. We shall restrict ourselves to the goal itself: the supernatural person or Christ in the person. This supernatural goal does not exclude the natural goal but includes it. "Thus the true Christian is not obliged to renounce the things of this world or to lessen his natural abilities. On the contrary, inasmuch as he incorporates them into his normal life in a disciplined manner, he develops and perfects them; he thereby ennobles the natural life itself, supplying efficacious values to it not only of the spiritual and eternal world but also of the material and earthly world."[40] In this concise formulation, the natural and supernatural goals have thus been combined according to the principle that grace perfects nature. If we wish to explain this further, we must keep in mind the teaching of faith on the *natura integra, lapsa et redempta.*[41] But that entails the development of what we are given in the account of Creation and the Fall of Man, the Commandments of God, the gospel of Jesus Christ, and the living example of the God-man.

The first man was created perfect. That means his nature was not designed for development but was already fully developed in all things of which human nature is capable. For the present, however, we must disregard what was given to him through grace here on earth and what final glorification awaits him in heaven. He was destined to transmit pure nature to his descendants not as a fully developed state but in essence, whose perfection would be attained through the course of their lives. Thus the nature Adam was endowed with meant for them the goal of development. Integral nature, that is original nature, meant: the body's perfect strength, health and beauty, the perfect functioning of all its organs and its perfect obedience to the mind—which is to say to the will as enlightened by reason. The perfect functioning of bodily organs depends on flawless sensory functions and infallible sensory perceptions. The perfect mental state depends on the creature's unerring rational grasp of other creatures and of the Creator; a perfect harmony of reason and will; the unswerving focusing of the will on the highest good, and the willing submission of the lower instincts to these higher and highest aspirations.

Is pure human nature also the goal of our development? Must it also be the goal of our educational work? No longer is it the goal of development in the same sense as before the Fall because our natural state no longer suffices to attain it; rather, development may even be impeded by our predispositions even though an inherent striving to this goal is still present in fallen nature. But pure human nature must be the goal of our educational work although we cannot attain it perfectly and completely by our own power. (For instance, we need only think of the perfect strength, health, and beauty of the body.) Pure nature can be attained only through grace; its perfection only through the perfection of grace in eternal glory. But we may not rely on grace to guide fallen nature to integrity because justifying grace does not restore fully nature's integrity; rather, only with our cooperation can grace initiate this integrity and make it possible.

Adam was not only the integral man but also the child of God: clinging to God in faith and love; knowing him in a more perfect way than man after the Fall; called to His eternal vision although not yet seeing Him directly. The loss of man's divine sonship was the direct consequence of his turning away from God through original sin. His loss of integrity was only a further consequence, although the fact that Adam turned away from God was rooted in a disturbance of social justice. Thus the restoration of sonship to God is also the immediate goal of redemption; the restoration of perfect integrity is also a possible further effect of grace. Divine sonship and its highest perfection in glory is placed before us as a goal by the two orders of creation and redemption, and it is linked by them to our free cooperation. Therefore, educational work must also embrace the supernatural goal.

Through the redemptive work of Jesus Christ, man wins his return to divine sonship, the expectancy of the eternal beatific vision, and the perfect restoration of nature. This is accessible to each individual through his personal contact with the God-man, and through his membership in the Mystical Body of Christ. By his own action, he is able to have a share in the redemptive work in himself and in the whole

Mystical Body under the leadership of its Head. Thus, incorporation into the Mystical Body must be the goal of educational work which aspires towards a perfect humanity.

2. NOTION OF PERFECTED WOMANHOOD

Humanity was created as a unique organism and recovered organic form through its tie with Christ who is the head of this body. Each member shares *one* nature of the whole body; but, as a *member,* he also has his place in the organism corresponding to his special nature. At the same time, the whole body shows a symmetrical structure: it has, as it were, a double nature whose halves complement each other in order to build up the harmonious whole and to make possible its works. The goal of educational work must be to preserve for each member his unique character while maintaining the symmetry of the whole structure.

"He created them as man and woman" and created woman for man as a "helpmate as if side by side with him" *(eser kenegdo):*[42] She was created as his other half in which he could see his own image and find himself reproduced. She was to take her place with him in their dominion over all other creatures of the earth among which none could be his *equal.* Together with him by the act of procreation, she was to build up the whole organism of humankind. I would like to clarify here what I think St. Thomas means when he calls man the *principle and end of woman.* First of all, a *principle* is that from which something else follows. Thus it signifies that woman was made from man. It signifies further the principle as primary and that which follows as subordinate. (The term that Paul used, that man is head of woman corresponds to the Thomistic concept.) The "end" as St. Thomas uses it means, first of all, that to which another strives, that wherein it finds peace and fulfillment; hence this signifies that the meaning of the feminine being is fulfilled in union

with man. End signifies further that for whose sake another
exists. Thus, it means that because man needs woman to fulfill the meaning of his being, she was created for his sake. It
does not seem to me that this means that woman was created
only for the sake of man; for every creature has its own
meaning, and that is its particular way of being an image of
the divine being. Also, if the sexual relation is not justified
by its own meaning and value, it was very possible indeed to
assure human propagation by other means. Nor do I understand that woman is denigrated by having been created "for
man's sake" unless it is misunderstood as it very well could
be after the degeneracy of both sexes as a result of the Fall,
i.e., that she is to serve man's own ends and satisfy his lust.
That was not intended for the companion standing *side by
side with him* over all other creatures. Rather, by her free,
personal decision to be his *helpmate,* she enables him to
become what he is intended to be. For "man is also not
without woman," and that is why he must "leave father and
mother in order to cling to his wife."

Thus, girls' education should lead to the development
and affirmation of their unique feminine nature. Relevant to
this is her God-willed place by man's side; she is not to be in
his place but also not in a degrading role unsuitable to the
dignity of the person.

It is already obvious that the meaning of the specifically
feminine being is not to be understood only by her relation
to man. Since the sexual relation is very closely involved
with procreation, we must refer to her characteristic relation
to posterity in order to understand her being. Moreover, it
has already been emphasized that all creatures relate to God
in their divine likeness; thus it is befitting the feminine nature
that her characteristic function is to reflect the divine. Finally, we must ask whether the latter meaning of the feminine
being can be realized only in marriage and motherhood or in
other ways as well.

From the account of creation we learn only that man

and woman together are called to procreation. We learn only
by God's judgment after the Fall, when the pains of childbirth were inflicted upon her, that woman is assigned a particular role in this function. Man's punishment, however, is not
linked to his relation to posterity but to his relation to other
creatures. Eve is called *mother of the living;* she calls herself
happy because God has given her a son. The women in Israel
who were mothers, especially of sons, were honored and
praised, whereas the barren woman was scorned and regarded
as if she were afflicted by a curse. That God turns the barren
woman into a happy mother is extolled by the Psalmist as a
special sign of His goodness (Ps. 113).[43] The place of the
spouse and mother in the family is highly regarded. Her
repute travels far beyond the confines of her home. She
cares for the well-being of her home and of all its members
but also for the needy. The heart of her husband is entrusted
to her; even her mature sons marvel at her and listen to her
counsel: "She opens her mouth in wisdom, and on her tongue
is kindly counsel." Praise is due to her because she fears the
Lord.[44] This is the secret both of her energetic works and of
all her success. Wherever the Old Testament tradition is still
somewhat alive in the family, the woman still holds this royal
place. It is her exalted duty, not only to bring children into
the world and care for their bodily development, but also to
raise them up in the fear of the Lord. This high esteem of
motherhood is stipulated by the consoling promise imparted
to the first woman along with her expulsion from paradise:
she and her posterity were destined to crush the serpent's
head. It has been woman's mission to war against evil and to
educate her posterity to do the same; this has been true of
woman including the Mother of the Son who conquered death
and hell, but it will have to remain so until the end of the
world.

Mary stands at the crucial point of human history and
especially at the crucial point of the history of woman; in her,
motherhood was transfigured and physical maternity sur-

mounted. Just as the goal of all human education is presented to us in a concrete, vital, and personal way through Christ,
so also the goal of all women's education is presented to us
through Mary. The most significant evidence of the eternal
meaning and value to be found in sexual differentiation lies in
the fact that the new Eve stands beside the new Adam on the
threshold between the Old and the New Covenants. God
chose as the instrument for His Incarnation a human mother,
and in her He presented the perfect image of a mother. From
the time that she learns she is to bear a son she is completely
at the service of this mission. He is given to her by God and
in fidelity to God she must look after Him. Her existence
until the hour of His birth is one of composed expectancy;
then in a life fully surrendered to service, she takes careful
note of all words and signs which anticipate something of His
future course. With all reverence for the divinity hidden in
Him, she still maintains authority over Him when He is a
child; in true perseverance, she participates in His work until
His death and beyond it. But before the annunciation of her
election, this woman called to the most exalted maternity
had not wanted marriage and motherhood for herself; and
this was against every tradition of her people. She was
determined to live free of marital obligations. As *handmaid
of the Lord* she bore God's Son and was mindful of the man
placed at her side for the protection of her child and herself.
She did not become *one flesh* with him; this marriage was not
meant to propagate his heirs or to carry on the human race.
In Mary we meet the image of virginal purity. What else could
have induced her decision to remain a virgin than her desire
to be *wholly the handmaid of the Lord,* to belong only to
Him and to be at His command? And how could such longing
in a person be explained otherwise than through divine inspiration and vocation?

And thereby, as co-redeemer by the side of the Redeemer, she emerges from the natural order. Both mother and Son
spring from the human race, and both embody human nature;

yet, both are free from that relationship which makes possible the fulfillment of life's meaning only in union with and through another person. Union with God replaces this relationship in both; in Christ through the hypostatic union, in Mary through the surrender of her whole being to the Lord's service. Are they both separated so much from the rest of humankind that we can no longer hold them as models? In no way is this true. They have lived for the sake of humanity, not only to effect our redemption through their power, but also to set an example of how we should live in order to participate ourselves in redemption. By his choice of the Virgin Mother, Christ did not only show God's good pleasure and the redemptive power of virginity freely chosen, but He has pronounced most distinctly that others are also called to virginity for the sake of the kingdom of heaven. We shall still have to discuss to what degree such a calling constitutes a special vocation.

First, we must establish whether or not virginity is a specific form of the feminine being so that it can be recognized as a goal of women's education. It seems to me that this is self-evident because it was proposed to us not in Christ alone but precisely in Christ and Mary.

God the Lord Himself meets us in Christ. The Eternal Word is the image of the Father by which the Father looks upon Himself; in the Incarnate Word, the image of the Father becomes visible to our human eyes: "Whoever sees me sees the Father." The human Christ reveals the transcendence of the Lord over all creatures in distancing Himself from all individual creatures. His humanity is entirely the instrument of His redemptive work, and it is given to him completely to dispose of in a free and personal way. His virginity is constitutive. This does not mean that He was not free to choose but that there was no question at all of choice. In this He is exalted above all human beings; there is the possibility of choice for everybody else, as, indeed, nobody can attain union with God other than through free choice. In this respect, Mary's freely chosen virginity is the example for all humanity, men and women alike. In another respect, however, we see a specific connotation: in the statement "I am the handmaid of the Lord," Mary's whole being is articulated. It bespeaks her readiness to serve the Lord and excludes every other relationship. Of course, the celibacy of priests also is founded in their undivided readiness to serve the Lord. The difference between the two can be seen in the way the Lord permits the readiness to become actual service. He makes the priest His proxy and permits us to see the Lord Himself in the priest. In Mary we do not see the Lord, but we see her always by the Lord's side. Her service is rendered directly to Him: through the prayer of intercession, she intercedes with Him for humankind; she receives from His hands graces to be bestowed and does indeed transmit them. She does not represent the Lord but assists Him. Her position is thus analogous to that of Eve by the side of the first Adam. But Mary is beside Jesus not for His sake but for ours. She is the mother of the living not because all succeeding generations come from her but because her maternal love embraces the whole Mystical Body with Jesus Christ its head. In her virginity, she is the pure prototype of womanhood because she stands beside Him who is the prototype of all manhood and because she leads all humanity to Him.

In this *womanhood* devoted to the service of love, is there really a divine image? Indeed, yes. A ministering love means *assistance* lent to all creatures in order to lead them toward perfection. But such love is properly the attribute of the Holy Spirit. Thus we can see the prototype of the feminine being in the Spirit of God poured out over all creatures. It finds its most perfect image in the purest Virgin who is the bride of God and mother of all mankind. Next to her stand the consecrated virgins who bear the honorary title *Sponsa Christi* and are called to participate in His redemptive work. But her image is also perpetuated by the woman standing beside a man who is Christ's image and helping to build up His body the Church through a physical and spiritual maternity.

Since Mary is the prototype of pure womanhood, the imitation of Mary must be the goal of girls' education. Since the dispensing of graces is entrusted to the hands of the Queen of Heaven, we will find our way to the goal not only by keeping our eyes raised to her but by maintaining a personal trusting association with her. But the imitation of Mary is not *fundamentally different from* the imitation of Christ. The imitation of Mary includes the imitation of Christ because Mary is the first Christian to follow Christ, and she is the first and most perfect model of Christ. Indeed, that is why the imitation of Mary is not only relevant to women but to all Christians. But she has a special significance for women, one in accord with their nature, for she leads them to the feminine form of the Christian image.

3. CONCEPT OF INDIVIDUALITY

Our consideration of the redemptive order has already shown us that there is not *one* fully undifferentiated goal for all women. Mary herself is the most significant example of this because in choosing virginity, she alienated herself from what was held up as woman's vocation by the tradition of her people. Although her vocation is a unique one in human history, we see time and time again throughout history women who distinctly have a special mission to fulfill: in the Old Testament are Judith and Esther who are viewed as prefigurements of Mary; to name only a few in the history of the Church whose efficacy was particularly striking and removed from the usual life of woman, we have for example Catherine of Siena, Joan of Arc, and the great St. Teresa.

But to have a special vocation is not a peculiar distinction of a chosen few whose names are recorded in world history. Each human soul is created by God; each one receives from Him a character which distinguishes it from every other soul, and this individuality is to be developed within the broader context of humanity in general and of womanhood in particular. There is a correspondence between the uniqueness of the individuality and the suitable activity to which she is called; the development of such uniqueness must be established as one of the goals of girls' education.

It is not possible to generalize about individuality as one might generalize concerning the image of perfected humanity or perfected womanhood. But we must understand clearly that these two general categories do not constitute fully the goal of girls' education. Rather, this goal can be reached only in the concrete wholeness of an individual person. A flexible variety of educational methods is needed to bring about a combination of an authentic humanity and womanhood with an unspoiled individuality. But especially needed are faith in one's own being and courage regarding it, as well as faith in one's individual calling to definite personal activities and a ready willingness to follow this call.

Thus we can specify as the goal of individual educational work the formation of a person who is what *she* is supposed to be personally, who goes *her* way, and performs *her* work. *Her* way is not chosen in an arbitrary fashion; it is the way in which God leads her. Whoever wishes to guide others towards the pure development of their individuality must guide them towards a trust in God's providence and towards the readiness to regard the signs of this providence and to follow them.

B. Distinction to be Made Between Two Goals: one, that characteristic of the eternal order; two, that characteristic of contemporary challenges

It is impossible to delineate the diversity of individualities in a conceptual form; also, it is hardly possible to depict each person's individual educational goal. Yet we have seen that we can discern types; and so, in the interest of girls' education, we can establish also a differentiation of goals corresponding to these types. We will have an opportunity to discuss the contemporary challenges as we consider these types. But first we must recognize that a differentiation showed itself even in our description of pure womanhood.

First of all, we found that the *mater-virgo* was the ideal of the type of woman described in the Old Testament: she stands beside her spouse, managing her home, and raising up her children in the fear of God. Then, there was the prototype of the *Sponsa Christi* whose home is the kingdom of God and whose family is the communion of saints.

First we must ask if this is a matter of either-or and how extensively this may be so. If the *mater-virgo* is the prototype of pure womanhood, then in a certain sense *both* of the above concepts must be the goal of *all* women's education. Indeed, not only the consecrated virgin but the whole Church and every Christian soul are called the *Spouse of Christ* just as Mary is the paragon of the whole Church and of all the redeemed. To be the bride of Christ means to belong to the Lord: it means to put the love of Christ before all things, not merely by theoretical conviction but in the tug of the heart and in practical life. To become so one must be detached from all creatures, free of a fixation on oneself and on others; and that is the deepest, most spiritual meaning of purity. The wife and mother must also have this *virginity* of soul: indeed, only from this does she get the power to fulfill her vocation; from this source alone flows the ministering love which is neither servile subjugation nor imperious self-assertion and imposed self-will. This ministering love is not only the essence of *maternity;* in the love of Christ it must needs devote itself to all creatures coming into its ken. It is for this reason that the woman who is not wife and mother must also be true in thought and deed to this spiritual maternity.

But the distinction between the two feminine types and

their life styles is not cancelled out by their mutual obligation to the ideal of the Virgin Mary. Indeed, whether or not a woman is a spouse and mother is neither an unimportant or negligible matter. It signifies the extension of the whole person into a larger psychosomatic organism. Body and soul must be suited to that purpose in order for this process to be rightly fulfilled, and by their integration, a definite formation and character are attained. On the other hand, a life style other than marriage also requires a definite aptitude and on its part gives a certain character.

Thus we find here a parting of the two ways indicated by natural aptitudes. There are girls who seem to possess a natural tendency for family life: they have strong vitality and are warm-hearted; they need to have close relationships with other people within a communal way of life; they have an empathy for the care of children and are inclined to diverse practical activity. Girls whose sex drives are weaker, who have a propensity toward contemplation and solitude would seem to be more readily adaptable to the unmarried state. But natural disposition alone is not decisive, for perfect suitability for either course of life is not automatically *given* along with the disposition. Marriage and family life require not only full development but also an extensive curtailing, control, and transformation of natural vitality and of social instincts. This is likewise true of the other path. Yet, life does not always lead to the path indicated by natural inclination; in fact, the vocation followed could be contrary to natural aptitude.

Thus on the one hand, we perceive the necessary inclusion of both goals in our educational program; on the other hand, we see how difficult it will be to strive at the same time for both.

I see here the main problem of a practical education for girls; and in the solution to this problem, I see our Catholic response to contemporary questions. The fruit of an ideal educational program, i.e., a relevant one, should be that each girl would be fit for both marriage and celibacy. This would come about, on the one hand, through bodily strength and health, through ingenuous natural feeling, through a willingness and capacity for sacrifice and renunciation. On the other hand, a strengthened spirituality must subdue the sexual drive.

Today we need more urgently than ever mothers who exemplify the ideal of the *mulier fortis*. And since we must consider the calling to physical maternity as the usual situation, the normal type of girls' schools and their curricula should be established towards that end.

Yet even those girls with a natural gift for physical maternity cannot be certain in any way that they will attain this state; thus all must be prepared for the other course as well. Natural inclination for celibacy is exceptional. But it is not always the case that a calling comes only to those naturally disposed to consecrated virginity. And today it is often the case that girls who would seem to be suited to marriage by nature and inclination are often destined to lead a single life. Educational work must take such cases into consideration so that God's call to celibacy, which can be made known just as distinctly through external coincidences as through individual feelings, will be obeyed willingly and not accepted rebelliously nor in weary resignation.

If the call to *virginity* is consented to full-heartedly and joyously even in the absence of a specific religious vocation and even when the call is opposed to natural inclination, it would seem certain that the feminine nature would not atrophy or be morbidly spoiled. The basis for this guarantee is the intention of the *ancilla Domini*[45] which should be the goal and fruit of religious educational work. But moreover, the faculties must be directed towards a fruitful cooperation with nature.

The educational goal for the girl with a natural aptitude for the domestic and maternal life should be to fit her for this vocation which suits her abilities. Indeed, when this vocation is predominant, she might also be trained for jobs in housekeeping, agriculture, horticulture, possibly for business or nursing, education, and social work. For the type of girl engaged in intellectual activities, the goal must be training for creative or useful intellectual work of a scientific, artistic, or managerial kind. Thus a selection takes place on common ground. This goal of professional efficiency so necessary for a sound development of the individual personality corresponds at the same time to the need of society as a whole for the utilization of feminine abilities.

Giving girls a clear picture of the structure and laws of state and society must be accepted as a goal of their education. This must be done so that personal activities may be integrated appropriately into society as a whole; an understanding of the social significance of their personal activities will heighten their readiness and joyousness to do so.

Thus, by situating our goal within the external order of human existence, we are confronted once again with contemporary challenges: aptitude for marriage and maternity, professional know-how, political and social responsibility, and, finally, readiness to serve the Lord which is the foundation for everything else.[46]

Of course, it is only these contemporary claims as they ensue from *our* view of the times which must be harmonized with the eternal order. This eternal order likewise demands a categorical rejection of the claims raised by another Weltanschauung.[47]   It demands rejection of a social order and of education which deny completely woman's unique nature and particular destiny, which disclaim an organic cooperation of the sexes and organic social patterns but seek rather to consider all individuals as similar atoms in a mechanistically ordered structure. Such a society and educational system consider humanity and the relationship of the sexes merely on a biological basis, fail to realize the special significance and the higher level of the spiritual as compared to the physical, and, above all, are lacking completely in any supernatural orientation. Against these contemporary currents there is today no other bulwark than the Catholic faith and a meta-physical, social and educational system founded upon it.

If we can institute an independent Catholic system of education for girls, we shall be defending in this way not only the threatened position of the woman in cultural life but also we shall be taking part in the great struggle of the spirit against materialism and biologism in the struggle for Christ's kingdom against all unchristian and anti-Christian movements and trends.[48]

IV. EDUCATORS AND OUR CULTURAL HERITAGE

Significance of Educational Communities and of the Objective Cultural Heritage in the Program for Girls

In earlier papers on the problems of women's education, we discussed education as the goal-orientation of the person. The nature of woman was treated as the material to be formed. We discussed the goal which should be attained through educational work. The question still remains: Who should do educational work? By what means are its goals to be attained?

A. Communities as Educators

1. THE FAMILY

Can human beings form themselves to fulfill their allot-ted destiny? Yes and no. As rational, free, and responsible beings, they have the ability and, therefore, the responsibility to help in their own formation. But they do not have the use of their reason and of their freedom from the moment of birth; and until they do, others must help with their forma-tion. Later, self-education and external educational work must be coordinated. Others remain responsible for mature persons as well—for their understanding, freedom and development. This can be accepted because humanity shares a common responsibility and because the individual is a member of this most comprehensive oneness and also of the concrete communities in which this oneness is structured. That is why the encyclical on education reads: "Education is necessarily a work of the community," and it names "three necessary communities in which each person exists";[49] two natural social orders—family and state, and one supernatural order—the Church.

The family has as its immediate goal the rearing and education of its offspring. Thus it has the inalienable right and at the same time the strict obligation regarding the education of its children: "a right prior to every right of the nation and of the state and which is, therefore, an inviolable right superior to every worldly power."[50]   Thus, Canon Law *(Kirchenrecht)* reads in Canon 1113: "Parents have the strict duty to concern themselves according to their means for their offspring's religious and moral education as well as their physical and civic upbringing and temporal well-being." The educational right and duty of parents as expounded mainly in the conclusion of the encyclical are based on the teachings of St. Thomas:[51] the child is like unto the father by nature and is subject to paternal care prior to the use of reason; that is why it would be contrary to the law of nature if, before the children reach the age of reason, they be taken away from the parents' care or if in some way decisions be made on their behalf against the parents' will. Here the basic concept is that the family is to be considered as an organism with the father as its head. But if, as the encyclical on marriage reads, woman is the heart of this organism, it is therefore evident that her attribute is not to be considered inferior to that of the head regarding the education of its members. Indeed, we have already established previously that she is to achieve the most essential factors in the education of her children according to her natural vocation, although under the protection and with her husband's support.

In our time the natural right of the family is most decidedly contested and actually curtailed or completely abrogated in the name of the all powerful state. Now it is rightly an urgent task to be engaged even more deeply and comprehensively in supporting the family. But we cannot dwell on this now. We take it as a given fact that a share in educational work falls to the family. We will ask only what it consists in and by what it is limited.

We must therefore keep in mind the comprehensive idea of education as explained in an earlier passage:[52] Education as the orientation of the whole person towards the goal for which he or she is destined. This process embraces body, soul, and mind with all their faculties. And in great part, it is an instinctive process taking place spontaneously in compliance with the person's inner form.

Consequently, a great part of educational work consists in allowing the process to take place as smoothly as possible and in keeping it free of interruptions and obstructions. This is especially true of physical and spiritual development in the first period of life. Here the work consists essentially in providing proper and punctual nourishment and cleanliness, light, air, and sun, and opportunities for free movement. And beyond that, there is the need for restraining those interventions and influences which at the least are superfluous and frequently also harmful. With these procedures, of course, substantial educational gains are achieved: the physical organs are accustomed to regular functions; the sensual drives already becoming active and even getting out of hand are restrained. All this prepares for the formation of the will. Furthermore, the soul, especially in its imaginative and emotional faculties, is protected from impressions received which might become fixed and perhaps strongly influence the person's later life before their meanings are even understood.

The physical and spiritual faculties attain their proper

development only by participating in activities suitable to them. The body and its senses can best take care of themselves, at least in the early years. On the contrary, the higher faculties—the intellect, emotions, and will—need certain spiritual and intellectual subject-matter as stimuli, and they do not necessarily find what suits them on their own. And, moreover, their action is subordinate to the laws of reason. And these laws of reason are not the laws of nature but are rather based on logical, aesthetic, ethical and religious norms. This means that thought, emotion, and volition do not proceed in an unchanging course but can go astray; they must be guided first in compliance with these norms and then made accustomed to them. Thus, to educate the higher faculties, broader tasks are required than those involving the lower ones: making available suitable subject-matter and introducing it to standard procedure.

Heavy demands are made on the persons wishing to accomplish these tasks: a knowledge of human personality, of its structure and development; an understanding of the uniqueness of the person and his or her needs, and, particularly, an understanding of the specific characteristics of woman; knowledge of the cultural traditions with which young people are to be brought into contact; finally, knowledge of the norms suitable for the intellectual and spiritual life, and the application of these norms to their own personal life; for one can only teach what one practices oneself.

Moreover, even the most exemplary family will not be able to carry on all these tasks. If the mother exemplifies the feminine ideal as previously described, she will be better qualified than any other person to grasp the unique nature of her children and to sense what they need for their most perfect development. And her life, conforming to the moral and religious norms we have described, will be an example to them.

Only in rare instances will she be able to introduce them even indirectly to the cultural traditions they need; and even where the father and perhaps other family members cooperate with her, she cannot be fully successful. For "the family is an imperfect society" which "does not in itself possess all the means necessary for its own perfection."[53] Hence it needs replenishment through contact with other educational groups. So the educational work of the family has its innate limitation. The nature of the children themselves constitute another limitation: Their laws for development must be observed; and their freedom which enables them to liberate themselves from their family's influence and, indeed, makes it necessary for them to do so, must be respected.

2. THE STATE

The encyclical names the state as the second important natural society, describing it as a "perfect society," "incorporating all the necessary means for the attaining of individual goals."[54] Material concern for public welfare may be considered as its purpose. Here sovereignty forms an essential attribute of the state:[55] this implies the right of self-determination including the right to rule its subjects and the power to be able to exercise its sovereignty effectively. It also has the capability to set goals for itself in addition to those mentioned (for example, the greatest possible enhancement of its power). But here its sovereignty and thereby its existence is conditioned by the recognition of its sovereignty by its subjects, i.e., the people in its sphere of influence. It will always be working towards its own downfall if it withdraws from its natural purpose and sets for itself goals which arouse the resistance of its subjects.

As an organized power, the state has the potential possessed by no other social structure to draw all worldly purposes into its realm and either to further or to suppress them. The family's existence and prosperity depend on its protection. It also has the potential of getting involved in the educational system and in cultural affairs. In a certain sense, this even appertains to the safeguarding of existence: training in citizenship, i.e., concern for the civic consciousness of youth. The state's existence depends on its success in making youth recognize its power and its rights and in preparing them to perform willingly their civic duties. But it is also in its interests to form future citizens who will be energetic and healthy, well-adjusted and achievement oriented. Whenever this takes place thanks to the action of another educational group such as the family, it is reasonable for the state to protect and further the action of such a group according to the means at its disposal. Should this not come about through the action of another group or should it be achieved inadequately, then it is rational and appropriate for the state itself to create suitable institutions to do so. But it follows from what we have said that the state has only an indirect role to play in the formation of youth since this is not its immediate purpose but belongs rather to the family.

3. THE CHURCH

The role of the Church in the education of youth is completely different. It is one of her direct obligations. Like her whole origin, her claim here is supernatural and rests on two canonical titles: that of the *universal teacher,* a title bestowed upon her by her divine founder,[56] "that she may teach mankind the divine faith, keeping pure and intact for them the store of faith entrusted to her, guiding and forming mankind with its alliances and actions to moral integrity and purity of life in accordance with revealed teachings";[57] then *supernatural maternity* by which as the bride of Christ, "with her sacraments and her teachings, she gives birth to souls, nourishes and educates them to the divine life of grace."[58]

In her origin as in the practice of her rights, the Church

is independent of every earthly power. To instruct souls in the faith and to educate them to a life of faith is her immediate mission. But in order for her goal to be attained, she must go further. "Because the Church as the perfect society has an autonomous right to the means towards her goal, and because every teaching just as all human action stands in a necessary dependent relationship to the ultimate end of mankind and hence cannot evade the norms of divine law of which she is guardian, expounder, and infallible teacher," she has with regard to all other aspects, from the time she undertook her educational role, the right to make use and particularly to judge these aspects to the extent that they are beneficial or harmful to Christian education."[59]   And again: if adequate educational work is not achieved by other channels, public or private, or one not in harmony with supernatural goals, it is thus the right of the Church to set in place her own institutions and to undertake the total educational work, as, for example, she has done in mission territories.

4. FURTHER EDUCATIONAL FACTORS
RELATIONSHIP OF THE VARIOUS FACTORS

There are other educational factors, however, in addition to the three we have described. Everything that is truly absorbed into the depths of the soul educates and forms the whole person. Consequently, every human contact can have its educational effect. (We will disregard for the time being the external cultural heritage.)

For instance, take the example of adults whose conduct towards young people as well as towards other adults automatically has an impact even when there is not the least educational intention involved. Formal education will always have to take into consideration these unintentional influences and it should attempt to control them. But such education can also be undertaken by agents other than the three educational *communities* already named: by individuals or by groups who take human formation as their goal—perhaps as teachers, writers, or organizers. They are able to assist or to impede the work of competent educational institutions. Their power should not be underrated: one need only think of how decisively the people of our time have been formed through the influence of political parties, the youth movement, and the feminist movement. It is a significant social problem to determine how really *competent* these movements are, how they have done and will continue to do work which professional educational groups have failed in.

The contemporary Church, state, and family cannot attain their goal today if they do not reach a genuine consensus in the understanding of these factors to which we have referred. As for the relation of the three educational communities to one another, no clash will arise as long as each one limits itself to its own functions and goal. But when one of them extends its power arbitrarily, a conflict can hardly be avoided. The secular state is most likely to permit such arbitrary encroachment. With the family, the principal danger is when it fails to assume its duty; then it is taken over by the other educational groups. When the family is interfered with for reasons other than this, then unfortunately, it lacks the strength to defend itself. It would have to seek protection from one or the other great corporate body.

The greatest clashes through the ages have taken place between state and Church: in Germany such clashes have been designated as "Kulturkampf."[60] They are usually caused by the state's excessive claim to power, and by its interventions into the Church's universal teaching mandate. But it cannot be denied that this universal right can be exercised wrongfully by the representatives of the Church and that conflicts can be caused or intensified thereby.

We must now consider by which means the different educational communities are able to define and carry out their functions, with particular reference to the education of girls.

5. THE FAMILY, CHURCH AND STATE
AS AGENTS OF GIRLS' EDUCATION

The most essential factor in personal development is the mature person by whom immature persons are guided and cared for as long as they are physically dependent and by whom they are still guided later on in their intellectual and spiritual lives. Their inner lives are awakened and directed onto positive paths because children think and feel in harmony with the diverse attitudes of adults. The human environment in which children grow up does much to determine their character and form it according to its own image. Such guidance is indispensable for personality formation, but this alone does not suffice. The adult must bring the intrinsic nature of children to fruition. They must become extensively free of the mere "going along with others" and "aping of others." Among other things, this can be accomplished through discussion with different kinds of people, perhaps with contrasting personalities, furthermore through tasks to which they are assigned—we would provisionally restrict these tasks to the service of other people. The family, which indeed finds its immediate goal in the formation of the person, is completely suited to this purpose; the conditions for personality development through other people are proffered in the child's intimate life with parents and relatives. The Church likewise possesses such vital agents for human development suitable to its original purpose: first of all in the parents themselves as far as they as Church members are called upon and equipped to educate their children as children of the Church; then in the priests who, in their ministry of forming individual souls, work directly on a person to person basis (although we disregard at this time their homilies and dispensing of the sacraments in relation to objective educational method); finally, in all those who set as their goal the education of youth in the spirit of the Church. The state does not possess such natural agents for human development.

Should it raise educational work to a national goal, it would first have to create for itself agents for that purpose, i.e., teachers who are civil servants.

Earlier in our discussion, we considered the mother the most essential agent of a girl's formation in the family. If living with those who are what one should be is the basic and most efficacious factor in human development, then the most essential factor in the formation of pure womanhood must be growing up near a woman who embodies it. And the mother who does *not* embody this fails in her mission. A mother's example is also fundamental because pure womanhood cannot take shape without pure humanity also being developed at the same time.

Finally, it has already been emphasized also that the mother is called and equipped to detect her child's individuality and the needs which arise from it. The mission of being a prototype of pure humanity holds for the father in like measure (even if he brings the ideal of perfection to fruition along other paths). In order to further the girl's formation to authentic womanhood, her relationship to the father must needs pave the way for trustful association, for a loving self-subordination and readiness to serve. Although an understanding of individuality and its claims is generally less true of man than of woman, it is yet the father's duty to consider it reverently, to try to understand it (possibly with the help of the mother's more sensitive faculty of empathy), and to meet or at the least to allow the necessary practical measures for the girl's development. It is incumbent on both parents that, in mutual agreement and by suitable methods, they counteract in the child's nature all those urges which impede their goals. Living together with brothers and sisters is also of extraordinary significance for bringing about the threefold goal, particularly for cultivating the specific womanhood we have described: discussion with diverse personalities and regard for them; finally, performance of acts of kindness which they need. What priests and the educators working in the spirit of the Church achieve by direct action must simultaneously be paternal and maternal educational work. Because they are agents of Mother Church, they must project the image of a self-forgetful, ministering love and find in this love the intimate access to souls as well as to their individual uniqueness. Because they represent Christ, the Head of the Church, they must imitate His perfection. Acting with paternal authority, they must stimulate and guide the member to perform the ministry to which he is called for the Head and for the other members. Should these duties surpass natural human powers, they become possible in the divine power of the Head.

If the state is to engage in authentic educational activity, it must find persons who are suitable to perform it and who are ready to function *in loco parentis*[61] under its direction. The state can create institutions to train them for the function, but will succeed only if they have the necessary educational qualifications. They lack the intimate solidarity which is the natural foundation of guidance offered by the family. Also, if they do not have a deeply rooted faith, then they also lack the supernatural enhancement of power needed for their duty. However, a special personal gift for educational work can compensate for the lack of family solidarity, particularly if it is accompanied by a knowledge of human nature, by skill in dealing with people, and, in some cases, with an intellectual affinity. Nothing can compensate for the lack of charisma. The responsibility for educating without either family tie or spiritual strength, which is to say the natural way, is so great that one can endure it only when one does not think about it or is not fully conscious of it. The more the goals of official state institutions in the education of girls approximate the ideal of the family, the sooner they will be able to achieve their purpose. This involves the decisive role of authentic women, paternal guidance on the part of men, and a family spirit among the students. Indeed, on this last point, the school with its greater human diversity may have an advantage over the narrow family circle.

B. Education and Our Cultural Heritage

1. WHY SHOULD THE SCHOOL EXIST?

What induced the state to build up a widely ramified school system? Also, why has the Church always wished to establish its own schools rather than to accept as sufficient the education provided by priests in their pastoral care? And why would parents decide to send their children to school even if they were not coerced to do so? The frequent inability of the family to perform its educational mission is *one* reason but not the essential one. The meaning and function of the school goes beyond its role as a proxy of the family, the state, and the Church. Intellectual life does not depend only on contact with intellectual people. It also depends on discovering impersonal forms of intellectuality which we might call *works of the objective mind,* that is to say, *culture.* The human mind is designed to understand and to enjoy works of culture. It cannot be developed fully if it does not come into contact with a multiplicity of cultural disciplines. And the individual human being cannot attain his destined calling if he is unable to discover the cultural domain suited to his talent.

When a nation reaches a certain degree of differentiation, it commands a cultural treasure that the individual can no longer discover at a glance. Familiarity with a single cultural discipline then requires special training and only those who possess this knowledge of a field of culture can guide others to it. An adequate introduction to the entire cultural life represents a higher level of development than that made possible by the family. The school's specific task is to introduce the student to the various areas of culture and to make them effective in the development of the individual human being.

2. EDUCATIONAL VALUE OF OBJECTIVE
INTELLECTUAL DISCIPLINES

We will now have to investigate what cultural traditions —more broadly understood, what objective intellectual disciplines—can serve to procure the goals of girls' education. As stated, we understand the "objective mind" to be all impersonal objects or manifestations which *potentially* contain mind; this mind is actualized in contact with persons who are intellectually open and interested.

a. Word and Language

The *word* is the most direct "incarnation of the mind." The mind of God as well as the mind of man are manifested and reflected in the word. Through the word we have access to both. Let us, for the time being, put aside the divine word —and especially that objective treasury of the divine texts in which God speaks to us—and limit ourselves to the human word. *Luther* has said felicitously that languages are "the scabbard in which the blade of the intellect is inserted." It is so even when separated from the concrete context of a living, speaking personality as in books or in manuscripts or inscriptions; they are to be preserved although seemingly "dead" themselves. The *grammatical forms* of language reflect its intellectual structures and the systematic inquiry of this is the function of *logic*. That is why every introduction to the knowledge of grammatical categories and every exercise in their differentiation are not easily replaced by other means for training in logic.

On average, girls do not apply themselves to such abstract thought. But it is necessary that they be educated to think clearly and keenly in order to establish the priority of the intellect in their formation as is proper in the structure of the human personality. Without such a formation, the human mind cannot be a likeness of the mind of God. Furthermore, such intellectual work is of great importance as a remedy for the weakness of fallen human nature which is particularly characteristic of woman: her mental clarity is often dulled by her emotions, desires, and libidinal drives. The young girls' antipathy toward abstract and grammatical subject-matter can be overcome if the philosophical meaning of the forms is opened up to them: it is shown that they give us an insight into the whole structure of the mind and, at the same time, of the formal structure of the objective world (an early understanding of this context can be reached by younger girls through language training).

Connections with personal intellectual life become even more significant. By being initiated into different languages, one is able to indicate how the particular type of national mentality is expressed through the preference for this or that form. And with the study of individual literary works, the intellectual uniqueness of the individual personality can be shown. Finally, should we consider the *content* of speech patterns, what expressive values are added to the vernacular in the living flow of conversation; through this means we are brought to an understanding of the full profusion of human and national life to which feminine interests are drawn naturally. Here there is ample opportunity to train and to care for the natural predisposition to understand the singularity and intrinsic value of human beings and their institutions, an opportunity as well to strengthen those close human and national ties within woman's soul.

b. Human Works

The human mind is manifested in its *works:* in the creations of works of art, of things of daily use, of means by which nature is controlled and modified, i.e., by technology, in social and political institutions, and in scientific theories. A knowledge and understanding of human art and of human life as well is made possible by initiation to all these fields. Moreover, the introduction to art (both theoretical and practical) is primarily suited to awaken joy in beauty and perhaps to stimulate existing practical and creative talents. History and civics are able to build an understanding of one's own duty in community life. Mathematics and the natural sciences, as characteristic ways of intellectual activities, could be brought closer to human and personal concerns through the humanities. Introduction to their own methods which are abstract and exact (here we refer especially to the "exact" natural sciences) would appear again to be somewhat alien to the mentality of the young girl. However, to eliminate these disciplines from girls' education would, first of all, disadvantage those individuals possessing an aptitude for them. Then, apart from grammatical instruction, they offer the best opportunity for training in keen and clear thought; finally, they give a characteristic explanation—from the philosophical point of view—of the human mind focused on the world. Moreover, they are so important for an understanding of man's place in creation that they can scarcely be dispensed with as a foundation for a consistent view of life. Just as the liberal arts and the exact sciences when methodically considered give an insight into the achievements of the human mind, so does the description of nature reveal the direct work of divine creation, the cosmos; both together reveal the totality of the created world. But the desire to construe a consistent world view, i.e., the *metaphysical tendency,* is fixed in the human mind itself, and is strongly apparent even in the mind of the young girl. Authentic educational work could hardly be spoken of wherever this tendency is not considered. That is why religious instruction must be offered in the upper-grades of secondary schools, and supplementary to it, an introduction to philosophy as well—the culmination and integration of the entire theoretical structure.

The human mind is revealed in the *design of the human personality* itself. What a person is, what lasting special character he takes on in the course of his life, his insights, his accomplishments, the enduring principles of his behavior, are to a large extent the consequence of what others have made of him and what he has made of himself. Because *human development* is the *most specific and exalted mission of woman,* studies in *anthropology* and *theory of pedagogy* are essential to girls' education. Thus, all these foregoing remarks indicate *that no achievement of the human mind can be dispensed with in the system of girls' education.* Naturally, that is not to say that just anything at all which is considered as a method for the suitable formation of women's intellect must be accepted in the curriculum of every school. Universal cultural traditions must be structured in suitable ways in a system of different kinds of schools according to age levels and types of aptitude. But every school, from which the pupils go out into the world, must guide them to a consistent view of life. This world view will be suitable to the age level and intellectual type, here more elementary and there deeper and more comprehensive. And in any case, it will be only a ground plan giving rules for the structure of the student's own future lifework.

C. View of God as the Educator of Man

We have briefly surveyed the significance attributed to the achievements of the human mind. But the *objective mind* passes beyond human culture. It has already been said that the mind of God and of man are expressed in the Word. But the divine Word is not the only deposit of the divine mind and not the only means which God uses to educate man. We shall devote a separate analysis, a conclusive one, to the question of the totality of woman's education as God's work. But first we must complete our discussions of human educators and their methods by considering the institutions within which their methods may be put to use.

V. METHODS OF EDUCATION

A. Home and School: Boarding Schools—Day Schools

We have already seen that fundamentally nothing can replace the educational competence of the home; yet, the family is unable to exercise the educational function alone. Disregarding for the time being the educational functions of the Church, we see then that the cooperation of home and school on an advanced cultural level is evidently both natural and desirable.

The ideal home is a place where the children grow up under the responsible care of both parents, in a circle of brothers and sisters, and in an environment adjusted to the physical and spiritual needs of the child and the adolescent. When this is so, the home will naturally transmit what we have come to regard as the formation of the person through other persons: a formation which is silent and persistent, which in part operates unconsciously in harmony with the natural laws of growing up and in part works consciously under the guiding and forming influence of the environment.

It has already been stated that nothing can replace the girl's growing up near a mother who embodies authentic womanhood. If in her early years, the child has experienced that caring love which is aware of everything she needs even before she herself knows what she lacks, then the vital solidarity between mother and daughter has become a spiritual-intellectual tie scarcely to be severed: the child has thus been given a love capable of counsel, help and consolation in all predicaments, of sharing joy and sorrow and yet meeting with unyielding firmness the disordered urges; this love is able to build those virtues which are acquired in later life only with difficulty or not at all: cleanliness and order, obedience, truthfulness and consideration. This tie between mother and child will overcome the first crisis which occurs when the child begins school and enters into a new world; the mother will build the bridge into this new world and avert the pitfall of alienation by her understanding and her child's trust in her. And if the veracity of the mother and the child's confidence in her has endowed the child herself with self-reliance and veracity, then the second and more difficult crisis will also be surmounted: the time of puberty. Now is the time when the child's individuality and womanhood arrive at the point of breakthrough; when the adolescent cannot understand herself, when she becomes an independent personality and stands up to others, when she would like to be respected by others and yet is conscious of what she lacks, and when for all these reasons she would like to withdraw into herself and yet longs for understanding and guidance. If the maternal style of up-bringing stands the test here, if she silently takes into consideration that the child is no longer a child and therefore treats her accordingly, if she does not try to coerce the child's confidence and yet conveys the idea that she is cognizant of the child's inner struggles, and, finally, if she knows how to give advice and can reveal the highest meaning of this course of events—then she has won for good. The mother's example and judgment will be the child's guiding principle for life. We cannot consider again here the significance of the father, brothers, and sisters in regard to the child's direct formation.

Thus the child already experiences in the home as well a formation through the cultural heritage if a sympathetic or, indeed, creative interest in cultural life is evidenced in the home. And the child's instinctive venturing into the world of the objective mind is also something which is scarcely compensated for by systematic instruction. Yet, education through cultural heritage remains the subordinate goal in the family, while for the school it is the primary and more important goal. For the latter, on the other hand, education through cultural tradition must be imparted by persons: the school exposes impressionable young people to the daily influence of adults; being formed through these persons is inevitably a direct educational action. At the same time, this makes it important that the teacher is a responsible educator.

The contemporary view of education as the *foremost* purpose of the school is justifiable in *principle* by two factors: all educational work, even that imparted through objective forms, aims at personality formation: and the whole course of instruction must be structured in view of this goal. But the decisive fact remains that today, to a large degree, the home no longer fulfills its natural purpose; often it achieves nothing, and what educative work it does achieve is negative. Thus it is incumbent on the school to act by mandate in place of the family or, indeed, with the authorization of the great corporate bodies, the state and the Church, who beside the family are responsible for the education of youth.

Wherever the home and school share in educational activity, they should function in cooperation, "hand-in-hand," rather than in mutual indifference. In regard to girls' education, there is danger that the child may be led into conflict and confusion and the direct educational process may be curtailed or even neglected if the teachers' influence counteracts that of the mother; the teachers' personalities and views may work against the goal to which the mother aspires or unknowingly initiates. But wherever parents and teachers work together responsibly, both parties will take pains to be at least enlightened concerning each other's influence and, if an understanding cannot be reached, to handle these influences in appropriate ways. And if on one hand, there is a conviction that the other's influence is impeding the goal, then an attempt will be made to eliminate it: responsible parents will not permit their children to attend a school which, according to their conviction, jeopardizes the goal in dangerous ways; and responsible teachers will endeavor to liberate children from a home in which they are endangered.

There are times when schools to which parents can entrust their children simply are not available. Such a situation can be caused by family circumstances or the home may be unable to assume its educational function. These circumstances will either stress exclusive education in the home or in an institution. The advantage of the one or of the other vis-à-vis their combination is obviously the possibility of a consistent and self-contained educational program. Yet, each alone will always remain provisional.

We have already indicated the priority, indeed, the primacy, of education through the family. However, it has its disadvantages. First of all, the family often does not come into contact with broader cultural life. This limitation may cause an atrophy of talents and faculties which can be stimulated only through such broader cultural influence. (Nevertheless, this danger can be avoided in families where a high cultural level exists and where suitable private instruction is available. Indeed, since it permits greater flexibility and a greater potential for individual adaptation, it may have advantages over the schematization of institutional instruction.) A second danger of education through the family exists in the strong ties to particular people of the family. This could enchain the individual for life and possibly could even impede the free development of her personality; for instance, the family may arbitrarily decide that a girl is of a feminine type which might not correspond at all to her own inclinations. Finally, there is a danger of inadequate preparation for social life which makes later adaptation more difficult and perhaps even impossible.

An institutional education has the advantage of being in the hands of people who have chosen education as their life work, people who are theoretically prepared and properly qualified. Their way of taking charge, their personal influence and instruction are able to focus on a readily grasped and unanimously desired goal. Furthermore, the interchange between teacher and student, more extensive than in the family, gives better opportunities for the development of both individual tendencies and social qualities.

However, institutional education presents serious dangers. First of all there is a lack of the close personal tie, of the heart-warming natural love which envelops the child in

her home.   Individuality suffers neglect or even oppression
through an institutional system.   Often it lacks the authentic
type of maternal woman by whom or according to whom the
girl should be formed.   Finally, the girl is limited by the very
narrowness of the institutional community, where there is
often a lack of association with broader outside groups which
employ successfully more contemporary concepts.   The more
clearly one is conscious of the dangers and the greater the
attempt to approach the kind of community for which one
must compensate, the more easily the dangers of one and the
other can be avoided.

It is correct to say that, in general, it is even more critical for girls than for boys to break away from the family and
to transfer to a purely institutional education. We can understand this because of the difference in their natural vocation.
If it is true that a man's primary work is professional activity,
it will be to the youth's advantage if, at an opportune time,
he becomes accustomed to a life style which is in some way
suitable to the social circumstances of his later life; this could
take the form of objective work in competition with his comrades on the same level, under the direction of his superiors.
(An "opportune time" means that he should not be initiated
too soon to this competitive way of life before acquiring that
strength to get along without the family's loving care.   And
there is also the danger here that by breaking away premature-
ly from the family, the aptitude for family life will suffer and
also the aptitude for establishing a family in later life and for
its accompanying domestic tasks.)   And if the woman's foremost vocation is that of spouse, mother, and housekeeper,
then no better preparation for these roles can be given than
maturing in a family in which she accustoms herself to performing such duties. And an environment and life style which
do not accustom her to such duties implies a hazard to the
fulfillment of her later vocation. On the other hand, after a
more secure groundwork is laid for the duties of domestic
life, an *occasional* breaking away from the home is desirable

for many reasons: to release the girl's personality from excessively close ties to the family; to avert the danger of a too rigid commitment to one's family type; to initiate a greater adaptability to varying characters and circumstances (this is important for setting up one's own family as well as for the single life); and to prepare for a vocation outside of the home and for social duties.

Boarding schools exclusively operated for the education of girls will not be able to do justice to their job before they have the character of a large family as a whole and are structured into family-like sections. This happens more readily in convent schools if the girls are admitted as members of the monastic family; unfortunately, it so often happens that the girls are separated completely from the religious community as part of a constructed "institute" with its own regulated system. This family-like character is possible elsewhere if the directress is more "mother" than "director" or "prefect" in relation to her students and colleagues and if the "faculty" evidence less of the solidarity between officials and more of mutuality in a responsible and ministering love. A family-like structure requires the incorporation of a small circle under a maternal leader; it requires a fellowship between older and younger girls which enables the older ones to take care of the younger. But such boarding schools should now and then be able to adapt themselves to the methods of the day schools; day students indeed live with the family, but they do not experience there the education which they need. Today, the role of public schools is widely recognized in this respect. This leads us now to a consideration of the various types of schools. But first there is still something else to be explained.

Up to now we have discussed the problem of the boarding and day schools with specific regard to woman's education, but our attention has been focused on the goal of the "maternal woman" alone. However, we have seen the perfect ideal of woman exemplified by the *Virgin Mother*. If this perfect ideal must be the goal of the entire education of girls in a spiritual sense, it will naturally be embodied in the woman who is the actual mother in a more intense and urgent way. In the other instance, the ideal of virginity is best exemplified where a virgin life is led. That is why an obvious conclusion follows: just as the family is the best educational institution for girls called to maternity in the family, just so the convent boarding school is the best for the others.

At the present time, this differentiation is not so simple. First of all, to be sure, girls today are by no means entrusted to cloistered schools by their parents in order to prepare them for the religious life; they must try to adapt themselves to the tasks required of the majority of girls. On the other hand, an authentic Catholic education must include the ideal of virginity even if it takes place in the family or in worldly institutions. And, finally, in no way today does the life of chastity mean only the cloistered life. And for many girls the ideal of virginity can have a different meaning: for them, it is approached independently from the tie to the vocation of life in a convent.

Yet, in cloistered institutions, the possibility of stimulating an understanding of the ideal of virginity should exist. And when it does happen, no matter which road the girl takes for her future life, it will be an advantage for everyone. But this ideal becomes credible to girls only where girls see for themselves virginity embodied in an active and visible way. Virginity is not negative in its highest and ultimate sense. It is not empty resignation, a renunciation of something to which one's desires stay fixed. (Were it only that, it could have only a deterrent effect on young, healthy people with natural feelings.) Certainly it is not a denial of something which holds no meaning. (A disparaging opinion of love and marriage is, first of all, thoroughly contrary to Catholic belief; and, moreover, such a rejection would cause the natural feelings to protest.) It is the highest positive thing: union with Christ in a continuing life companionship. This union must be marked above all in the love of Christ which determines the total activity of the true *Spouse of Christ,* and must, of course, be especially effective in the teacher's relations with the students. It must be apparent in the instinctive, radiating joyfulness bestowed on a life spent with and for Christ, and the obvious readiness to make sacrifices and in the inner peace which no external vicissitude can disrupt. It evidences itself in the fulfilling of divine truth living in Scripture; it acts as a self-evident guiding principle in the making of decisions for all theoretical and practical questions. It is seen in the joyful enthusiasm which also accompanies the life of Christ in the Church: in attention given to the liturgy, the sacrifice of the mass, and choir duty, in a devotion to the entire Church year but quite particularly to the holy days.

Children who witness such a truly dedicated and God-filled life will not be able to evade its persuasive power. Even if it does not induce them to choose the life of a religious, they will take this spirit of authentic virginity into marriage or into their "worldly" vocation. It is evident that it is the specific task of cloistered institutions to attain this goal, and if they do not attain it, they fail in their "raison d'être." But it is also evident that wherever the same goal is lived and worked for, it can be attained.

B. The Organization of the School System Into Various Types of Schools

We have discussed the threefold goal of woman's education: perfected humanity, pure womanhood, and a fully developed individuality. In addition, we have given consideration to the vast area of cultural tradition. Thus we see that they are both coordinated with each other and that we can eliminate from the total system of women's education neither that which educates intellectually nor that which forms humanly. But by this we do not mean to say that every human soul would be capable of embracing both of them in their

entirely nor that it is necessary to make that understanding
accessible to everyone. In the first place, each person possesses a limited power of comprehension depending on individual
faculties. Individuals are receptive to a greater or lesser degree
to different cultural fields, and many are not receptive to
them at all. That which the soul cannot receive and assimilate has no formative power: it holds no educational value
for the soul; indeed, it is rather superfluous and harmful. In
all of this, practical results depend on the choice of the right
methods to be used. We must use the means leading more
perfectly to the goal; from that which would clearly affect
our goal, we should choose that which is really serviceable in
the given circumstances.

We need a basic, standard type of girls' education suited
to the future which awaits the majority of them and to which
the majority of them are called. In Irmgard Liebster's small
pamphlet *Feminine Types—Feminine Education,*[62] she makes
a very simple distinction between the *uncultured* woman and
the *responsive* woman who is *conscious* of life's problems.
Uncultured women—who constitute the great majority—have
a faculty for maturing early into well-rounded personalities
with simple, clear, and fixed characteristics which do not
change. Women who are aware of life's problems—a relatively
small group—are versatile and adaptive; growing up, they
retain a youthful receptivity and ability to learn from those
people whom they accompany on life's path; they mature
successfully through much experience and sufferings to become wise mothers.[63] There are exceptional women of both
types who perform objectively and creatively in particular
ways. However, in general, the strength of woman is her
receptivity,[64] and this necessitates that her respective faculties be cultivated. I do not wish to develop this line of
thought any further at this time. Also, I will not speculate
now about whether the system is too simple, especially for
women who are not uncultured. It seems to me that we have
encountered an essential problem in the uncultured type of

woman, and I would like to discuss it. Let us ask: what must
we do, what can we do for this great majority? Most girls will
have to take care of themselves practically in later life. If
they develop along healthy lines, as we would wish, most of
them would be housewives. But in all likelihood, many of
them will be practicing a vocation as well, working not only
at home but outside of it as domestics, factory workers, sales-
persons, or as clerks in the offices of large concerns. Most
girls have practical ability while only a selective few have an
aptitude and interest in purely theoretical matters. How
should this majority be formed then so that they will be able
to take their place in society?

Wherever they may be at any time, they will not be able
to do their job until they possess the hierarchy of faculties
appropriate to pure human nature: i.e., the libidinous drive
is controlled by the will; the intellect, the eye of the soul,
guides the will and guides us along life's path. We know that
the educational process alone cannot establish this hierarchy,
but it can and must cooperate with other forces to bring it
about. The intellect and the will must be disciplined in order
to obey and to rule. Elementary public schools are designed
to meet the most immediate needs of practical life; first-rate
methods are used to achieve the maximum development of
the intellect and thereby to endow it with an ever stronger
vitality: that is, formal training in grammar, in arithmetic,
and in the catechism. We do not need to prove that all of
these disciplines form the child's abstract intellectual ability.

But perhaps it is not entirely superfluous to comment
that such training does fit the most urgent demands of practical life. It is clear that the housewife, as well as every other
woman in practical life, should be *skilled* in arithmetic (even
more than is generally the case today). However, the importance of a formal mastery of language is not so obvious.

To begin with, it may seem as if the ability to express
oneself, so important for practical life, is one which either
develops on its own or is acquired by practical exercises

rather than by abstract and formal instruction. In fact today, free and unaffected self-expression is the first thing one tries for in instruction for beginners. First of all, the children are allowed to be completely plain-spoken. They are permitted to use the vernacular and popular means of expression. They are encouraged to speak about their own feelings so that they express themselves spontaneously and willingly; this is to free them from any inhibitions which would check the soul's free and natural self-revelation taking place in oral speech. Psychologically this builds the confidence necessary concerning the entire educational process and maintains or regulates the natural expressive function which is the prerequisite of all speech formation.

But then the educational process must set in. Finding a *suitable term* for what one has to say and understanding correctly what others say must be the purpose of education; a sensitivity to *the beauty of speech* is to be awakened; language is to be *used correctly*. I would like to eliminate here the aesthetic view, not because I consider it unimportant but because it seems impossible to do it sufficient justice in a brief aside comment. By "a suitable term" I do not mean a term which is correct according to the rules of an artificial written language but rather one which captures the concept as one wishes to say it. Relevant to this is a rich vocabulary acquired by listening and talking, reading and writing. Yet there is another matter involved also without which an acquired vocabulary is harmful: the attempt to employ phraseology rather than to utter candid speech—i.e., to clothe inward thoughts with outward speech.

Thought and speech are connected most closely; basically, they are *one* process. Where a thought ripens into perfect clarity and meaning, it is organized by way of logical-grammatical categories and is articulated. And where a thought is not successful in finding the right expression, the thought process has not attained completion. What one cannot express remains dark and gloomy in the soul, and whoever is unable to express himself is imprisoned in his own soul; he is unable to liberate himself and cannot relate to others. Differentiation of grammatical categories (naturally, not anything superficial but those pertinent to meaning) is an exercise in forms of thought; it is a way of perceiving the two-fold essential significance of speech: it expresses what lives in the soul and thereby reveals oneself to others; it is a way of releasing one's soul and mind. To be able to express oneself appropriately is thus something which belongs essentially to perfected humanity. But woman also needs it simply for her practical duties. If she is to cooperate in developing human-ity, if she is to guide people in their activity or to have busi-ness dealings with them, it will always depend on whether or not she can really express what she wants to say and what suits her purpose.

To speak appropriately has yet another meaning: to make the right use of speech. When one has grasped the essential import of speech, one knows that it signifies a responsibility taken upon oneself and that one must have reverence for words. Intentionally or not, the word always reveals the speaker's own soul. It is released from the soul's innermost depths like a ripened fruit and discloses the soul's inner activity; an unrestrained verbal outburst betrays the soul's seething and raging; thoughtless speech testifies to superficial dealings. And speech always has its repercussion on other souls. The word can enrich other souls, stimulate and guide them; it can injure them and cause them to retreat into themselves; it can make a deadly mark on them. Every person, and above all every future mother, should be led to understand why we will be judged on our every word. And the teaching of language can help to attain this understanding.

Considering that formal speech training is important in regard to the goal of education and that, on the other hand, the pursuit of abstract matters is suitable to the natural gifts and tendencies of only a small minority of girls, we must ask "How is it possible to interest the majority of girls in the study of language and to assure the success of such training?"

This can be attained sometimes through exercise in the use of a living, concrete speech. At other times consideration should be given to individual uniqueness in the means of expression, to the differences in dialects, or to the characteristic distinctions between the mother language and a foreign tongue (where a knowledge of foreign languages does exist). All this is interesting from human and personal aspects. And at the same time, it is a suitable approach to the study of the general character of language and to its status in intellectual life; the relationship of the individual to the community should also be introduced—to be sure, this should be done according to the age level in a more elementary or more advanced manner; a brief explanation should be given of the ethical and practical significance of the mastery of language. But these are all, in addition, methods of stimulating for one thing, the girls' eagerness for lessons and exercises which may seem alien to them: they can be introduced in this way to the universal human meaning of language, its philosophical implications and practical value. In a comparable fashion, their interest in mathematical instruction is stimulated by a concrete and practical presentation of the lesson material.

The capacity for abstract thought is acquired in religious instruction as well. Catholic dogma functions thanks to a distinct well-defined conceptual apparatus. This first-rate means of education should not be waived but rather used fully. Catechetic instruction should not accompany Biblical readings like a necessary evil but should be incorporated in them as captivating and effective material. Just as it is fatal to learn dogma by mere rote, just so is it fruitful and even essential to actually penetrate into the distinctions of faith perceptively; it is fruitful in strengthening our educational goals. The more clearly and distinctly the student understands the relation of the Creator and the created, the facts concerning the Fall of Man and Redemption, the deep mysteries of the divine inner life of the Trinity, the nature of Christ, the essence and the exalted calling of the Mother of God, the deeper will be her union with divinity, the Redeemer, and the Queen of Heaven.

One can see clearly in the lives of the saints that their advancement in personal sanctity and in a more profound insight into the truths of faith postulate and promote each other reciprocally. This is also precisely true of those saints without a scholarly education. And one need not believe by any means that these deep mysteries exceed the child's powers of comprehension. The strong desire to be introduced to the mysteries of God is often stronger in small children than in adults. And if children are responded to in the right manner with no arbitrary force, then their joyful awareness of getting to know God and of coming closer to Him will be accelerated up to the most intensive thinking and living with Him. Thus, it is so much more than a formal schooling in the thinking process: a most serious formation of their souls and persons is attained.

I had intended to emphasize precisely this point because, in general, it deserves much more attention than it receives today. Indeed, one need hardly say that adequate, substantial education has been underestimated: i.e., introduction to the best German linguistic tradition, familiarity with the great literary figures and with sacred and secular history which generally appeals to the majority of girls. Moreover, it has always been recognized that literature and subjects of national culture introduce students to the life of the world and of man and, at the same time, prepare them for the work of human formation in the family and in professional life. Certainly, from an administrative point of view, theoretical schooling is well-founded if religion, German language and literature, and history remain its fundamental subjects. These subjects must be studied before the students graduate from school into life in order that they may attain a liberal, lasting outlook concerning their life duties: i.e., they should be given simple, clear instruction and guidance which are philosophical, psychological, and sociological in nature. Because this instruction is basically significant to form them for their future life, it is desirable to postpone their departure from school as much as possible in order that the educational process may continue during their most impressionable years *after* the puberty crisis.

Since an over-loaded curriculum is the greatest danger to an effective educational process, we must ask ourselves what material can be eliminated without detriment to overall effectiveness. In all branches of study, a great many individual facts which are important and interesting for the specialist but absolutely unnecessary in elementary education can be dispensed with. In addition to that, I believe that instruction in the natural sciences may be carried out very simply. The majority of girls are seldom urged to work in abstractions. However, such abstract studies are in no way completely dispensable: they are important in formal education because they are the best schooling for the authentic observation and description of reality; and they contribute much that is necessary to girls who have to take care of themselves later on in practical life. And then, this scientific study corroborates the individual's natural innate knowledge of God. Besides, these disciplines are necessary in every technological period so that the technological aspects of domestic and public life may function effectively. However, one must restrict oneself to what is indispensable for these purposes; and, if possible, this material should be tied into the practical categories of study as it is basically done today. In the beginning of the public school system, one could detect the specifically "feminine" characteristics of the practical courses, especially in needlework and in home economics. Today we are beyond that. On the other hand, we realize what significance is attributed today precisely to the technical categories (including drawing and gymnastics) for the practical duties of housekeeping, of decorating, of wholesome and legitimate body culture and the formation of social life.

There must be ample opportunity for all this in the school since activities we have mentioned, once the concern of the family, are no longer considered to be so.

Thus we have clearly established the content and the goal of a basic education for girls. Subsequent "higher" education should proceed from here. The longer period of time involved can be spent in developing and reinforcing the different categories of studies according to the attitude and inclination of students and with consideration to their later vocation. If foreign language instruction is added to that of the mother tongue, language training as well as entrance into the life of the world and humanity could be essentially enriched and deepened. The classics merit priority *in principle* because of their potentially higher educational power as formal education and because of the basic significance of classical antiquity for German culture. However, in consideration of individual aptitude and future choice of vocation, a type of school with predominantly modern language instruction is of course required. Other types of schools are to be adapted according to other abilities. But such adaptations should never take place at the cost of the basic subjects essential to the goal and to the structure of the basic type of school.

In addition to the secondary schools which emerged as a means of preparation for university education, we now see another type, the non-classical secondary school for women, whose approach is focused on specifically feminine abilities. This is certainly a great gain. And it could become a point of departure stimulating other schools as well to undertake programs which take into consideration the specific feminine nature.

Chapter VI

The Church, Woman and Youth

I. WOMAN'S POSITION WITHIN THE CHURCH

The goal of religious training must be to make young people a part of the *corpus Christi mysticum* in that place reserved to them by the eternal order of God. All who are redeemed become *children of the Church,* and here there is no difference between men and women. The Church is not only the community of the faithful, but it is also the Mystical Body of Christ. As such, it is an organism in which individuals take on the nature of members and organs according to their nature and gifts, and they are correlated to make their specific individual contribution to the overall purpose of the whole. Thus woman achieves a particular *organic position* in the Church; and, lastly, she is called upon to embody in her highest and purest development the essence of the Church— to be its *symbol.* The training of girls and the guidance of youth must lead to these three levels of spirituality, i.e., as child, as organ of the Mystical Body, and as symbol of the Church.

Clarity concerning the essence of the Church is the first condition for an understanding of this task. The notion of the Church as community of the faithful is the most accessible to human reason. Whoever believes in Christ and His gospel, hopes for the fulfillment of His promises, clings to Him in love, and keeps His commandments must unite with all who are like-minded in the deepest communion of mind and heart. Those who adhered to the Lord during His stay on

230

earth were the early seeds of the great Christian community; they spread that community and that faith which held them together, until they have been inherited by us today through the process of time.

But, if even a natural human community is more than a loose union of single individuals, if even here we can verify a movement developing into a kind of organic unit, it must be still more true of the supernatural community of the Church. The union of the soul with Christ differs from the union among people in the world: it is a rooting and growing in Him (so we are told by the parable of the vine and the branches) which begins in baptism, and which is constantly strengthened and formed through the sacraments in diverse ways. However this real union with Christ implies the growth of a genuine community among all Christians. Thus the Church forms the Mystical Body of Christ. The Body is a living Body, and the spirit which gives the Body life is Christ's spirit, streaming from the head to all parts. The spirit which Christ radiates is the Holy Spirit; the Church is thus the temple of the Holy Spirit.

In spite of the real organic oneness of head and body, the Church stands by the side of Christ like an independent person. Christ lived prior to all time and all humanity as Son of the eternal Father. Mankind came into being by the act of creation before Christ assumed its nature and entered into it. By entering into creation, He brought His divine life into it. From Himself, He generated human nature anew, in that, through His redemption, He made humanity receptive to His grace and fulfilled it by grace. The Church is that humanity newly created and redeemed through Christ. The original cell of all redeemed mankind is Mary, in whom first took place the purification and sanctification through Christ and impregnation by the Holy Spirit. Before the Son of Man was born of the Virgin, the Son of God conceived of this very virgin as one full of grace, and He created the Church in and with her. Thus the Church stands as a new creation beside

Him, although it is indissolubly bound to Him.

Every soul purified through baptism and raised to the state of grace is thereby conceived through Christ and is born for His sake. Yet the soul is conceived in and born through the Church. Each new soul is formed and endowed with divine life through the organs of the Church. The Church is thus the mother of all the redeemed. But it is so because of its most intimate union with Christ, because it stands at His side as the *Spouse of Christ* and cooperates with Him in His work, the redemption of humanity.

We may consider the Church as a supernatural mother of whom woman is an essential organ. First, because of her physical maternity. The human race must reproduce itself in order for the Church to carry out its mission of attaining her destined number of members. The life of grace presupposes the life of nature. The physical-psychic organism of woman is fashioned for the task of natural maternity, and the procreation of offspring has been sanctified by the sacrament of marriage and woven into the vital fabric of the Church itself. However, woman's participation in the supernatural maternity of the Church is more extensive. She is called upon to cooperate in awakening and furthering the life of grace in children. Consequently, she is an essential organ of the supernatural maternity of the Church and thereby shares directly in it. And her action is not necessarily limited to her own children. The first obligation of husband and wife in marriage is the mutual furthering of the life of grace. Over and above this, it is the task of the mother of the house to take into her maternal care everyone who is living under her roof. Finally, the vocation of every Christian is to awaken and further the life of grace in souls wherever the possibility exists. But woman assumes this vocation in a special way, thanks to her special relationship to the Lord who has destined her for it.

Genesis places woman by man's side as a suitable helpmate to him in order for both to be able to work together as a single nature. The Letter to the Ephesians describes this

relationship as that of head and body, and thereby as symbol
of Christ's relationship to the Church. Accordingly, woman
is to be understood as symbol of the Church. The creation of
Eve from the rib of the first Adam becomes a prefigurement
for the emergence of the new Eve—by that is meant Mary,
but, at the same time, also the whole Church—from the
opened side of the new Adam. The woman who is bound to
her husband in true Christian matrimony, that is, in an indissoluble union of life and love, represents the Church as God's
bride. Even more impressively and perfectly, the Church is
personally embodied in the woman who as *Spouse of Christ*
has consecrated her life to the Lord and has entered into an
indissoluble contract with Him. She herself stands at His side
like the Church, and assists in His work of redemption like its
prototype, the Mother of God, in whom it has its origin. The
complete surrender of her entire life and being is to live and
work with Christ; but that means also to suffer and die with
Him—that fruitful death from which springs the life of grace
for all mankind. And so the life of God's bride becomes
supernatural maternity for all of redeemed humanity, whether
she works directly with the soul herself or whether she only
brings forth through her sacrifice the fruits of grace, of which
she and perhaps no other have knowledge.

Mary is the most perfect symbol of the Church because
she is its prefigurement and origin. She is also a unique organ
of the Church, that organ from which the entire Mystical
Body, even the Head itself, was formed. She might be called,
and happily so, the heart of the Church in order to indicate
her central and vital position in it. The terms *body, head,*
and *heart* are of course simply metaphors. But their meaning,
nevertheless, is somehow absolutely real. There is a distinctive
coherence between head and heart, and they certainly play an
essential role in the human body; all other organs and limbs
are dependent on them for their existence and function. Just
as certainly, through her unique relation with Christ, Mary
must have a real—that means have a mystic—relationship with

the other members of the Church. This relationship extends far above that of the other members in intensity, nature, and importance; it is analogous to the relationship which a mother has with her children, a relationship surpassing that which the children have amongst themselves. The title of Mary as our mother is not merely symbolic. Mary *is* our mother in the most real and lofty sense, a sense which surpasses that of earthly maternity. She begot our life of grace for us because she offered up her entire being, body and soul, as the Mother of God.

That is why an intimate bond exists between Mary and ourselves. She loves us, she knows us, she exerts herself to bring each one of us into the closest possible relationship with the Lord—that which we are above all supposed to be. Of course, this is true for all humanity, but most particularly for women. The maternity and bridehood of the *Virgo-Mater* is continued, so to speak, in their maternity, natural and super-natural, and in their life as brides of Christ. And just as the heart sustains the other organs of woman's body and makes it possible for them to function, so we may genuinely believe there is just such a collaboration of Mary with every woman wherever that woman is fulfilling her vocation as woman; just so, there is a collaboration of Mary with us in all works of the Church. But just as grace cannot achieve its work in souls unless they open themselves to it in free decision, so also Mary cannot function fully as a mother if men do not entrust themselves to her. Those women who wish to fulfill their feminine vocations in one of several ways will most surely succeed in their goals if they not only keep the ideal of the *Virgo-Mater* before their eyes and strive to form themselves according to her image but if they also entrust themselves to her guidance and place themselves completely under her care. She herself can form in her own image those who belong to her.

The stages which lead to a divinely-ordered incorporation of woman into the Church are thus indicated: child of God, organ of the Church in her natural and supernatural maternity, symbol of the Church, and child of Mary on all levels. What can we, especially women, do to guide young women along this path?

II. GUIDANCE OF YOUTH IN THE CHURCH

As the maternal organ of the Church, woman is called upon to educate youth and especially young women.[1] Her foremost duty is to form young women as children of God, baptism being the first and most essential step. This is generally the priest's concern, but above all it is the concern of the parents. The child of God is born through baptism and so becomes the child of the Church. But grace in the child is like a hidden little flame which must be painstakingly tended and nursed. To guard and nourish it in the early years is above all the duty of the mother.

To protect the life of grace means to defend it against any influence that could extinguish it, such as loss of faith or sin. These, of course, endanger the child only when he arrives at the age of reason and freedom. Nevertheless, the child needs protection even before this for poisonous matter can penetrate into the soul even before the life of reason has begun. The child's soul receives impressions from what he sees, hears, and touches; indeed, even experiences before birth can leave impressions upon the soul, and these impressions can have unpredictable consequences in later life. Therefore, the mother must keep pure the atmosphere in which the child is living. Above all things, she herself must remain pure and faithful; she must try, as much as possible, to keep far from the children those people whom she cannot trust implicitly. Before the age of reason is reached, this nurturing of the flame of grace is ensured through the prayer of the mother, and it is also ensured because the child is thus confided to the protection of the Mother of God. With the age of reason, direct influence becomes possible. The child must learn to know and to love the Father in heaven, the child Jesus, the Mother of God, and the guardian angel. With increasing understanding, a deeper and more extensive penetration into the world of faith is possible. The pure, uncorrupted child's heart has no difficulties in this and asks for more and more. The sources of grace provided by the sacraments must also be made accessible. They are the strongest nourishment of the life of grace and the most efficacious safeguard against the dangers which come about almost unavoidably in this very time when, in many instances, various and uncontrollable influences encroach upon the influence of the mother and of the strictest family circle.

If in these first years a firm and secure basis for religious education is laid, the school has an easy task. But we all know how seldom today the mother fulfills her duty. How many children come to school without any knowledge of the faith? How many are already prejudiced because of lack of faith in the family or on the street? The purity of many children is sullied by all that they must see and hear in the most tender years of childhood, and the path of divine truth is thereby obstructed. Nevertheless, the task is in no way hopeless if the child finds in the school what the home lacks: introduction into the life of faith by a maternal, pure, God-centered teacher. The heart of the child, even the one already contaminated by sin, has a strong desire for purity, goodness, and love, a yearning to be allowed to love and to trust. The teacher who approaches these little ones like a true mother wins them quickly and can guide them wherever she wishes. It is almost inevitable that the child should become personally dependent on her. But that is not enough. Her goal must be to establish a direct, firm relationship to the world of faith, one which endures after her instruction ceases and which resists dangerous effects counteracting from another direction.

Bible stories, animatedly presented, make a deep impression on the youthful imagination during the early school years. The cultivation of beautiful religious customs is to be initiated with love and care: connection should be established between the festivities of the Church year such as Advent and Christmas and the May altar and May songs, etc.; communal Church attendance should be practiced, with well-planned liturgical prayer and song. But it would be dangerous to rely on imagination, feeling, and force of habit. This could result in an underestimation of the overwhelming power of primitive passions and the great life crises. There could also result misjudgment of the feminine nature in which imagination and emotion appeal quite easily and may often dominate that nature for some time. (Certainly weighty decisions should not be determined on the basis of feelings and moods.)

Religious education must be objectively anchored for it to last, and the strongest realities of nature must be confronted with the even stronger realities of the supernatural. The earliest possible preparation for the sacraments is necessary for this, and guidance towards frequent communion, ideally daily reception. Equally important is the preparation of the soul for a meaningful reception of the sacraments so that the great supernatural reality which is inherent in them, lives in them, and works through them in the soul will be clearly understood. Therefore, religious training must build from the beginning on the foundation of clear and thorough dogmatic instruction. (Objectivity in respect to supernatural realities is required not only on this issue but in general.) To be sure, life built on faith should be the fruit of religious formation. Faith, however, is not a matter of imagination or pious emotion; but, on the contrary, it is an intellectual recognition (if not a rational permeation) and a voluntary acceptance by the will; a complete development of faith is one of the most profound acts of the individual, one in which all his powers become acute. Sentient observation and imagination stimulate the activity of the mind and are indispensable as the point of departure. Emotional responses are the impetus which move the will to concurrence and are, therefore, valuable aids. But if the matter rests there, if the intellect and the will are not utilized to their highest effect, then an authentic and full life of faith fails to materialize.

And who would deny the intellect and will of girls? That would be questioning their full humanity. On the average, *abstract* and *mere* intellectual activity is not suitable for them; they want to understand reality completely, and they want to comprehend not merely with the intellect but also with the heart. And precisely because they are driven by nature to put their whole person into each act, that act of faith which involves the whole person with all her powers *suits* them, and they are easier to lead to a life of faith than boys. Penetration into the mystery of faith is as fruitful as memorization of an uncomprehended catechism is dangerous. There is a desire to learn to know Mary and the Christ child more intimately and deeply if the gospel of Christmas, and its festival with gifts of the Christ child, and the mysterious spell of the holy night have invited understanding and won hearts. And then the time has come to introduce the children to the mystery of the Incarnation and the exalted vocation of the Mother of God. They can now understand for the first time what the union with transcendental powers means and what this trusting union means for their entire lives. Just so the story of the Last Supper introduces the meaning of the Eucharist, and the account of the Passion and Easter for the meaning of redemption, of suffering, of death, and resurrection. And penetration into the mysteries of Christianity must always lead to transformation in the ways of life. This will only be successful when the people who introduce the children to the mysteries are themselves permeated and their lives formed by these mysteries. And only when liturgical prayer is the expression of liturgical life will it really contribute fruitfully and formatively in the process of religious education.

It has often been said that women are more easily penetrated by the whole life of faith because of the greater unity and tenacity of their nature. One may then conclude that they will be more able to give an animated, life-forming religious instruction. In any case, women will more easily succeed in decisively influencing *girls*. This does not imply the elimination of the priest's influence. However, the significance of the guidance of youth by women should be emphasized. Such guidance lays the basis for the religious life (and it is indeed here that it should be laid), and instruction by women is especially fruitful towards that end; it can also be fruitful in the school's complete curriculum as well as outside of the school.

The more the child is exposed to dangers outside of the school (in the home and on the street), the more it is necessary for the Church member to care for the child outside of school time; this is particularly true if the school is not parochial. *Child care,* organized on an even greater scale than it is already by private initiative, should become the foundation for all youth work because the firm basis for the work of religious education must be laid in childhood. Every spiritual director and teacher knows how hard educational work is, and this is especially true of the religious education of girls in the critical years of puberty. If good training capable of prevailing over these storms does not *already* exist, there is little prospect for success. Work in the youth movements is unsuccessful when the work is initiated too late and in a very unfavorable time of development.

Naturally, a staff of youth advisers would be important if fruitful work is to be performed in child care on a large scale. It would not be impossible to acquire these young feminine leaders if the great number of unemployed young teachers could be interested, and if they could be given the basic religious, psychological, and pedagogical training. (Of course they would be carefully screened before they would be allowed to work with youth.)[2]

Guidance to the condition of being a child of God should be carried out in the first years of childhood, although later it must be constantly renewed and deepened. Then the period of maturation would be free for a further task which should begin exactly at that time—preparation for the woman's place in the Church. It is precisely the crisis which takes place in the body and soul of the girl and absorbs her so intently which should be utilized in order to disclose to her the great and sacred meaning of that which she herself experiences.

Here, also, it would certainly be the mother who has the primary calling to do this. But how few mothers, even the good and conscientious ones, are able to do it properly! The priest who is catechist or moderator is also faced here with an almost insolvable task. He may have studied psychology, and he may have had extensive experience in directing girls; but the girl's soul will always remain for him in great measure *unknown ground* (and the better grounded his psychological training has been, the more he will be aware of just this fact). Thus he will not have the necessary self-possession precisely in regard to these delicate questions, and therefore he will not have the necessary freedom and lack of constraint. Even if the priest did have the candor, the girls would not; and communication would be difficult to establish. Even mature women almost always find it very difficult to speak calmly and unreservedly about sex, because for them it is almost indefinably bound up with the most intimately personal considerations. Calm and objectivity concerning these matters are found in genuine scholarly occupations, especially the medical. But there is a much more radical liberation through supernatural insight, which makes what is intimately personal accessible in calm, objective consideration. Half-grown girls who are still unsure about themselves and the general facts of sex, for whom the subject itself has the character of the mysterious and sensational, and who, over and above this, are likely to feel embarrassed by seeing the man in the priest are going to make it very difficult for the priests to bring them to the proper frame of mind.[3]

The female leader can instruct the girls properly if she

herself has that great freedom and candor which results from consideration of natural facts in the light of faith. And when, after long association, the woman knows the girls intimately and possesses their full confidence, then she will be able to raise these intimately personal questions and talk about them in a general and objective manner so that there is no impression of an indiscreet and impertinent desire to penetrate into personal matters. And yet this should be carried out in such a way that every girl can find the response to her own personal questions and will be eventually encouraged to seek help for her particular difficulties in private dialogue. In these years, girls should be brought to a clear understanding of marriage and motherhood in the full Catholic sense. In this light, girls should understand their own development as preparation for their vocation; that would help them in overcoming the crisis, and later they would themselves be able to give support to the following generation as mothers and youth advisers.

To be developed in its full sense, maternity must be interpreted as supernatural as well as natural. And here it should be made clear that it is also possible for supernatural maternity to be disassociated from natural maternity. For the many who will not marry, this is an absolutely necessary perspective relevant to their future way of life. They must commence professional life ready to uphold this perspective during the entire span of their authentically formed feminine life. This attitude should first be instilled in school; as often as possible, the question concerning later life should be raised in religion classes and other classes as well. And this concept of spiritual maternity should also play a very serious role in the choice of profession. But it can be developed practically in the best way during their years in a youth group. It is of greatest importance that the girls see in their leader a living example of virginal maternity and that they should witness her magnanimity.

A deepened awareness of Mary's virginal maternity and

the significance of her maternal aid is of extraordinary importance precisely as preparation for girls in their feminine vocation and for women in the exercise of their vocation. I
would like to stress even more in relation to Marian devotion
what I have said about the basic significance of dogma in all
religious formation. In order to develop to its full efficacy,
the devotion must be set much more forcefully on a dogmatic
basis. The traditional forms of Marian devotion as they are
usually practiced in parishes seem to me to be ineffective
today. The poetry of Marian songs and May devotions, the
symbolism of Marian colors and flags, certainly exercise a
charm on childish minds; moreover, the devotion is a fitting
expression of genuine love for Mary, and, frequently, it has
also been even the gate of grace for sinners and unbelievers.
But experience teaches us that, in innumerable instances, the
devotion cannot ward off the dangers to which the young girl
is exposed. Faced with really violent temptation and passion,
the restrained methods of psychology and aesthetics fail.
Only the fully developed power of the mystery can maintain
victory here. Only the girl who has understood the grandeur
of virginal purity and union with God will fight earnestly for
her purity. Only the one who believes in the unlimited power
of the *Help of Christians* will surrender to her protection, not
only in communal repetitive prayer but in an act of inner
surrender; and Mary will protect whoever stays in her care.

Introduction to Marian dogma is at the same time introduction to the concept of the *Spouse of Christ.* For a perfect
Christian formation, it behooves us to be filled with the sublime vocation of standing at the Lord's side and leading our
life in union with Him.

No woman's life which has been illuminated by this
supernatural joy can be destitute and empty. The ultimate
goal of all work with girls should be to inspire them to form
their lives as a symbol of the mysterious union which Christ
entered into with His Church and with redeemed humanity.
The girl who gets married should know that marriage has this

exalted symbolic significance and that she should honor the image of the Lord in her husband. Whoever understands that and takes it seriously will not enter into this union lightly and will examine herself and her partner to see if they are fit for such a holy mission. And the one who decides for marriage will know that she must persevere; she must struggle during her entire life to guide to completion the image of God in her husband and herself; she may not surrender in the worst situation, even in the most hopeless humiliation and defamation; she will know that she receives her children from the Lord and must rear them for the Lord. And the other women who must renounce the idea of marriage, either by free choice or because of conditions of life, should rejoice in the faith that the Lord has chosen them for a specially intimate relationship with Himself. They should know the various forms of a God-dedicated life, whether it be the life of a religious order or professional life in the world. The best and easiest impression of convent life will be received through observation of active orders in hospitals, schools, and social work; there the girls themselves witness feminine tasks being performed and thereby the love of Christ being made effective. But visiting an abbey as a group can also be useful; such a hike or trip instills fervent praise for God in His total beauty and majesty. And in conjunction with this, it is possible to develop an appreciation of a lifestyle in which the Liturgy of the Hours takes first place. The life of little Thérèse of Lisieux can be an introduction into the closed garden of Carmel, an initiation into the mysteries of sacrifice and of the work of co-redemption accomplished through the vicarious suffering of expiation. We have also today numerous biographies of women in contemporary life and from the past, women in the midst of the world who are yet in the most intimate union with the Lord and who manifest the most highly developed perfection. There is an inexhaustible treasury which can be opened up to girls through reading material and by intimate personal conversation with them. But this requires leaders who know the sources and are able to delve into them and who carry in their own souls the fire which they wish to enkindle in young spirits.

Those who have done practical work with youth and are familiar with the whole scene of need and delinquency from which the children come into schools and youth groups may find too great and irreconcilable the difference between the human material they have to work with and the high ideal that I have designated. But if the goals which God has set are clear and unassailable, and I believe that they are, then the training work must be directed to these goals; otherwise it is senseless and lost effort. The Christian vocation is holiness, and the Christian's life work is to rise from the depths of sin to that holiness.

Of course, there does seem to be a terrifying contradiction: on the one hand, we have young girls who are giddy, superficial, pleasure mad, filled with thoughts of beautiful clothes and love affairs; and on the other hand, we have the most exalted mysteries of the faith. The youth leader who has these girls with her for only a few hours on Sunday, and who furthermore considers that it is her duty to give them harmless joys in order to keep them away from dangerous pleasures, will not be able to achieve very much. For the life outside will attract more strongly than the innocent joys in the well-chaperoned circle, and anyone who has tasted of those other joys will no longer relish the innocent ones. But the goal is not unattainable if youth work is initiated in early childhood and is more persistently rendered in communal activities. The goal is not unattainable if all the radiant joy of God's creatures is brought into the child's life; but, at the same time, the sure foundation is laid in the unspoiled heart for that edifice of life which is to rise to heaven, and then this edifice is built further, day by day and year by year. The very highest goal is attainable because with every bridge built to the beyond, a way is laid for the powers that come from above to help us, powers that can accomplish everything which all human endeavor cannot achieve.

Millions of children today are homeless and orphaned, even though they do have a home and a mother. They hunger for love and eagerly await a guiding hand to draw them out of dirt and misery into purity and light. Who else than our great holy mother the Church should open her arms wide to take these beloved of the Lord to her heart? But for this she needs human arms and human hearts, maternal arms and maternal hearts.

Youth work and particularly work among girls in the name of the Church is perhaps the greatest task to be solved at the present time in Germany. If it were solved, then we could hope that a generation of mothers would grow up whose children would again have a home and would not have to be treated like orphans. Then, once again, there could arise in Germany a morally wholesome and faithful Christian people.

Chapter VII

The Significance of Woman's Intrinsic Value in National Life

Honored guests, dear colleagues! Please let me begin with a short personal observation. Two days ago, I traveled from Beuron, where I was permitted to spend Holy Week and Easter Sunday, to Ludwigshafen into the midst of preparation for the convention. One can hardly imagine a greater contrast: there, the quiet valley of peace where, unconcerned with everything that happens abroad in the world, praise to the Lord is sung day after day, year after year—*a custodia matutina usque ad noctem*[1]—and this assembly which has gathered to speak of burning contemporary questions.

This was almost like dropping from heaven to earth.[2] But perhaps this contrast is a direct symbol of the problem which we all have. Within the last week, we have all gone the way of the cross with our Savior; all our hearts still exult in the paschal "Alleluia." And in a week we must return to our ordinary duties. But the efficacy of the Passion and Easter should not be an incidental holiday disposition dissipated by ordinary life; on the contrary, it is a living power of God within us which we interweave into our professional life. And this convention ought to help us to do so.

Now to the topic. For me, this topic in its precise working indicates how much the image of the feminist movement has changed recently. Even twenty years ago, it would have scarcely occurred to anyone to pose such a question. The big slogan in the beginning of the feminist movement was *Eman-*

246

cipation. That sounds rather lofty and revolutionary: liberation from the chains of slavery. The demands were more
practical: removal of the fetters which prevented women from
entering into the same educational and professional activities
as men. Woman's personal capabilities and powers, often
dwarfed without these opportunities for action, were to be
liberated. Hence the goal was one of *individualism.* Outside
the extreme left, this demand met lively resistance. "Woman's place is in the home!" resounded from every side. It was
feared that granting women's demands would jeopardize feminine singularity and woman's natural calling. On the other
hand, these opponents maintained that woman was not qualified for *masculine* professions because of her singularity. The
Suffragettes violently opposed this view; and, in the heat of
battle, they went so far as to *deny* completely the feminine
singularity—that women were any different from men. Consequently, one could not speak of an *intrinsic feminine value.*
(As a matter of fact, their only goal was to insist that women
were equal to men in all fields.)

The Weimar Constitution recognized women's claims to
such a degree that the most audacious pioneers of the feminist movement would not have believed it possible for it to
take place so soon. And with that a change commenced. The
heat of battle cooled. One was again capable of judging calmly and clearly. Besides, today we can speak from years of
experience concerning the future of the professional woman;
whereas earlier, the arguments of both factions were à priori
judgments, if not completely arbitrary ones. So the contemporary situation is characterized primarily by feminine *singularity* being accepted as *self-evident.* We women have become
aware once again of our singularity. Many a woman who
formerly denied it has perhaps become aware of it, painfully
aware of it, if she has entered one of the traditionally masculine professions and sees herself forced into conditions of life
and work alien to her nature. If her *nature* is strong enough,
she has perhaps succeeded in converting the *masculine* profes-

sion into a *feminine* one. And this *self-awareness* could also develop the conviction that an *intrinsic feminine value* resides in the singularity.

And finally, a contemporary trend became decisive for the acceptance of feminine singularity also. The individualistic disposition of the nineteenth century has yielded more and more to a social disposition. Today, that which is to be of value must be made fruitful for the community. And our theme upholds that this possibility also exists for the intrinsic value of woman.

The first task now is to sketch briefly the *singularity* of women, for it is indeed only by doing this that the intrinsic value can be made comprehensible. During the last few decades, psychology has been much occupied with the psychical differences between the sexes; certainly, experiment and statistics have not revealed much more than what ordinary experience already teaches. I would like to emphasize only two criteria differentiating man from woman from those which are usually mentioned since they have particular significance in helping us understand the intrinsic value of woman.

1. Man appears more *objective:* it is natural for him to dedicate his faculties to a discipline (be it mathematics or technology, a trade or business management) and thereby to subject himself to the precepts of this *discipline. Woman's attitude is personal;* and this has several meanings: in one instance she is happily involved with her total being in what she does; then, she has particular interest for the living, concrete person, and, indeed, as much for her own personal life and personal affairs as for those of other persons.

2. Through submission to a discipline, man easily experiences a *one-sided development.* In woman, there lives a natural drive towards *totality* and *self-containment.* And, again, this drive has a twofold direction: she herself would like to become a *complete human being,* one who is fully developed in every way; and she would like to help others to become so, and by all means, she would like to do justice to the com-

plete human being whenever she has to deal with persons.

Both of these characteristic impulses as they *emerge from nature* do not demonstrate yet any initial value; indeed, they can be harmful. But, correctly handled, they can become most valuable. Let us clarify the *value of the personal attitude and the tendency to completeness,* and then consider how this value can be developed from the raw material.

The personal attitude is objectively justified and valuable because actually the human person is more precious than all objective values. All truth is discerned by persons; all beauty is beheld and measured by persons. All objective values exist in this sense for persons. And behind all things of value to be found in the world stands the *person of the Creator* who, as prefigurement, encloses all earthly values in Himself and transmits them. In the area of our common experience, the human being is the highest among creation since his personality is created in the image of God. It is the *whole person* about whom we are speaking: *that* human being in whom God's image is developed most purely, in whom the gifts which the Creator has bestowed do not wither but bloom, and in whom the faculties are balanced in conformity to God's image and God's will—the will led by intellect, and the lower faculties bridled by intellect and will.

Each human being is called naturally to this total humanity, and the desire for it lives in each one of us. We may consider that the drive for this which is particularly strong in woman is well related to her particular destiny of companion and mother. *To be a companion,* that means to be support and mainstay, and to be able to be so, a woman herself must stand firmly; however, this is possible only if inwardly everything is in right order and rests in equilibrium. *To be a mother* is to nourish and protect true humanity and bring it to development. But again, this necessitates that she possess true humanity herself, and that she is clear as to what it means; otherwise, she cannot lead others to it. One can become suitable for this double duty if one has the *correct personal attitude.* As we have already stated, woman does not possess this by nature. The initial form of feminine singularity is primarily a debasement and blockage of this true attitude. On the one hand, it is a bias *to secure her own personal importance* by which she may busy herself and others; also, it is an inability to endure criticism which is experienced as an attack on her person. These yearnings for importance, yearnings towards unlimited recognition, are extended to everything unique to the person. Her own husband must be recognized as the very best husband, her own children must be known as the most beautiful, clever, and gifted. This is blind feminine love which dulls realistic judgment and renders her completely unsuitable for the designated feminine vocation. Along with this excessive vindication of her own person goes an *excessive interest in others,* a perverse desire to penetrate into personal lives, a passion of wanting to confiscate people. Excess of interest in both her own and in the stranger's personality merge in feminine surrender, the urge to lose herself completely in a human being; but in so doing, she does justice neither to self nor to the humanity of another, and, at the same time, becomes unfit for exercising other duties.

Also connected to the false pursuit of prestige is a perverted desire for totality and inclusiveness, a mania to know everything and thereby to skim the surface of everything and to plunge deeply into nothing. However, such superficiality can never be true humanity. Whoever controls a matter thoroughly stands closer to true humanity than he who never stands on firm ground. Among those who have a thoroughly objective formation, there are certainly more men than women. However, in the *small flock* that approaches the goal of full humanity there seem to be more women than men.

How is it then possible to extricate the purified valuable feminine character from the raw material of feminine singularity with all its faults and weaknesses, of which, as daughters of Eve, we all have a share?

In the first instance, a good natural method for this is *thoroughly objective work.* Every such work, no matter of what kind, whether housework, a trade, science or anything else, necessitates submitting to the laws of the matter concerned; the whole person, thoughts just as all moods and dispositions, must be made subordinate to the work. And whoever has learned this, has become *objective,* has lost something of the *hyper-individuality* and has attained a definite freedom of self; at the same time she has attained an inner depth—she has attained a basis of self-control. Indeed, every young girl should receive a basic vocational formation for the sake of these great personal gains, quite aside from any economic compulsion; and after this formation, she should hold a position which completely fulfills her. No other environment than the life of the *high school* girl of the old style and that of the unoccupied woman from affluent circles provides a more fertile soil for the debasement of the feminine singularity and for hysteria, its sickly enhancement. Because objective work, which we view as a remedy for the faults of feminine singularity, is something to which the average man is naturally inclined, it can thus be said as well that an allowance of masculine nature is the antidote for the *hyper-feminine nature.* But with this, we in reality propose that, after all, the matter cannot rest there. It would be to attain thereby only an analogy to the masculine species, as, in fact, it frequently was in the beginning of the feminist movement; and that would be neither a greater gain for us or for others. We must advance further from the objective outlook to the proper personal one, which is also the attitude that is actually most highly objective. But relevant to this personal outlook is a realization of true humanity, i.e., of its ideal image, and a perception of the predispositions towards it as well as departures from it within ourselves and in others, a freedom of insight, an autonomy within ourselves and in others, and a power for enforcement of the needed practical precautions that cannot win at all by human means. No book learning can give this acuteness of vision to our blind sight, no straining of the will can provide the energy to clip the wild shoots within ourselves and in those people dear to us. Supernatural means must now come to our help.

To begin with, where do we have the concrete image of total humanity? God's image walked amongst us in human form, in the Son of Man, Jesus Christ. If we reflect on how this image speaks to us in the simple account of the gospels, it then opens our eyes. The better we get to know the Savior, the more we are conquered by His sublimity and gentleness, by His kingly freedom which knows no other obligation than submission to the Father's will, and by His freedom from all living creatures which is simultaneously the foundation for His compassionate love towards each living creature. And the deeper this image of God penetrates into us, the more it awakens our love. In just this way, we become the more sensitive to all falling away from Him in ourselves and in others; our eyes are opened, free of all extenuations, to true knowledge of human nature. And if the power fails us to endure the sight of human weakness in ourselves and in others, only a look at the Savior is again needed; indeed, He has not turned from our misery with horror, but He came to us exactly because of this misery and took it upon Himself— *vere languores nostros ipse portavit et livore eius nos sanati sumus.* Thus He Himself has the remedy if we do not know where to find redress. Through His sacraments, He purifies and strengthens us. And if we turn confidently to Him, which is His will, His spirit penetrates us more and more and converts us; through union with Him, we learn to dispense with human props and to gain the freedom and strength which we must have in order to be the support and mainstay for others. He Himself guides us and shows us how we should guide others. We therefore achieve total humanity through Him and, simultaneously, the right personal attitude. Whoever looks to Him and is concentrated on Him sees God, the archetype of all personality and the embodiment of all value. The surrender to which feminine nature inclines is here appropriate; on the other hand, we also *find* here the absolute love and surrender for which we seek vainly in people. And surrender to Christ does not make us blind and deaf to the needs of others—on the contrary. We now seek for God's image in each human being and want, above all, to help each human being win his freedom. Accordingly, we can now also say: the *intrinsic value of woman* consists essentially in *exceptional receptivity for God's work in the soul,* and this value comes to unalloyed development if we abandon ourselves confidently and unresistingly to this work.

Only now have we come to the second part of our theme —the significance of woman for national life. This significance presents itself as a simple conclusion from what has been said. What is, then, the great sickness of our time and of our people? There is an inner disunion, a complete deficiency of set convictions and strong principles, an aimless drifting. Therefore, the great mass of humanity seeks for an anesthetic in ever new, ever more refined delights. Those who wish to maintain a sober level of life, in order to protect themselves from contemporary turmoil, frequently annihilate this level by one-sided professional work; but even they cannot do anything to escape the turmoil. Only whole human beings as we have described them are immune to the contemporary sickness: such beings are steadfast on eternal first principles, unperturbed in their views and in their actions by the changing modes of thoughts, follies, and depravities surrounding them. Every such individual is like a pillar to which many can fasten themselves, thereby attaining a firm footing. Consequently, when women themselves are once again whole persons and when they help others to become so, they create healthy, energetic spores supplying healthy energy to the entire national body.

They are able to do this above all in their vocation as *mother*. These are mothers who have a firm philosophy of

life, who know *to what purpose* they should rear their children, who have an open vision of the developmental possibilities of their children. But also they have an incorruptible
perspective of the dangerous drives in them which must be
curtailed and which must be seized with a powerful hand at
the right moment. And these also must be mothers who
know their place, who do not think that they are able to do
everything themselves but, on the contrary, are able to let go
of their children and place them in God's hand when the time
comes, when the children have outgrown them. Such mothers are probably the most important agents for the recovery
of the nation. Also, woman frequently has the duty to help
all humanity towards victory in relation to her spouse. He
generally has the need "to be an individual also" when he
comes from his professional activity, but often he no longer
has the strength to be able to do so on his own. The wife's
concern must therefore be to take care that he does not look
for compensation in shallow or dangerous diversions. A fine
home creates an atmosphere in which the soul can freely
breathe. And then the values which she longs for are materialized naturally. Tact and delicacy must discover what is to
be settled at a given moment. Often the proper relationship
between the father and children, which is of greatest significance for both parties, must above all be mediated by the
mother. And in countless cases, it is the difficult, thorny
duty of the woman to win back to the faith a husband who
is indifferent to religion or who rejects it. This is a task of
greatest responsibility which only very few—even with proper
good will—know how to handle in the right way. For here, in
most cases, more is lost rather than gained by much talk or
even with scolding. Even in apparently desperate cases,
weapons which have led to victory are to go one's own quiet
and unperturbed path (along with the greatest of all loving
cooperation and civility), and, in self-surrender, to pray constantly. The battle is not always won, for here it is a question
of God's mystery which we cannot penetrate.

Close to that of spouse and mother, the profession of *teacher* has always been valued as a truly feminine vocation. The teacher certainly has to shape mankind. And in our times in which the home breaks down so frequently, the future of our people depends more than ever on the teaching body. And with this comes a grave responsibility. Certainly, the school in many instances can no longer rectify the wrongs committed in the home. But it must try to do this by every means. And today, when we recognize at last that the primary school must be "the training school of our people," we may hope that by degrees this will also be accomplished in the high schools as well, and that the curricula will undergo the necessary reshaping and improvement in order to free forces for the educational task of the school. And what is efficacious for the mother is naturally efficacious for the educator as well, and in an enhanced degree. She must *be firm:* confusion in young heads and hearts is produced by wobbly and untested perspectives, by undigested and undigestible fruits of reading, a confusion which many times can be remedied no longer. And particularly when the teacher has to deal with older children, her theoretical basis must be well-grounded because she will meet interferences and objections which occur less frequently at home. The teacher thus needs a basic education in dogma and asceticism. Apologetics is certainly also good, but the former seems more important to me: ready arguments, as right as they may be, often do not have penetrating force. But she whose soul is formed through the truths of faith—and I call this ascetic formation—finds words which are proper for *this* human being and for *this* moment respectively.

And in one respect the teacher has it more difficult, for the natural bond of love which exists between mother and child from the beginning does not exist between her and the children. Love and trust are, however, necessary rudiments for every educational influence in depth. On the part of the teacher, this love and trust must be won by means of a nature

which loves consistently. And truly supernatural forces are
needed to offer such equal, motherly love to *all,* even to the
unlovable, the difficult, the intolerable children—and especially to them because, indeed, they are in most need of it.

Woman's vocation as teacher has never been disputed.
But even other professions, which were considered earlier as
masculine monopolies, have changed through usage and have
shown themselves in keeping with feminine individuality;
these professions are so constituted that they can be mastered
through truly feminine handling, in the right sense. I am
thinking of the profession of the medical woman. I have
made the gratifying observation that women who have once
been in the care of a woman doctor do not willingly give
themselves again to other treatment. It may be that a feeling
of shame contributes to this fact. But I believe that something else is even more important. As a rule, the sick who
visit or send for a doctor do not seek merely to have a particular organ healed of a particular trouble; one feels himself
"out of line" in his entire system; one seeks healing for body
and soul, and one also desires a friendly, comprehensive sympathy. This was to be found in the house doctor of the old
school.   But this beneficial service has become just about
extinct, ousted through specialization.   This development
naturally cannot be revoked. Medical science has adopted
such proportion that it is no longer actually possible to master
fundamentally all its divisions. But in specialization it should
not be forgotten that in most cases it is not only the organ
but, on the contrary, it is the entire person who is sick along
with the organ. Just as in the knowledge of the illness, so is
it also not a matter of indifference as to what kind of person
the doctor is facing in regard to the medical treatment. The
symptoms are not exactly the same with each individual, and
even much less can every remedy be of value for each one.
And, as we have said, it is, moreover, consideration of the
whole being which approaches the spiritual needs of the sick
person. As we have seen, such a regard lies in the nature of

woman. And if she exercises her medical vocation in this manner, she can thus attain much more than healing the actual illness. She receives insight into diverse human situations; she necessarily gets to see material and moral need. This is a wide area for authentic feminine activity, and it signifies Christian charity at the same time.

We have arrived at the large range of social vocations which have in most part been formed only in recent years or are still in the process of formation. They all require womanly hands and, naturally, also women who are whole persons: the vocations of social worker, welfare worker for young people, nursery school teacher, administrator in a jail or factory, etc. Everywhere, the problem is to save, to heal endangered or demoralized humanity, to steer it into healthy ways. In order not to entrench upon later papers, I do not want to examine these vocations more closely here. I do want to say only a few words on scholarly work for women because you perhaps expect something from me precisely on that subject. I believe that in reality there is less occasion here for the effect of feminine intrinsic value. Scholarship is the realm of the most austere objectivity. Hence, feminine singularity will only fructify where the subject deemed worthy of research is in a personal direction, i.e., in the humanities: history, literature, etc. Whoever chooses one of the abstract sciences—mathematics, natural sciences, pure philosophy, etc.—finds that as a rule, the masculine-intellectual type predominates in at least whatever is related to pure research. However, woman may perhaps assert her singularity anew in such areas of knowledge by the way she instructs; this is a helpful way which brings her into close relationship with people.

In addition, I would like to speak of the intrinsic value of woman in *political life*. In *legislation*, there is always danger that resolution "at the official level" will be based on the elaboration of the possibly most perfect paragraphs without their consideration of actual circumstances and consequences in practical life. Feminine singularity resists this abstract proceeding; woman is suited to act in accordance with the concrete human circumstance, and so she is able to serve as redress here. She has also already proved herself as a blessed counterbalance against another deterioration of *masculine objectivity*. The intention of the politician's party is often the *object* which is of primary importance for him, one to which he has dedicated himself. And somehow, this can result in the highest unobjectivity by the manipulation of a bill's draft. Thus, years ago on the deliberation of youth laws, the danger did exist that the project would end in failure by party opposition. The women of the differing parties at that time worked together and reached an agreement. The authentic feminine longing to remedy human need was thus victorious over the dilemma of party viewpoint. Just as in legislation, feminine singularity can also work beneficially in the application of the law in *bureaucracy,* provided it does not lead to abstract validation of the letter of the law but to the accomplishment of justice for mankind.

Finally, woman's intrinsic value can work in every place and thereby institute grace, completely independent of the profession which she practices and whether it concurs with her singularity or not. Everywhere she meets with a human being, she will find opportunity to sustain, to counsel, to help. If the factory worker or the office employee would only pay attention to the spirits of the persons who work with her in the same room, she would prevail upon trouble-laden hearts to be opened to her through a friendly word, a sympathetic question; she will find out where the shoe is pinching and will be able to provide relief. Everywhere the need exists for maternal sympathy and help, and thus we are able to recapitulate in the *one* word *motherliness* that which we have developed as the characteristic value of woman. Only, the motherliness must be that which does not remain within the narrow circle of blood relations or of personal friends; but in accordance with the model of the Mother of Mercy, it must have its root in universal divine love for all who are there, belabored and burdened.

Thus I can summarize, that a high vocation is designated in feminine singularity—that is, to bring true humanity in oneself and in others to development, but hazardous germs also lie in feminine singularity which endanger the essential value in its development and, thereby, the realization of mission. The dangers can only be conquered through rigorous discipline in the school of work and through the liberating power of divine grace. Our mission is to become flexible instruments in God's hand and to effect His work to which He leads us. If we fulfill our mission, we do what is best for ourselves, for our immediate environment, and together with it, what is best for the entire nation.

Chapter VIII

Challenges Facing Swiss Catholic Academic Women

Most honored university chaplains, Most honored guests, My dear women in academia!

We have come together to clarify the responsibilities of the Catholic academic women of Switzerland, and we do this in order to act more resolutely in the future. My task now is to evaluate the general scope of the present challenge for women.

I shall start by discussing the nature of Catholic academic women. What are the responsibilities they face in their profession and in their society? What are their responsibilities for leadership in a supernatural sense? What are their apostolic duties?

Two Preliminary Observations: Permit me to be candid and dispense with flattery. What we want to do is clarify what has happened in the past and what has not happened in order to find what *must* happen in the future.

Second Remark: The problems are so immensely varied that I can only glance at them here, reserving a fuller treatment for later conferences. I will single out particular topics in order to deal with the question in greater detail.

The Woman Academic: Simply defined, she is a woman with a university education. She has achieved a harmonious inner development, bringing together a well-schooled intellect and deepened knowledge, which is not limited to one field, together with a strong will. She is capable of purposeful action and is motivated by a broad outlook and lofty goals.

260

The Catholic Academic Woman: Does this status imply narrowness or inferiority? No! Rather, it confers an advantage! The academic is not destined blindly to favorable living conditions; no, God calls her to a mission in His service, and her duties far surpass her concrete professional obligations. She was either born or raised in a community which derives its highest character from the much used term, very nearly a misused phrase, *the Mystical Body of Christ.*

We are Catholic academic women: We *are!* Our first task is to cultivate our being, our individuality. I am not speaking of being formed in a collective sense; no, our personal being must rise to its highest form. But there is a potential danger here, the temptation of a certain rigidity, a cult of personality divorced from external action. Hence the highest, the greatest enhancement of individuality demands the greatest surrender. You know the lines of these most eminent individualists:

Goethe:
> And as long as you do not grasp this:
> "Die and become"—
> You are only an unredeemed sojourner
> Upon the gloomy earth.

Nietzsche, the most extreme of individualists, in *Zarathustra,* said:
> You must desire to be consumed in your own flame: how did you intend to become new if you were not ashes first?

Christ, "Being in Himself":
> The grain of wheat must die, only then does it bring forth fruit. Whoever wants to win his soul must lose it.

The abandonment of self on the part of the Catholic

academic woman, in fact of any Christian, does not involve a loss of personhood in the sense of disappearing into Indian nothingness or being absorbed in a Russian style collectivism. No, it is a surrender to *Being* (God), a sublimation of the person, a bursting of the chains of personality to achieve a union with infinite Being. (*Indeed,* this is "superhumanity.") This would lead back to the responsibilities involved with our subject (the teaching profession), with people (guidance), and with other souls (our apostolate).

The Woman Academic and Her Vocation: (Vocation as a Calling.) Here it would be well to distinguish three levels of academic women and their calling. The first calling is common to all women in the academic profession: the calling to be the image of God. In the second calling, i.e., in the academic profession itself, there are three different categories:

Category 1: *The married academic woman.*
Her primary calling is to be the image of God.
Her secondary calling is that of wife and mother.
Effect of professional acitivities becomes tertiary.

Category 2: The so-called *working woman.*
Primary calling: to be the image of God.
Secondary calling: devotion to the profession for the sake of the profession.

Category 3: *The woman consecrated to God.*
Primary calling: to be the image of God.
Secondary calling: vocation as the servant of God in the convent and in the world as she functions in almost all professions today.

The problems and duties of the academic woman in these three categories are different. Unfortunately, there is not enough time to give a complete picture of them. I would like to offer a few summary suggestions.

Category 1: The *married* academic.

Responsibilities: Motherhood and the profession.

Duties: 1. To sacrifice the third calling (professional activity) to the second calling (role of wife and mother) in order to achieve better the primary calling, to be the image of God.

2. To utilize the primary calling (to be the image of God) and the tertiary calling (professional activity) in order to become a better wife and mother.

Category 2: The *professional* academic.

Group 1

Responsibilities: Professional activity for its own sake considered as a substitute for marriage and as a means of livelihood is positively unsatisfactory if the occupation is not enhanced by typical feminine qualities or if it does not correspond to some extent to personal inclinations.

Duties: Let us disregard all professions which do not fall under the preceding categories! Instead, let us strive for spiritualization, enrichment, and a thorough and more conscious deepening of the teaching profession. Let us create new professions which serve the living and the personal.

Group 2

Responsibilities: A devotion to professional activity for the sake of professional activity, based on personal ability. This is positively unsatisfactory if the ability cannot be utilized suitably because of external obstructions.

Duties: To create the facilities necessary so that each person can make use of his or her personal qualities and gifts in the profession.

Category 3: The *consecrated* academic.

Group 1: In the convent.

Responsibilities: See *Journal for Asceticism and Mysticism* 1932 No. 1 and 3. The article which deals with these questions outlines an approximate picture.

Duties: The solution is best left to the academics in the individual convents.

Group 2: In the world.

Responsibilities: The lack of clarity concerning new paths. Particular requirements for candidates of this category: a deepening spirituality, perceptivity, pioneering blood.

Primary duties: To prepare herself to be an instrument of God.

The burning contemporary question of *woman and vocation* also belongs in this context. Certainly it is born out of necessity, but the approach is instinctive and ill-considered which wishes to solve the problem by suggesting: "Turn out the women from all vocations." Here it is up to the academic woman to distinguish between vocations in which women enrich humanity and those in which they perform their work half-heartedly and obstruct others. But this is a question for the academic to qualify *individually.* For individual aptitude does not often permit itself to be forced into the pattern of "man-woman." To clarify this issue, to steer the right course is a noteworthy, important task for academically trained, objectively thinking women.

The question of *academic women and scholarship* is also relevant in this context.

Do possibilities exist today in Switzerland for Catholic academics to work in a scholarly manner and to utilize their abilities for that purpose? Do available funds exist for subsidies to scholarly work so that the academic will not have to dissipate her energy in bread-winning? Unfortunately, they do not exist. Consequently, it is unjust to pass the judgment "scholarly unproductive" on academically trained women as long as the possibility to be scholarly productive is not open to them.

Do the Catholic academics of Switzerland exert themselves in this direction? Do they mutually encourage each
other? Do they support and help the young?

Does there exist a *Catholic women's training center*
where bibliographical sources are at hand: books, journals,
newspapers, etc.?

Does a center exist where academically trained women
can find stimulation and relaxation and contact with other
like-minded women, etc.? Should not such a place be created
eventually as a part of the so-called women's training center?
A place like shining glass which focuses intellectual light and
transforms them into sparks of fire. Something positive! And
not diabolic fire!

All this does not exist. It remains to be done!

The third area of responsibilities: the most immediate
factors of the *academic woman's environment* involved in her
leadership of others. We shall discuss this problem under
several aspects.

Academics and the Youth Movement: Do we share the
problems of today's youth? Apparently not! So at least we
must analyze the problems objectively in order to understand
them better. Understanding is, after all, the secret of every
form of leadership. Here we might read among other things
Günther Gründel's book *Mission of the Young Generation.*
Does it reflect a growing revolutionary attitude of our time?
Let us read it to get a glimpse of what is inflaming and shaping today's youth.

Are we aware of Russian youth, of its elite Komsomol,
a foreshadowing of the future? Don't think that our youth is
so different from them; Russian doctrines are already influencing them. We have an illusion that we are living on an island,
an "island of peace," unaware of the universal tumult all
about us which is already endangering it. Don't think such
tidal waves won't engulf us. We are asleep and like to call
our attitude *moderation,* perhaps even *virtue.* But is not the
uncomprehending life a basically defective one?

Academics and the Women's Movement: Perhaps we are thinking: "Such movements do not concern us. They are for the anonymous masses. We are different!" We feel that we are protected by our knowledge which is perhaps pseudo-knowledge!

Our scholarly existence and our lives would be misspent if our studies had evoked such pride! Academic women who feel that way could be overwhelmed by the very life which they so childishly reject. Are we responsibly trained women or are we children at play? The universities should eliminate the latter. The academic training of women is being challenged again today. Would this be possible to such a degree were it not that the greater part of the academically trained women have failed to assume leadership?

Let's get to the point: Are we Catholic academics in contact with organized workers, the Swiss Women's Movement, the Women's Union, and the Christian Socialists? We are not. Why? *Certainly* the fault lies on both sides, but it is equally certain it is indeed on *both* sides.

Academics and Social Consciousness: Do we grasp social problems, the burning problems of today? Do they concern us also? Or are we waiting until others find some solution or until we are submerged by the billows of chaos? Is such an attitude worthy of an *academic woman?* Must we not try to help in deed as well as in thought? I believe this is a theoretical matter primarily in that we should investigate connections and causes so that we may know what help is needed and how to give it. Concretely, we must proceed through *Caritas,* that means that our love of God must find practical expression. There are manifold ways to fit manifold needs. Let us not be stuck in a rut. We must get in touch with the social ferment of the masses and understand their physical and spiritual needs. (Examples here are the students of Zürich!)

Academics and Public Life: I have reached the core of a burning question, one on which Swiss academics differ. I do not want to impose my opinion here. Permit me only to pose a question and cite a quotation.

Question: Are we familiar with the work of the adversary? In the mine fields of today's society, can we justify looking backwards continuously while our adversary wages war against our views?

A quotation: A prince of the Church can answer this question better than I can. In Cardinal Faulhaber's commentary on the vesper psalms, he explains the middle verse of the "Magnificat." He writes:

> Who still dares to say that politics has nothing to do with religion and that souls directed towards God, especially women, should stay far from public life? If the quiet virgin of Nazareth, her soul resting completely in God her savior, could be concerned with the happenings on the world scene (middle verse of the Magnificat), then religious people, including women of course, dare not be indifferent as to whether the arm of God is seen in world events. They must not be unconcerned as to whether the God-willed spiritual, political, and economic order is established. Nor may they be unconcerned when dogmatic intellectuals confuse the people with their knowledge when political leaders strike out God's name from public life, or when capitalistic exploiters are upsetting the economic order..." (München, 1929, p. 333).

The example of *Mary* is relevant here. She is the ideal type of woman who knew how to unite tenderness with power. *She stood under the cross.* She had previously concerned herself about the human condition, observed it, understood it! In her son's tragic hour she appeared publicly. *Perhaps the moment has almost come for the Catholic woman also to stand with Mary and with the Church under the cross!*

Concretely: I am not asking the Swiss Catholic academic woman to decide today whether or not woman should take part in public life (it would even be childish presumption to ask for this). But I believe there is something that must be promoted in the name of sound human reason, in the interest of our families, our nation, and our Church. It is that you take an interest in the question, reflect on it, and study it objectively *in the light of contemporary development.*

Academics and the Apostolate: Catherine of Siena writes in a letter to the king of Naples: "Indeed, out of love for the crucified Jesus, we must be zealous, indeed overzealous for the holy Church."

Perhaps through the course of the centuries, our attitude in the Church has been too passive. Perhaps we have left it to exceptional people "to prove the exception to the rule," people like Teresa of Jesus, Hildegard of Bingen, Catherine of Siena, etc. The twentieth century demands more! I am thinking specifically of the atheistic movement. How can we oppose this phalanx? Pope Pius XI has already sanctioned the lay apostolate; in fact, he has summoned us to it. Should Catholic action stay a catchword and a cliché which resounds through the assemblies but does not ignite?

Do we understand what the so-called *Liturgical Movement* is all about? It is certainly not about *aesthetics.* No, it is about a deeper sharing in the life of Christ and witness to it by means of the Church. (I would say much more here, but I am afraid it would take too much time.)

Much has been done, but there is endlessly more yet to be done! *In hoc signo vinces*[1] runs youth's slogan. Could this not also be our slogan? We will not overcome this mountain of difficulties by our own power, but we will do it well through *that sign!* We will be *victorious* in the sign of the cross; that is, we will live our lives fully as Catholic academics —successfully or unsuccessfully—as a blessing of our society, our nation, and our Church.

Notes

EDITORS' INTRODUCTION

1.   At the Victoria school in Breslau, "a little less than five years after I took the final examination and left this institution." This appears in youthful reminiscences of the author now in the possession of *Archivum Carmelitanum Edith Stein.*

2.   In this text see pp. 130-133 and other passages.

3.   Taken from St. Thomas, *Summa Theol.* I, q. 1, a. 8, ad 2.

4.   From *The Idea of a University,* translated from English into German by Dr. Edith Stein. The two volume manuscript is in the possession of the *Archivum Carmelitanum Edith Stein;* its publication is intended.

5.   See among other testimonies that of Archabbot Raphael Walzer in the possession of the Carmel *Maria vom Frieden* in Cologne.

6.   See reminiscences and letters of Edith Stein, partly in the possession of the Carmel in Cologne, *Maria vom Frieden,* other documents held at the *Archivum Carmelitanum Edith Stein.*

7.   Cited from an essay on education which will appear in the following edition of *Edith Steins Werke.* The editor has selected these thoughts from the teachings of Forster and other leading pedagogues.

8.   "Mittelschule," the term cited here, designates the school which leads to the General Certificate of Education Ordinary Level. (Tr.'s note)

9.   Citations from the pedagogical essays which will appear in a forthcoming volume of *Edith Steins Werke.*

10.   See in this volume p. 86.

11.   See p. 182.

12.   See p. 183.

13.   See p. 119.

14.   See p. 230.

15.   These are the first two lines of Prov 31:10-31, cited by the editor in Latin (Tr.'s note):

> Mulierem fortem quis inveniet?
> Procul et de ultimis finibus pretium ejus . . .

16.   See p. 186.

17.   See p. 192.

18.   See p. 193.
19.   See p. 102.
20.   See p. 106.
21.   Ibid.
22.   See p. 213.
23.   See p. 107.
24.   See pp. 250-251.
25.   See p. 81.
26.   See p. 161.
27.   See among other passages in this volume pp. 151-152.

28.   Edith Stein gave the introductory paper at the Bavarian Catholic Women Teachers' Association, entitled "The Significance of Woman's Intrinsic Value in National Life." See Introduction pp. 32-37 for further data. The paper itself appears on pp. 246-259. (Tr.'s note)

29.   See *Kreuzeswissenschaft, Edith Steins Werke,* Vol. I, p. 282, note No. 2.

30.   See *Duden,* 14th edition (1954).

31.   Edith Stein has not specified this topic in the record but has indeed alluded to it at the end of her address. See below the review of the lecture by E. Vierneisel.

32.   See p. 100.

33.   See pp. 77-78.

34.   Similar studies of the marks of the typesetter allow us to assume that the manuscript was to have appeared in *Stimmen der Zeit.*

35.   Section II is missing on the note pad.

36.   The manuscript of "Challenges Facing Swiss Catholic Academic Women" is an outline of the ideas presented in the lecture. It was necessary for the translator to create sentences out of phrases, remaining faithful to content and sequence. (Tr.'s note)

Chapter II

THE SEPARATE VOCATIONS OF MAN AND WOMAN ACCORDING TO NATURE AND GRACE

1.   Gn 1:26.
2.   Ibid., 1:27.
3.   Ibid., 1:28.
4.   Gn 2:7ff.
5.   Ibid., 2:20.
6.   Ibid., 2:18.
7.   Ibid., 2:23.
8.   Ibid., 2:24.
9.   Ibid., 2:25.
10.   Gn 3:12.
11.   Ibid., 3:17.
12.   Ibid., 3:18.

13.   Ibid., 3:19.
14.   Ibid., 3:16.
15.   Ibid., 3:21.
16.   Ibid., 3:15.
17.   Mt 19:1-12; Mk 10:1-12.
18.   I Cor 11:3-4.
19.   Ibid., 11:5.
20.   Ibid., 11:7.
21.   Ibid., 11:8.
22.   Ibid., 11:9.
23.   Ibid., 11:11.
24.   Ibid., 11:16.
25.   I Cor 7:14, 16.
26.   Eph 5:22ff.
27.   Ibid., 5:22-23.
28.   Ibid., 5:24.
29.   Ibid., 5:25.
30.   Ibid., 5:26.
31.   Ibid., 5:27.
32.   Ibid., 5:28.
33.   Ibid., 5:29.
34.   Ibid., 5:30.
35.   Ibid., 5:31.
36.   Ibid., 5:32.
37.   Ibid., 5:33.
38.   I Tim 2:9.
39.   Ibid., 2:11.
40.   Ibid., 2:12.
41.   Ibid., 2:13.
42.   Ibid., 2:14.
43.   Ibid., 2:15.
44.   Gal 3:23-24, 28.
45.   I Cor 6.
46.   V. Borsinger, *Rechtstellung der Frau in der Katholischen Kirche* (Leipzig, 1931).

Chapter III

SPIRITUALITY OF THE CHRISTIAN WOMAN

1.   These are two citations from Goethe: "reine Menschlichkeit," i.e., "pure humanity," and "Ewig-Weibliches," i.e., "the eternal feminine." (Tr.'s note)

2.   This Thomistic concept (inner form) connotes the essence of being. (Tr.'s note)

3.   See the essay "The Separate Vocations of Man and Woman According to Nature and Grace," pp. 57-85. (Eds.' note)

4. This sentence is an allusion to the economic crisis and the emergency ordinances of the 1930s, which were of decisive significance for the total German educational system. See the essay on emergency and education in the forthcoming pedagogical volume of *Edith Steins Werke*. (Eds.' note)

Chapter IV

FUNDAMENTAL PRINCIPLES OF WOMEN'S EDUCATION

1. This subject was first presented in an address for the Educational Standing Committee of German Catholic Federation of Women, in Berndorf a. Rh. on November 11, 1930. (Eds.' note)

2. The following concepts are dealt with somewhat more comprehensively in a lecture on the concept of education. The text for these addresses will be assumed in a later volume of *Edith Steins Werke*. (Eds.' note)

3. The term "Gestalt" when used as a psychological term has many meanings; here it can be translated as "form" or "character." (Tr.'s note)

4. My Salzburg address, "The Ethos of Women's Professions" contains supplementary thoughts. See in this volume pp. 41-56.

5. A clarified theory of values and a respective explanation of perception of values would be an essential prerequisite for a justifiable and philosophical theory of education; this would explain which part reason and soul have in the perception of values and would illuminate their collaboration.

6. "Höheren Töchterschule" were high schools for girls. (Tr.'s note)

7. Literally, "Selbsttätigkeit" is the self-activity of the student, but it pertains to the free choice of curriculum and self-governance of the student. (Tr.'s note)

8. By the examination of the literary remains, sheets of manuscripts were discovered which contain supplementary thoughts to the above lectures. (Eds.' note)

9. This is an excerpt from the Latin hymn to the Holy Spirit, "Nunc Sancti Nobis Spiritus" ascribed to St. Ambrose and prescribed for the hour of Terce (9:00 a.m.) throughout the year in the Roman Breviary. A literal translation reads: "Let charity be inflamed with fire, and ardor enkindle our neighbors." (Tr.'s note)

Chapter V

PROBLEMS OF WOMEN'S EDUCATION

1. The initial wording of page 1 is retained in the fragmentary manuscript of the first chapter:

Survey of the problem of woman's present position.
The topic which was assigned to me for this semester
covers a great deal in a widely extended scope. A
complete and exhaustive treatment is not possible in
the few hours at our disposal: it is a question only of
how to set the limitations. I think that as a beginning for our work together, it would be good to
review the problematic area and to single out particular questions for an exchange of ideas in a possible
discussion.

The problems concerning the education of young
girls are actually determined by woman's present
position. Therefore, I would like to evolve the
problems from that focal point. Of course, there
immediately arises a difficulty in doing so . . . (Eds.'
note)

2.   Published by A. Salomon and M. Baum (Berlin, 1930).
3.   The three recognized social groups in medieval Europe were
the nobility, the clergy, and the city merchants. Stein's referral to the
fourth estate as dating back one century would place it with the
Industrial Revolution and may signify the working man as the fourth
estate. Today, the public press is commonly referred to as the fourth
estate. (Tr.'s note)
4.   This final examination at German secondary schools is the
equivalent of our university entrance examination. (Tr.'s note)
5.   The National Socialist party claimed superiority of the
Anglo-Saxon race and hence was desirous of continuing this heritage by
breeding. (Tr.'s note)
6.   Leipzig, 1931.
7.   "The Separate Vocations of Man and Woman According to
Nature and Grace"; in this volume pp. 57-85. (Eds.' note)
8.   See above under A.
9.   *Lebenserinnerungen* (Berlin, 1927).
10.   Luise Otto-Peters took a stab in this direction in literary
form already in the 40s; especially impressive is her 1848 address to the
Saxon ministry and the Commission for the Discussion of Industrial and
Working Conditions which met at that time in Dresden for the benefit
of working women. Elizabeth Gnauck-Kühne revived these attempts
in the 90s on the basis of detailed sociological studies. The social point
of view established the motive and guiding principle for the proletariat
feminist movement.
11.   For this purpose, the Lette Society served from 1865 in
Berlin for the furtherance of feminine business activity.
12.   Luise Otto at the Leipzig founding assembly of the General
Association of German Women.
13.   They were organized in the Women's Welfare Society, Association for Reform in Women's Education, and later in the League of
Progressive Women's Associations.
14.   Through the emergency decrees of recent years, the nation-

al education for girls has been highly restricted to a significant adjustment of their duties in life, and the existence of the schools has been threatened.

15. See above, p. 149.

16. The Association of Catholic Women Teachers is even somewhat older than the general societies as Catholic teachers' training preceded that of the non-Catholic.

17. See above, p. 150.

18. In the manuscript is inscribed the following passage crossed out by the author: "(The usual mode of expression, to be sure, distinguishes the masculine and female *genus*. But the question remains whether *genus* in this sense and *genus* in the sense of logic signify the same thing. And I cannot encumber our problem now with this question.)" (Eds.' note)

19. See O. Lipmann's text *Psychical Differences of the Sexes* (Leipzig, 1924) for a general and critical view, and a thorough study of this material.

20. In his paper "Sexual Psychology as a Prerequisite of a Sexual Pedagogy," Rudolf Allers has given a very clear explanation of this. See *Problems of Sexual Pedagogy* (Münster: German Institute for Scientific Pedagogy, 1931). His writings of the last few years indicate a general progression from psychology of the individual to anthropology.

21. "Maxim for the unsolvable riddle of the world"; see *Langenscheidt's Enzyklopädisches Wörterbuch*, I, p. 823. (Tr.'s note)

22. Whether it is more advisable to speak here of genus or of species can be determined only after an inquiry into the formal, ontological problem.

23. A sentence crossed out by Edith Stein follows here in the manuscript: ". . . a final account of this must be reserved for another occasion." (Eds.' note)

24. Once more I must decline to discuss further how far-reaching an inquiry has been made concerning this method of cognition. From the great flood of literature on women, i.e., the books and articles by men and women on the being or nature of woman, I would like just to single out one as a serious, scholarly, and, it seems to me, a pioneering achievement. Since its publication, it has been widely acclaimed: see Sr. Thoma Angelica Walter of the Poor Child Jesus, *The Rhythm of Being: a Study Concerning the Foundation of a Metaphysics of the Sexes (Seinsrhythmik. Eine Studie zur Begründung einer Metaphysik der Geschlechter)*, by Sr. Thoma Angelica Walter vom armen Kinde Jesu (Freiburg, 1932). Here an entirely new method sets out on the track of the ultimate meaning of the terms *masculine* and *feminine;* the problem of the sexes is brought to its radical ontological form, i.e., she inquires whether *masculine* and *feminine* are not basic forms of being, a double form occurring in all created being; and these basic forms are followed on all levels of created being, from the first creation—light— to the highest spiritual creatures. Her liberal treatment of the problem

and the authenticity and vigor of the ontological analysis give to this
work its fundamental significance. I am also convinced that it holds
enduring conclusions; but I must add that the work lacks a conclusive
justification for the method applied, and I attribute this lack to the fact
that not all of her assertions can be regarded as irrefutable conclusions.
The author is guided by a few fundamental truths from the philosophy
of St. Thomas as well as by some statements from the writings of E.
Przywara and R. Guardini. Besides, she uses a method which draws
near to the phenomenological intuition. [Here follows in the manuscript an addition crossed out by the author: "strongly evident of the
influence of H. Conrad-Martius' writings." Eds.] Finally, she occasionally makes use of the results of recent research of various scientific disciplines such as mathematics, physics and biology. But no justification
is given for the combination of these different methods and the order
of their relations. Of course, in order to make such justification, a
particular system of philosophy would have had to premise her analysis
of the problem of the sexes. In the short preliminary remarks on
method contained in the book's Preface, the author states that the
Catholic faith, as the most secure system of human knowledge, must be
accepted as the book's foundation. But she does not treat separately
what has been ascertained about the problem of the sexes from this
point of view.

    25. *Summa Theol,* I, 92, a. 1.

    26. The original wording of Edith Stein which was crossed out
in the manuscript reads: ". . . of St. Paul comes to mind as well. His
meaning therein is a specification regarding 'from where?' and 'where
to?' concerning the actual source and end of the female sex. We can
disregard here the question of the real origin because it is not directly
relevant to our perception of being. His statement concerning the end
of woman must be followed more closely. That means, it must first of
all be understood from the context . . ." (Eds.' note)

    27. We shall have to take up this problem once more when
treating the question of educational goals.

    28. The original, unshortened wording of the manuscript reads
". . . theological considerations. First of all, do nature and essence
signify something different or are they the same? With St. Thomas,
natura and *essentia* are used frequently as synonyms. Both denote that
which the thing is in itself. But this "what" can be understood from
different aspects: first, as that which is given to the thing in the act of
creation, as it was placed into existence and, therefore, as it was destined to function. And thus the term *natura* is suitable. Then, this
"what" can be understood as that which we find in the thing which is
proper and *necessary* in contrast to all external qualities, behavioral
patterns, and manner of appearance, i.e., which depend on the external,
accidental conditions of its existence. And for that the term *essence* is
suitable. The task of understanding essence is directly concerned with
what and how the thing *is* in fact present, i.e., with the help of possible

considerations (which modifications are conceivable without a thing ceasing to be its essence: tree or lion or, in fact, woman), to advance to that which belongs necessarily to its structure. Now, *nature* can be understood so that this necessity would not necessarily be taken into its inner structure. (For instance, we can think of lions which are different in many respects from what the nature of lions actually is according to the descriptions of experiential knowledge). So could the nature of woman, how she is suited to her destiny, admit of modification without woman's essence being annulled thereby. Thus, if it should appear that there are certain differences between philosophical statements and theological definitions, one could discern that those differences do not mean contradictions necessarily." (Eds.' notes)

29.   In this text, see pp. 57ff.

30.   In this previously mentioned text, *The Rhythm of Being,* the author tries to follow this differentiation through all grades of being. She emphasizes that this uniqueness of all created beings is that their existence ("Dasein") can be differentiated from *what* they are, and that it must endure through time in order to develop to that which they are. (Mother Thoma Angelica distinguishes between the terms *existence* ("Dasein") and *essence* ("Sosein"); I shall explain directly that my main reservation concerns her structure of ideas based on this antithetical pair and concerns *only* that. Each being has a force of being *("Seinsmacht")* to which a specific rhythm corresponds; what the being is unfolds in its existence according to this rhythm. Each grade differs in rhythm which, according to Mother Thoma Angelica, is double depending on what is predominant—that which wants to be formed into existence or the existence which wants to take on form. The element of existence is regarded as feminine, that of essential being as masculine. They are combined in all creatures. The predominance of life's plenty is considered as the distinctive attribute of the feminine rhythm of being, the predominance of the ability to form as the specific quality of the masculine rhythm of being. In the lower grades, there are not yet two parallel lines of forms, i.e., not yet actual sexual differentiation as they begin in the organic realm; rather, there are forms showing either the one or the other rhythm of being. Where the species (understood as plant or animal species) has a double form, it itself is to be regarded as the unity of both partial species. This unity finds its strongest expression in the fact that this kind of species is procreated and kept in existence by the union of individuals embodying the *member rhythms.* In the human being this double form does not show in individuals of different member rhythm; rather, in every individual throughout his or her entire physical-spiritual-psychic structure, it can be followed. (Thus in the soul, the will is regarded as feminine, the understanding as masculine.)

It is not possible to describe here in detail and to take a position regarding the *carrying out* of the rhythm of being. I would like only to comment on the ontological foundation to which my objections are directed and which must naturally have an effect up to the final conclusions. Obviously, the differentiation between *"Dasein"* and *"Sosein"* is supposed to reproduce the Thomistic differentiation between *"existentia"* and *"essentia."* The expression *"Sosein"* seems to me an unhappy one because it is suitable for accidental form rather than for substantial form which it is obviously meant to signify. (For the accidental also, further distinction needs to be made between *thus* ("So") and *accidental being* ("Sosein"): the accidental form and the being determined by way of the form.) However, the term *"Dasein"* appears to me to include much more than St. Thomas included under *"existentia."* If the whole text was intended to be oriented toward Thomistic ontology, then in addition to the pair of opposites *"Essenz"* and *"Existenz,"* a second pair *form* *("Form")* and *matter ("Materie")* as well as a third pair *act ("Akt")* and *potency ("Potenz")* should also have been taken into consideration. I have the impression that much which is ascribed to *"Dasein"* would be more suited to *"Materie,"* and much would fit the potential aspect of the being. Only on the basis of a close analysis of the entire ontological structure of created being do I consider the problem solvable whether *masculine* and *feminine* are actually to be understood only as *rhythms of being ("Seinsrhythmen")* or whether or not a difference of substantial form lies at the basis of the different rhythms of being.

31.   Mausbach, *Die Stellung der Frau im Menschheitsleben: eine Anwendung Katholischer Grundsätze auf die Frauenfrage* (München-Gladbach, 1906).

32.   Compare to Mausbach, *Die Stellung.*

33.   Compare to Denzinger-Bannwart, *Enchiridion symbolorum,* No. 981.

34.   "I believe that I may understand" and "Faith seeking understanding." (Tr.'s note)

35.   *Die Psyche der weiblichen Jugend* (Langensalza, 1930).

36.   "Fomes peccati"—inclination toward sin. (Tr.'s note)

37.   Compare to the foregoing on pp. 134ff.

38.   See above, pp. 161ff.

39.   The German text of Pius XI, *Rappresentanti* (Herder, 1930), p. 42.

40.   *Rappresentanti,* p. 44.

41.   "Nature—original, fallen, and redeemed." (Tr.'s note)

42.   This is the Hebrew term for "complementary helpmate." (Tr.'s note)

43.   This is marked Ps 112 in the text; in the contemporary standard edition of the Bible it is Ps 113. (Tr.'s note)

44.   See Prov 31:10-31. (Tr.'s note)

45.   "Handmaid of the Lord." (Tr.'s note)

46.   The following sentence appears here in the manuscript as crossed out by Edith Stein: "Incorporation into the Church must be considered specifically still once more at a later time." (Eds.' note)

47.   In the manuscript this sentence includes here an allusion to the imminent danger of National Socialism which was crossed out by the writer herself: ". . . are raised by another 'Weltanschauung' and with which we will perhaps have to come to terms practically very soon." (Eds.' note)

48.   The printing of this essay in *Benediktinische Monatschrift* (1933, No. 3/4) adds a complementary note not contained in the manuscript; "A valuable supplement to my statements can be found in the recent publication of *Mädchenbildung auf christlicher Grundlage* 29 (1933, No. 2) "Lebensformen der Erzieherin" by Dr. Maria Bienias. (Eds.' note)

49.   *Rappresentanti,* p. 7.

50.   *Rappresentanti,* p. 15.

51.   *Summa Theol.* II, 2, q. 10-12.

52.   See above section III A.   It is different from the much narrower, limited educational concept, for example that of Eggerdorf.

53.   *Rappresentanti,* p. 7.

54.   Ibid.

55.   Compare to my *Abhandlung über den Staat* in Vol. 7 of Husserl's *Jahrbuch für Philosophie und phänomenologische Forschung.* (Eds.: This study will appear in the series of *Edith Steins Werke.)*

56.   Mt 28:18-20.

57.   *Rappresentanti,* p. 8.

58.   Ibid.

59.   *Rappresentanti,* p. 9.

60.   This term was given to the struggle between Church and State under Bismarck, 1872-1887. (Tr.'s note)

61.   "In loco parentis" is "to take the place of the parents." (Tr.'s note)

62.   Leipzig, 1927.

63.   Compare this to the memorial issue for P. M. Hamann, *Die Christliche Frau* (May, 1932).

64.   In her essay on the intellectuality of girls, Maria Bienias has emphasized that it is preferable to call the feminine nature *productive* in contrast to the masculine nature which is *dispositive.* That which is incorporated into one's own being in the sense of an organic knowledge has a fruitful effect on other beings. See *Mädchenbildung auf christlicher Grundlage* (1931, No. 21/22).

Chapter VI

THE CHURCH, WOMAN AND YOUTH

1.   This sentence is missing in the first edition. (Eds.' note)

2.   In the first printing this paragraph concludes with the addition: "Likewise, there are many employed advisers already prepared in the youth movement who would most certainly be happy to extend

their work to younger children." (Eds.' note)

3. The first draft of this manuscript contains the following footnote: "Rudolph Peil stresses in his book *Concrete Pedagogy for Girls* (Honnef on the Rhine, 1932) that girls see the priest predominantly in his objective character as priest and precisely for this reason will reveal themselves to him more easily than they will to mother or teacher. I do not doubt that if the priest is entirely priest and if girls are religiously educated enough already, they can have this thoroughly calm and objective attitude. The only thing I do doubt is that the *concrete situation* of which Father Peil is here speaking is the average situation in which we have to deal in the training of girls." (Eds.' note)

Chapter VII

THE SIGNIFICANCE OF WOMAN'S INTRINSIC VALUE IN NATIONAL LIFE

1. "A watch from morning until night." (Tr.'s note)

2. A passage which was eliminated by the author from the original text reads: "I did not decline when the director of the Bavarian Women's Teachers' Association approached me to read this opening paper, but, nevertheless, I had strong reservations and even expressed them. Is a person who lives in the seclusion of the cloister, and who hears the surge of worldly life only from a great distance, well-called to say something concerning the significance of woman in contemporary life? Even so, when I think of the quiet oasis of peace where I spent Easter week and Easter Sunday, and now see myself in this great gathering, then the contrast seems almost irreconcilable." (Eds.' note)

Chapter VIII

CHALLENGES FACING SWISS CATHOLIC ACADEMIC WOMEN

1. "In this sign you will conquer." The slogan of the section of the Youth of the International Union of the Catholic Women's Leagues.

Index

This index lists all persons and places. The thematic listings record principal, significant references to Edith Stein's text. They are not intended to be all-inclusive or exhaustive.

281